Treatises Against the Anabaptists and Against the Libertines

John Calvin

Treatises Against the Anabaptists and Against the Libertines

Translation, Introduction, and Notes

Benjamin Wirt Farley
Editor and Translator

Baker Book House
Grand Rapids, Michigan 49506

ISBN: 0–8010–2476–5

Library of Congress Catalog Card Number: 82–72539

Printed in the United States of America

To

John Haddon Leith

Pemberton Professor of Theology

Union Theological Seminary

in Virginia

Contents

Acknowledgments

It was Professor John Haddon Leith of Union Theological Seminary in Richmond, Virginia, who first suggested, in the winter of 1979, that I consider translating Calvin's treatises *Against the Anabaptists* and *Against the Libertines.* Dan Van't Kerkhoff of Baker Book House concurred with the proposal, and both he and Professor Leith lent me support during my work on the project with their encouragement and interest. To each I am deeply grateful.

Work on the treatises soon involved me in various aspects of Reformation studies. George H. Williams's *Radical Reformation* (Philadelphia: Westminster, 1977) provided invaluable historical information and insight. My debt to his study is noticeable in both the introduction and the many footnotes in which his book is cited as a principal reference.

I must also cite the four-volume *Mennonite Encyclopedia,* edited by Harold S. Bender and C. Henry Smith (Scottdale, Pa.: Herald, 1955–1959), and commend readers to consult those articles which are relevant to the treatises in this volume. The editors have made accessible a wealth of research which illumines the work and ideas of the Anabaptists. Also worthy of mention is the *Mennonite Quarterly Review,* the articles of which supplement the *Encyclopedia.*

My appreciation goes to colleagues at Erskine College with whom I frequently consulted: to Professor John Miller Grier (modern languages), with whom I often discussed the French text of *Against the Libertines;* to Professors Hans G. Engler (modern languages) and William H. F. Kuykendall (Bible) for their assistance with the Latin texts and Herminjard's letters;

and to Professor Merwyn S. Johnson (systematic theology—Erskine Theological Seminary) both for his assistance with Wilhelm Niesel's "Calvin und die Libertiner" and for our discussion concerning the "moral licentiousness" problem posed by Niesel.

I am also grateful to the Erskine College Library staff, whose efficiency made my own work easier: to Professor John H. Wilde, Librarian; and to staff members Jack Pitzer, Edith Brawley, Alice Haddon, Beth Hawthorne, and Dorian Meaders.

I am indebted to Mary Lou Wilde and her work on Johannes Kessler's *Sabbata;* and to William H. Demuralt, a student from the Netherlands, who assisted me in my reading of W. Balke's *Calvijn en de doperse Radikalen.*

Appreciation is also due to Mrs. B. D. Aycock, Reference Librarian, Union Theological Seminary, for acquiring copies of the relevant *Calvini Opera* materials; and to the Reverend Palmer M. Patterson, who graciously proofread the manuscript and made many helpful suggestions.

Finally, I am most grateful to Dr. Jimmy A. Knight, Vice President and Dean, Erskine College, for his interest throughout the project and for making available funds to help offset the expenses of copying, travel, and related research.

Brief Instruction for Arming All the Good Faithful Against the Errors of the Common Sect of the Anabaptists

Editor's Introduction

The translation of Calvin's *Brief Instruction for Arming All the Good Faithful Against the Errors of the Common Sect of the Anabaptists* (1544)[1] is based on the text in the *Calvini Opera*, volume 7, columns 49–142. An old English translation, called *A Shorte Instruction for to warn all good Christian People against the Pestiferous Errours of the Common Secte of Anabaptists* (London, 1549), does exist; however, the current work is an entirely independent translation.

The Anabaptists and the Seven Articles

Calvin's *Brief Instruction* was written primarily in response to a translation into French and circulation of *The Schleitheim Confession*, or more accurately, the *Brotherly Union of a Number of Children of God Concerning Seven Articles*,[2] made at Schleitheim (near the Swiss-German border) in August of 1527.

1. *Brieve instruction pour armer tous bons fideles contre les erreurs de la secte commune des Anabaptistes*, par M. Iehan Calvin, a Geneve, par Iehan Girard, 1544, in *Ioannis Calvini Opera quae supersunt omnia*, ed. Guilielmus Baum, Eduardus Cunitz, and Eduardus Reuss (Brunsvigae: C. A. Schwetschkte et filium, 1863–1900), vol. 7, cols. 49–142 (hereafter cited as *CO*).

2. In German: *Brüderlich Vereinigung etlicher Kinder Gottes, sieben Artikel betreffend*, in *Flugschriften aus den ersten Jahren der Reformation*, ed. Otto Clemen (Leipzig: Halle, 1907–1911), vol. 2, pt. 3, as well as in other sources. See John H. Yoder's English translation in *The Legacy of Michael Sattler* (Scottdale, Pa.: Herald, 1973), pp. 34–43. (Hereafter references to the *Brotherly Union* are cited as *The Schleitheim Confession*.) See also J. C. Wenger, "The Schleitheim Confession of Faith," *Mennonite Quarterly Review* 19 (1945): 243–253.

The *Seven Articles*, as the *Confession* is also called, was largely the work of Michael Sattler[3] (1490–1527), an Evangelical Anabaptist.[4] He was born at Staufen in southern Germany (then under Austrian rule) and trained in the Benedictine monastery of St. Peter's near Freiburg. In time he became its prior, but in the early 1520s, due to Lutheran and Zwinglian influences, he left the monastery and married. In March of 1525 he joined the Anabaptist (Swiss Brethren) movement, which had scarcely begun two months earlier at Zurich. On November 18, 1525, he was expelled from Zurich and returned to work in Breisgau and Württemberg. In 1526 he visited Strassburg, but little else is known about his activities save for his literary works, his capture at Horb and imprisonment at Binsdorf (both in Württemberg), and his ensuing trial and martyrdom.[5] John H. Yoder, who has recently written a biography of Sattler and compiled his works, joins many previous admirers and critics alike in calling Sattler "the most significant of the first-generation leaders of Anabaptism."[6] As Yoder acknowledges, "The testing of this description best . . . [arises] out of the documents themselves."[7] This is notably true of the *Seven Articles.*

At the beginning of 1527 the Swiss Brethren movement stood in grave danger of disintegration.[8] Felix Manz[9] (ca. 1498–1527), one of its earliest leaders, had been executed in Zurich on January 5. Conrad Grebel[10] (ca. 1498–1526), the acknowledged

3. For brief accounts of Sattler's life, see Yoder, *Sattler*, pp. 10ff.; also "Sattler, Michael," *Mennonite Encyclopedia*, ed. Harold S. Bender and C. Henry Smith, 4 volumes (Scottdale, Pa.: Herald, 1955–59), vol. 4, pp. 427–434. The account in this introduction follows Yoder's.

4. For Sattler's classification as an "Evangelical Anabaptist," see George H. Williams and Angel Mergal, *Spiritual and Anabaptist Writers*, Library of Christian Classics (Philadelphia: Westminster, 1957), vol. 25, p. 31.

5. See Yoder, *Sattler*, pp. 10, 55, 66f.

6. Ibid., p. 10.

7. Ibid.

8. Ibid., p. 27.

9. See "Manz, Felix," *Mennonite Encyclopedia*, vol. 3, pp. 472–474.

10. See Harold S. Bender, *Conrad Grebel c. 1498–1526: The Founder of the Swiss Brethren Sometimes Called Anabaptists* (Scottdale, Pa.: Herald, 1950). It was Grebel who initiated the Anabaptist movement when, on the evening of January 25, 1525, after a prayer service at Zurich in the company of about fifteen evangelical Christians, George Blaurock (d. 1529) implored Grebel to baptize him "with the true Christian baptism," and Grebel did. See also "Grebel, Conrad," *Mennonite Encyclopedia*, vol. 2, pp. 566–575; and Williams and Mergal, *Anabaptist Writers*, p. 44.

founder of the Swiss Brethren and former associate of Zwingli himself, had died in the summer of 1526. The movement had also been suppressed in St. Gall, the canton immediately east of Zurich. And Sattler's own attempts to find a reception for an Anabaptist presence in Bucer and Capito's free city of Strassburg had failed. Disappointed, Sattler had returned to the Black Forest to nurture his group.[11]

Yoder suspects that Sattler was probably aware little time remained for him "to consolidate the movement he had planted."[12] From without they were threatened by the successes of the Reformers in both Switzerland and Germany as well as by the Catholics elsewhere. From within they were beset by antinomian and radical groups such as had flourished at St. Gall and Appenzell.[13] Above all, the period of the Zurich founders had passed.

It was these pressures that finally brought the Brethren together at Schleitheim, where they discussed their situation and adopted the *Seven Articles* defining their Brotherly Union. The seven articles consist of (1) a rejection of infant baptism, (2–5) statements on the ban, the Lord's Supper, ministers, and the need to separate from political abominations, and (6–7) rejections of the use of the sword and the oath.

It is recognized today that the Swiss Brethren, along with their Contemplative and Revolutionary counterparts,[14] wanted a more thoroughgoing reformation than Luther or Zwingli had achieved. Franklin H. Littell[15] and Frank J. Wray[16] have analyzed this Anabaptist concept of "restitution."[17] The Anabaptists regarded the golden age of authentic Christianity as having lasted from the time of the apostles to the era of Constantine. At Nicaea, however, the charismatic and congregational character of the

11. See Yoder, *Sattler,* p. 29.

12. Ibid.

13. See George H. Williams, *The Radical Reformation* (Philadelphia: Westminster, 1977), pp. 127–134.

14. For these classifications, see Williams and Mergal, *Anabaptist Writers,* pp. 28ff.

15. Franklin H. Littell, *The Origins of Sectarian Protestantism* (New York: Macmillan, 1964), pp. 79–108.

16. Frank J. Wray, "The Anabaptist Doctrine of the Restitution of the Church," *Mennonite Quarterly Review* 28 (1954): 186–196.

17. See "Restitution," *Mennonite Encyclopedia,* vol. 4, pp. 302–307.

church died. With Nicaea a long period of decline and fall ensued. This decline had lasted up through the great Reformers. Thus the Anabaptists saw themselves as participating in the church's restitution. Their aim was to restore the church to its primitive character as depicted in the Acts of the Apostles.

For this reason virtually everything associated with what the Anabaptists regarded as the fallen church came under suspicion. The union of church and state, compulsory religion, outward power, war among Christians, the territorial system, the influx of nominal Christians into the ranks of the church, and infant baptism, which in the Anabaptist view was no baptism at all, were seen as corrupt developments.[18]

In light of these suspicions modern readers of the *Seven Articles* can appreciate the Swiss Brethren's concern to disavow the sword and the church's connections with political authority, to abstain from oaths of allegiance that still bound one to the old political, social, economic, and legal structures of the age, and to use the ban as the only legitimate Christian exercise of censure. At the same time one can understand why the Reformers viewed such radicals as seditious revolutionaries or, in Calvin's own words, as "fanatics," "poor fools," "scatterbrains," "poor ignoramuses," and "enemies of government."

Events Leading to the **Brief Instruction**

William Farel[19] in the winter of 1544 was the first to implore Calvin to write against the Anabaptists.[20] Farel was in Neuchâtel, where a resurgence of Anabaptism had led to sharp confrontations between certain propagandists and the Reformed pastors of the canton.

More specifically, Anabaptist sympathizers had made favorable inroads in the area of Neuchâtel in the early 1530s. Gains were made especially among the inhabitants of Cornaux, a

18. Littell, *Origins*, pp. 64–72.

19. For the most part the account in this section follows *Guillaume Farel: 1489–1565*, ed. Comité Farel (Neuchâtel et Paris: Delachaux & Niestlé, 1930), pp. 536–539.

20. Farel to Calvin, February 23, 1544, in A.-L. Herminjard, *Correspondances des reformateurs dan les pays de langue française* (Geneva et Paris: 1866ff.), vol. 9, p. 174, no. 1332.

village near La Neuveville. This village had served as the residence of the parish priest of Saint-Blaise but in 1536 became Protestant. The pastoral gifts and judgment of Antoine Thomassin, the Reformed minister who took over in the village, appear to have been unequal to the difficult parish he was called to serve, for some of his parishioners never accepted the Reformed cause and others became indifferent to religion itself. Thomassin's own lack of ability compounded the problem.

In 1539 or 1540 one of the village women was imprisoned at Neuchâtel for blasphemy. She was accused of having denied Christ's resurrection and of maintaining that the human soul, which in her view was no different from an animal's, dies with the body.

In the meanwhile the Anabaptists enjoyed further gains among the parishioners who had become estranged from Christianity, and managed to turn them against Thomassin. The principal leader was a native of La Neuveville, Pierre Pelot (or Pelloux), who was aided by his brother-in-law, Antoine Jacottet. Tension between the two sides increased, and finally Georges de Rive, the governor of Neuchâtel, intervened. As a result Jacottet was imprisoned and Pelot banished.

Hostilities continued, however. On March 11, 1543, Michel Mulot, a pastor of Saint-Blaise who had exchanged pulpits with Thomassin, was verbally challenged when he attempted to baptize an infant. Parishioners demanded, "Where is it found in Holy Scripture that infants should be baptized?" Upon Thomassin's return, relations only worsened. These events alarmed the Neuchâtel pastors, who launched an investigation and sought to repress any disorder.

The turning point came at the beginning of 1544, when Pelot, in collaboration with an affiliate at Neuchâtel, had a certain Anabaptist booklet translated and circulated throughout the canton. Herminjard,[21] Williams,[22] and others[23] have identified this booklet, a copy of which Farel was to have sent Calvin in February of 1544,[24] as Balthasar Hubmaier's *Von der christlichen*

21. Herminjard, *Correspondances*, vol. 9, p. 173, no. 1332, n. 14.
22. Williams, *Radical Reformation*, p. 596.
23. *Guillaume Farel*, p. 538.
24. Herminjard, *Correspondances*, vol. 9, p. 173, no. 1332, n. 14.

Taufe der Gläubigen (*Concerning the Christian Baptism of Believers*).[25] W. Balke,[26] however, disagrees and argues that the booklet in question was *The Schleitheim Articles*, attributed to Michael Sattler. Farel's own letter to Calvin seems to bear this out, as Farel's description of the *libellus* he was to have sent to Calvin closely resembles Calvin's later description (in *Brief Instruction*) of a booklet which he notes he received and which he specifically identifies as the *Seven Articles*.[27]

John H. Yoder also surmises that a French translation of the *Articles* and of a piece on the "martyrdom of Michael Sattler" existed in early 1544.[28] It was this book or booklet (i.e., containing the *Articles* and the martyrdom piece) which Pelot had translated and circulated, a copy of which was secured by Farel and sent to Calvin.[29] Further, it is this document which Calvin identifies and to which he devotes his attention in *Brief Instruction*.[30] If the book Farel sent to Calvin had been Hubmaier's *Concerning the Christian Baptism of Believers*, it is strange that Calvin makes no mention of it whatsoever.

In Farel's letter to Calvin of February 23, 1544, Farel writes of the *libellus* that "the brothers consider it necessary to reply to it, not because the book is worthy of it, but because of the simple [people] who still fear God. They ask you, therefore, in the name of the Lord, to charge yourself with this task."[31] Farel then urges Calvin to translate his *Psychopannychia* as well.[32]

Matters at La Neuveville continued to deteriorate. On March 28, Bernese officials encouraged the council of La Neuveville to seize copies of the book and to arrest those responsible for

25. See William R. Estep, Jr.'s translation of *Concerning the Christian Baptism of Believers* in his *Anabaptist Beginnings (1523–1533): A Source Book* (Nieuwkoop: B. De Graaf, 1976), pp. 66–98.

26. W. Balke, *Calvijn en de doperse Radikalen*, 2d ed. (Amsterdam: Ton Bolland, 1977).

27. Farel's description: "Et quamvis *libellus* adeo ineptus sit, non solum interpretis vitio . . ." (Herminjard, *Correspondances*, vol. 9, p. 173, no. 1332)—"And however inept this little booklet be, not only in respect to its faulty translation. . . ." Calvin's description: "ce livre, . . . tant il est inepte et sotement escrit" (*CO* 7, cols. 49–50)—"this book, . . . as well as being inept and haphazardly written."

28. Yoder, *Sattler*, p. 14.

29. Ibid.

30. *CO* 7, col. 54: *"en sept articles."*

31. Herminjard, *Correspondances*, vol. 9, p. 174, no. 1332.

32. Ibid.

its circulation. On March 31, Farel sent a second and more urgent letter to Calvin, pressing him to refute the Anabaptists "as soon as possible."[33] In the meantime, Farel held a colloquy at La Neuveville (in April or May) with the Anabaptists in the hopes of vanquishing them. Neither the precise dates nor the results of this colloquy are known, but Calvin commends it in his preface to the *Brief Instruction.*[34]

In any event, Farel's pleas did not fall on deaf ears. By June 1, 1544,[35] Calvin's treatise *Against the Anabaptists* was a reality.

Calvin's Knowledge of the Anabaptists

Calvin's acquaintance with Anabaptists was scarcely as second-hand as the above events suggest. A decade earlier Calvin was aware of the Anabaptist movement.[36]

It has often been thought that there is a connection between Calvin's earliest contacts with Anabaptists and his first work as a Protestant, the *Psychopannychia,*[37] in which he dealt with the "wakefulness of the soul." Although not published until 1542,[38] Calvin had drafted it in 1534.

The traditional view of the Catholic church with respect to the state of the soul after death had been reaffirmed at the Council of Florence (1439)[39] and by the Fifth Lateran Council (1513).[40] This view held that the soul remains awake and conscious after death, neither dying (thnetopsychism) nor lapsing into unconscious sleep (psychosomnolence). Calvin shared this patristic view.[41]

33. Farel to Calvin, March 31, 1544—Herminjard, *Correspondances,* vol. 9, pp. 193f., no. 1341. See Balke, *Calvijn,* p. 179.

34. *CO* 7, cols. 51f.

35. The date of Calvin's preface to the *Brieve instruction* in *CO* 7, col. 52.

36. The summary in this section follows closely Williams, *Radical Reformation,* pp. 581–598; and Karl H. Wyneken, "Calvin and Anabaptism," *Concordia Theological Monthly* 36, no. 1 (1965): 18–29.

37. *Psychopannychia,* in *Quellenschriften zur Geschichte des Protestantismus,* ed. Walther Zimmerli (Leipzig: Deichert, 1932).

38. See Williams, *Radical Reformation,* p. 583, n. 5.

39. "Florence, Council of," *New Catholic Encyclopedia* (Palatine, Ill.: Publishers Guild, ———), vol. 5, pp. 972f.

40. "Lateran Councils," *New Catholic Encyclopedia,* vol. 8, p. 409.

41. Calvin identifies this as the view of the early church, Tertullian, Irenaeus, Chrysostom, and Augustine.

In 1534, while at Orléans, Calvin came in contact with two groups who espoused variant views of the soul's state after death. He describes one group (psychosomnolents) as holding the unconscious sleep of the soul and the other (thnetopsychists) as teaching that the soul "perishes along with the body," though the soul is revived when the whole man is raised.[42]

Calvin lumped both these groups under one rubric, the psychopannychists. In the prefaces to the 1534 and 1536 editions of the *Psychopannychia* he designated them as Anabaptists,[43] calling them Catabaptists[44] in the body of the work. However, it is doubtful that the psychopannychists were, strictly speaking, Anabaptists. Indeed, it is difficult to know to what extent either of these positions was espoused by the Anabaptists of Cornaux or La Neuveville. It is possible that French-speaking Anabaptists maintained belief in some form of psychosomnolence,[45] but the Mennonite scholar Christian Neff denies that the sleep of the soul was ever a tenet of the Anabaptists anywhere.[46]

Karl H. Wyneken's observation that the term *Catabaptistae* was one of Calvin's favorite designations for "the radicals of his earlier years"[47] should be kept in mind here. Wyneken also points out that Calvin twice labeled his opponents *Catabaptistae* in his 1536 edition of the *Institutes*, once in the preface (sect. 7), and the second time in a section in which he refutes rebaptism (4.15.16).[48]

If Calvin did mistakenly identify the psychopannychists of 1534 with all Anabaptists, he was nonetheless familiar with the general views of the Evangelical Anabaptists—although he would not have designated them by this term. W. Balke has amply documented this familiarity in his study of Calvin's 1536 edition of the *Institutes*. Balke points out no less than thirteen areas in which Calvin was aware he differed with the Anabaptists.[49] Among these are the nature of the church, the role of

42. *Psychopannychia*, in John Calvin, *Tracts and Treatises in Defense of the Reformed Faith*, trans. Henry Beveridge, ed. Thomas F. Torrance (Grand Rapids: Eerdmans, 1958), vol. 3, p. 419.

43. *Psychopannychia*, in *Quellenschriften*, pp. 17, 19.

44. Ibid., p. 108.

45. See Williams, *Radical Reformation*, p. 597, n. 41.

46. Christian Neff, "Sleep of the Soul," *Mennonite Encyclopedia*, vol. 4, p. 543.

47. Wyneken, "Calvin and Anabaptism," p. 19.

48. Ibid., pp. 19f.

49. Balke, *Calvijn*, pp. 37–70.

discipline, infant versus believer's baptism, the rightful place of the oath, civil authority, taxes, laws, the problem of pacifism, and opposition to tyranny. Wyneken has made a similar though less exhaustive comparison.[50]

During his first stay in Geneva Calvin appears to have made his initial significant contacts with Anabaptists. The occasion was the arrival of a group of Netherlandish Anabaptists in early 1537.[51] Two of these missionaries, Herman of Gerbehaye and Andrew Benoît of Engelen, were brought before the city council on March 9, 1537. The two requested a public disputation with Calvin and Farel. Their request was granted, but Calvin did not participate. Though the two men held their own against Farel, the council decreed them defeated and banished them. George H. Williams reports that in addition to the subjects of baptism and the ban, psychosomnolence was also discussed.[52]

Soon afterward, on March 29, a second disputation was held. Calvin participated and debated two other missionaries, John Bomeromenus and John Stordeur, both from Liège at the time. They too were declared defeated and were banished on March 30.

On April 23 of the following year Calvin himself was ordered to leave the city. He journeyed first to Basel but later, at Bucer's invitation, moved to Strassburg. Either while in route or upon his arrival Calvin learned of the work of certain fanatics at Metz, and in a letter to Farel[53] reported that there, too, "the plague of the Anabaptists, as it were," had arisen. He noted that two of them had been drowned in the Moselle River and a third banished "with the brand of ignominy." He concluded, "So far as I could ascertain by conjecture, that barber who was the companion of Herman was one of them. I fear that this pestilential doctrine is widely spread among the simple sort in that city."[54] Of further interest is Herminjard's footnote to this letter: citing *Les Chroniques de Metz,* he notes that the "barbier" clearly preached "the sleep of the soul."[55]

50. Wyneken, "Calvin and Anabaptism," pp. 20f.

51. Williams, *Radical Reformation,* pp. 586f.

52. Ibid.

53. Calvin to Farel, September 11, 1538—Herminjard, *Correspondances,* vol. 5, pp. 109–113, no. 743. There is an English translation in *Letters of John Calvin,* ed. Jules Bonnet, vols. 1–2 trans. David Constable; vols. 3–4 trans. Marcus Robert Gilchrist (Philadelphia: Presbyterian Board of Publication, 1858), vol. 1, p. 82.

54. Ibid.

55. Herminjard, *Correspondances,* vol. 5, p. 112, no. 743, n. 12: "Il . . . tenoit que

In Strassburg Bucer encouraged Calvin to publish his *Psychopannychia.* Calvin did have intentions of doing so, as he noted in a letter (October 1, 1538),[56] to a former friend of Orléans days, Antoine Pignet, who was at this time a pastor near Geneva. For unknown reasons, however, Calvin still did not carry out his plan to completion.

Calvin's sojourn in Strassburg soon brought him into firsthand contact with Anabaptism. Balke places heavy emphasis on the fact that many Swiss Brethren had passed through Strassburg.[57] At one time or another, a formidable group of Anabaptist leaders had visited the city, among them Hans Denck, Sebastian Franck, Caspar Schwenckfeld, Pilgram Marbeck, and Peter Riedemann. Riedemann arrived while Calvin was still in the city.[58]

The Strassburg city fathers early assigned Calvin to work with the French-speaking Protestants, largely refugees, as well as the French-speaking Anabaptists.[59] Although Calvin had difficulty distinguishing between the radical types and the quieter Evangelicals, Balke notes that the Genevan was very successful.[60]

While participating in a city synod of 1539 Calvin converted Herman of Gerbehaye and either John Bomeromenus or John Stordeur to the Reformed faith.[61] In a letter to Farel (February 6, 1540),[62] Calvin explained that Herman finally admitted his errors concerning infant baptism and Christ's humanity. Calvin also mentions that a certain John—most likely Bomeromenus—submitted his son for baptism.[63]

Three weeks later, in still another letter to Farel (February 27, 1540),[64] Calvin reflected on Herman's conversion. He was deeply pleased that the former Anabaptist had "accepted instruction on the freedom of the will, the deity and humanity of Christ, rebirth,

---

quand la personne s'en va mourir, qu'il dort et qu'il ne va ni en paradis ni en enfer, et qu'ils reposent là où il plaît à Dieu et n'y entreront point jusqu'au jour du jugement. . . ."

56. Calvin to Pignet—Herminjard, *Correspondances,* vol. 5, p. 126, no. 749.
57. Balke, *Calvijn,* p. 126.
58. Ibid.
59. Williams, *Radical Reformation,* p. 590.
60. Balke, *Calvijn,* p. 133.
61. Ibid., p. 131.
62. Herminjard, *Correspondances,* vol. 6, p. 165, no. 846.
63. See Williams, *Radical Reformation,* p. 591, n. 32.
64. Herminjard, *Correspondances,* vol. 6, p. 189, no. 854.

infant baptism, and other matters."[65] Only on the subject of predestination did Herman hesitate, having difficulty distinguishing between *"praescientiae et providentiae."*[66] Calvin reports that he then baptized Herman's two-year-old daughter and mentions that John (either Bomeromenus or Stordeur) had finally "come to his senses." Calvin was also successful in reconverting Paul Volz, a former pastor of the St. Nicholas Church. In August of 1540 Calvin married Idelette de Bure, the widow of John Stordeur.[67]

It is also likely that during his Strassburg sojourn Calvin became familiar with Melchior Hofmann and his "celestial flesh" theory of Christ's incarnation. Hofmann (1495–1543),[68] whom Williams classifies as a "Revolutionary Anabaptist,"[69] had been with Nikolaus von Amsdorf (1483–1565) at Wittenberg. In the course of his extensive travels across Europe he had visited Strassburg on numerous occasions, and at the very time of Calvin's sojourn was imprisoned in the city. It is highly unlikely that Calvin was unaware of his presence or uninformed of his Gnostic views. Balke speculates that Calvin may well have had a meeting with him.[70]

Hofmann held, in the words of Williams, a Valentinian view, stating that Christ passed through Mary's womb "as water through a pipe."[71] This famous phrase of Hofmann's is even cited by Calvin in the *Brief Instruction.*[72] According to this view Christ took nothing from Mary's body. More specifically, in Hofmann's words, "The eternal Word of God did not take our nature and flesh from the virgin Mary but himself became flesh (John 1:14), that is, our Lord Jesus has not two natures but only one nature."[73] In all likelihood it was this theory that Herman of Gerbehaye held prior to Calvin's work with him.

In addition to making these Anabaptist contacts while in

65. Williams's translation in *Radical Reformation,* p. 591.

66. Herminjard, *Correspondances,* vol. 6, p. 193, no. 854.

67. See "Idelette van Buren" in Balke, *Calvijn,* pp. 134ff., for a complete background.

68. See "Hofmann, Melchior," *Mennonite Encyclopedia,* vol. 2, pp. 778–785.

69. Williams and Mergal, *Anabaptist Writers,* p. 29.

70. Balke, *Calvijn,* p. 129.

71. Cited by Williams, *Radical Reformation,* p. 329.

72. *CO* 7, col. 105.

73. Cited by Williams, *Radical Reformation,* p. 331.

Strassburg, Calvin prepared and published the second edition of his *Institutes.* The expanded 1539 edition makes it very clear that he was now familiar with many Anabaptist views, including those of Grebel's, Hubmaier's, and Sattler's groups, all of which are noticeable in Calvin's enlarged sections. Again the studies of Balke and Wyneken, as well as the footnotes to the McNeill edition of the *Institutes,*[74] document this development.

For example, such matters as Sebastian Franck's concept of the inner Word (the question of Word and Spirit), the legitimate use of oaths, the proper relationship between the two Testaments, the refutation of Libertinism, the illusion of perfection in the church, the error of chiliasm (associated with the Revolutionary Anabaptists), and the true understanding of infant baptism all receive attention.[75] Most notably, Calvin added an entire new chapter on infant baptism, which demonstrates that, if not fully cognizant of Hubmaier's *Concerning the Christian Baptism of Believers,* he was at least familiar with its arguments, though he might not have identified them as being Hubmaier's per se.

Finally, toward the close of his years at Strassburg, Calvin was motivated to publish his old manuscript of the *Psychopannychia,* along with its earlier prefaces of 1534 and 1536. The book did not appear until 1542; by then Calvin had returned to Geneva. Because of the emergence of a militant Anabaptism at Neuchâtel, Calvin was not only favorably inclined but theologically prepared to provide Farel with a definitive refutation of Anabaptist errors.

Theological Content of the **Brief Instruction**

Calvin divides his *Brief Instruction* into three major parts. After opening with a preface and a brief introduction, Calvin proceeds in the first division to refute the *Seven Articles,* in the second to rebut the "celestial flesh" Christology of the Melchiorites, and in the third to provide a popular and less technical version of his *Psychopannychia.*

74. *Institutes of the Christian Religion,* trans. Ford Lewis Battles, ed. John T. McNeill, Library of Christian Classics (Philadelphia: Westminster, 1960), vols. 20–21; see especially the footnotes to 4.16.

75. See Balke, *Calvijn,* pp. 97–124; Wyneken, "Calvin and Anabaptism," pp. 23–26.

The Preface and Introduction

It should be noted that the preface is addressed to the "ministers of the canton of Neuchâtel." Calvin explains how the *Seven Articles* was sent to him with the request to refute its errors. What is of interest is his almost word for word agreement with Farel that the book is "inept and haphazardly written" and has the capacity to "misguide the simple."[76]

Calvin lists two reasons that have prompted him to address his treatise to the Neuchâtel ministers: (1) that he might witness to their unified stand against the Anabaptists, and (2) that through them his treatise might be called to the attention of others. He concludes the preface by commending Farel for his diligent efforts to offset the false teachings of the Anabaptists.

The introduction is even more enlightening. In it Calvin (1) classifies the Anabaptists, (2) clearly identifies the booklet Farel sent him as the *Seven Articles,* and (3) comments on the methodology used in the treatise.

Calvin divides the Anabaptists into two sects. The first group comprises those who accept the Scriptures and theologize, albeit errantly, in a coherent and understandable manner. It is clear from the content of his treatise that Calvin includes in this sect not only the Evangelical Anabaptists, or Swiss Brethren (i.e., Grebel, Hubmaier, and Sattler), but also the Netherlandish Anabaptists, the Melchiorites, and possibly a few radical Revolutionaries.[77] Calvin focuses principally on the views of the Swiss Brethren and the Melchiorites in the first two divisions of the treatise.

The second sect is comprised of the Libertines and radical Spiritualists, whom Calvin prefers to reserve for rebuttal in a second treatise. Calvin is confident that these two groups will not be confused, since there are few similarities.

In his comparison of Zwingli's *Refutation of the Tricks of the Baptists* (1527) with Calvin's *Brief Instruction,* Richard Stauffer praises Calvin's introduction for having "considerable theological and historical weight." Rather than faulting the Genevan for not recognizing the kinds of classifications that are known today,

76. *CO* 7, col. 50.

77. See Calvin's refutation of article 6 in the *Brief Instruction;* Balke, *Calvijn,* p. 133. Also see Balke's list of radical groups who comprised the left wing of the Reformation (pp. 1–3).

Stauffer applauds him for distinguishing his "two sects"[78] and for "his theological perspicacity."[79]

The significance of Calvin's distinction is better grasped when his introduction is compared with Zwingli's *Refutation*.[80] The Zurich theologian, in contrast to Calvin, includes among his Anabaptists not only the Swiss Brethren, as well as Hans Denck (ca. 1500–1527), Ludwig Hetzer (ca. 1500–1529), and Jakob Kautz (1500–?),[81] but also the violent, radical Spiritualists of St. Gall.[82] However, the Zurich-St. Gall situation was far different from anything Calvin personally experienced, so he could make distinctions Zwingli could not.

As for his methodology, Calvin explains that he intends to limit this present work to "a remonstrance of the falsities contained in the greater part of these seven articles" and to examine them all, lest he be accused of "unjustly defaming" the sect. Calvin observes how difficult it is to agree with the Anabaptists insofar as their interpretation of Scripture lacks a kind of normative principle, thus permitting them to deduce conclusions that are actually contrary to Scripture. As Calvin warns, "We are commanded to test the spirits to know if they are of God."[83]

Calvin specifically singles out three doctrinal differences between himself and the Anabaptists which make their hermeneutics "repugnant" to Scripture: "free will, predestination, and the cause of our salvation." In Calvin's view they expound their texts so improperly as to complicate a true exposition. Calvin's astuteness here again earns him Stauffer's commendations, for Stauffer calls him a true "homo theologicus." "For Calvin," Stauffer observes, "the principle of *sola Scriptura* is inseparable from that of *sola gratia*."[84] After pointing out these hermeneutical hurdles, Calvin now begins to examine the *Seven Articles.*

78. Richard Stauffer, "Zwingli et Calvin, critiques de la confession de Schleitheim," in *The Origins and Characteristics of Anabaptism*, ed. Marc Lienhard (The Hague: Martinus Nijhoff, 1977), p. 129.

79. Ibid., p. 130.

80. See *In catabaptistarum strophas elenchus* in *Corpus Reformatorum* 93, cols. 1–196. For the English translation see *Refutation of the Tricks of the Baptists*, in *Ulrich Zwingli: Selected Works*, ed. Samuel Macauley Jackson (Philadelphia: University of Pennsylvania, 1972), pp. 123–258.

81. Zwingli, *Refutation*, pp. 146–148.

82. Ibid., passim.

83. *CO* 7, col. 56.

84. Stauffer, "Zwingli et Calvin," p. 145.

Part One: Refutation of the ***Seven Articles***

Although the *Seven Articles* has already been discussed, at least four matters deserve brief attention here: the mechanics of Calvin's procedure; the relationship between Zwingli's and Calvin's pieces; the ethical, practical, and normative bent of the *Articles;* and Calvin's general criteria for rejecting Anabaptist concepts.

The mechanics of Calvin's procedure are simple. In the case of the articles on baptism, the ban, the sword, and the oath, Calvin begins by quoting significant portions of the article in question from the French translation Farel had sent him. A comparison of these articles with the original German text reveals them to be adequate for Calvin's task.[85] When not quoting directly, the Reformer for the most part paraphrases accurately and avoids distortion. The articles on the breaking of bread, the separation from abomination, and shepherds in the congregation are not quoted and are only briefly treated. In part this is owing to Calvin's agreement with the Anabaptist position on the breaking of bread and shepherds in the congregation.

The relationship between Zwingli's and Calvin's refutations is intriguing. Seventeen years separate Zwingli's *In catabaptistarum strophas elenchus* (1527) and Calvin's *Brief Instruction.* The inevitable question is whether Calvin knew of Zwingli's work or had ever read it; unfortunately, we cannot determine the extent of Calvin's familiarity with Zwingli's treatise.[86]

What has most impressed Stauffer is not so much the two Reformers' similarities but their differences. This has led Stauffer to venture that Calvin worked independently of Zwingli. Stauffer's conclusion seems satisfactory:

> If his judgments frequently crosscheck with those of the Zurich Reformer's, it is simply because the Anabaptist movement had put in question a certain number of attitudes and doctrines which were central to the Reformation in its entirety. . . . Hence both emphasize that circumcision prefigures infant baptism, that pedobaptism is not an invention of the pope, that the Anabaptist exegesis of Matthew 18:17 is erroneous, that baptism as administered

85. See Balke's comparison of Calvin's French quotations with the German text of the *Articles* (*Calvijn,* pp. 192–194).

86. See Stauffer, "Zwingli et Calvin," p. 145.

> by their adversaries is a rebaptism, and that the oath is a sacred act.[87]

Moreover, Stauffer notes that whereas Calvin did concur with two of the articles (the breaking of the bread and shepherds in the congregation), Zwingli attacked them all.

Perhaps Stauffer's most incisive contribution other than his discussion of the hermeneutical issues mentioned above is his analysis of Calvin's refutation of the Anabaptists' rigorous practice of the ban. Though Zwingli's own insight is penetrating,[88] Stauffer credits Calvin with the realization that the Anabaptists had made the ban a defining characteristic of the church. This introduced a form of perfectionism that Calvin inveighed against; hence he avoided the snare of making discipline a "third mark" of the church.[89]

A third item to be noted is the ethical, practical, and normative character of the *Seven Articles.* As H. W. Meihuizen[90] has pointed out, the Anabaptist concepts that underlie the *Articles* are "decisive doctrines." The *Articles* was a document "intended to delineate how everyone who wished to be acknowledged a true Anabaptist had to conduct himself."[91] Hence the emphasis was laid on "practical consequences for life" rather than on dogmatics. Furthermore, as a creedal symbol the document unified the Evangelical Anabaptists and thus became a normative guide. It was meant to separate its adherents from those who had turned aside from the true faith, whether "false brethren" among their own ranks or the half-Reformed proponents of magisterial Protestantism.

Such an obvious threat to the Swiss Reformed movement (whether at Zurich, Neuchâtel, or Geneva) could not go unchallenged, nor did it, as Zwingli's earlier work, Farel's letters, and Calvin's response demonstrate.

Calvin's criteria for rejecting the theology of the *Seven Articles* also merit attention. In each instance, the critical issue is the hermeneutical one. With respect to infant baptism Calvin argues

87. Ibid.
88. Zwingli, *Refutation*, pp. 178–180.
89. Stauffer, "Zwingli et Calvin," p. 134.
90. H. W. Meihuizen, "Who Were the 'False Brethren' Mentioned in The Schleitheim Articles?" *Mennonite Quarterly Review* 41 (1967): 200–222.
91. Ibid., p. 201.

that the Anabaptists ignore the whole covenantal context of grace and election. They cannot see that sacramental signs precede the truth they affirm. To expect one to affirm the truth before the sign is administered is to deny the operation of grace and election as witnessed in the "perfectly clear and plain promises" of the Scripture which the Anabaptists want to allegorize.

As for the ban, at least three issues are at stake: (1) Is it essential for the proper functioning of the church? (2) Are only unintentional sins forgiven? and (3) Is banishment from the congregation the true aim of discipline? Calvin answers no, on the grounds of biblical reasons the Anabaptist hermeneutic does not permit.

Calvin's arguments are forceful and flow out of a profound biblical and theological astuteness. He accuses the Anabaptists of being "poor theologians," of ignoring the consequences of their own doctrines and therefore becoming "more severe than God" Himself, and of making "men and their morals" their theological norm rather than God. One can sense Calvin's deep indebtedness to Augustine's doctrine of man, to his opposition to the Donatists, to his theory of the two cities. and to his emphasis on the "invisible" nature of the church.

The Anabaptist attempt to separate from pollutions is "diabolical" and smacks of "blasphemy." The sword is God-ordained. To deny it is to contravene God. Not "to resist unjust violence" is evil itself.

Calvin's tone stiffens with the article on "Magistrates." The Genevan Reformer draws upon all his theological acumen. Again he faults the Anabaptists for an inconsistent biblical hermeneutic that permits them to praise "cobblers" while demeaning "princes," whereas the Bible nowhere legitimates cobblers but everywhere (Old and New Testaments) extols "kings" and "governors" and dignifies their high office. To profane what God has made holy by denying Christians the right to become magistrates is not simply naive theology but is detrimental to the very task of theology itself. Calvin condemns such a radical separation of the church and the state on the grounds that it will result in the secularization of the state and the eventual irrelevance of the church. Besides, sinful men (both Christians and otherwise) need the state and its order and opportunities for litigation, just as the state needs Christian magistrates to preserve true religion and faithfully exercise the office of the sword.

Moreover, to use the ban as the Anabaptists wish is to turn it into a form of punishment rather than a means of grace. Christ came to forgive sin. The state exists to punish sin. But the Anabaptist use of the ban makes Christ the punisher.

Calvin's refutation pulses with his strong sense of the unity of God's purposes and will throughout Scripture. Thus the New Testament does not so much introduce a "greater perfection" as a "restoration" of original divine intention. Hence the moral law of the Old Testament retains its normative function. Calvin's insight into this matter leads him to conclude that these "miserable fanatics" and "enemies of government" are guilty of "poor exposition."

Finally, Calvin states his objections to their rejection of the oath. He finds the Anabaptists "too hasty," faults them for failing to discern the "good" aspects of the oath, and discredits their exegesis of Matthew 5:33–37 on the grounds that they neglect the "occasion" that underlies the text, pointing out that the apostles also called upon God as their witness. The Genevan suggests that one should never condemn anything that "checks abuse," and charges that by rejecting the oath the Anabaptists are actually evading their moral accountability to the society to which they inescapably belong.

Something of Calvin's appraisal of his opponents is tellingly revealed in his pejorative epithets. Consider this list: "fanatics," "ignorant," "deluded," "poor dreamers," "poor fools," "foolish men," "scatterbrains," "without reason," "unreasonable," "insane," "harebrained," "obstinate," "poor ignoramuses." He shows no respect for their lack of intellectual acumen. Calvin realizes that the task of theology requires more than an ability to cite texts. It demands understanding, knowledge, insight, reason, an ability to think through a doctrine's consequences, an awareness of moral ramifications, and above all a devotion to the pure and plain Word of God in its true and natural sense.

If Calvin's epithets seem uncharitable, one ought to note that he refrains from calling them "heretics," "blasphemers," "scoundrels," "wretches," "mad dogs," or "asses," as he will call the Libertines.

How fairly does Calvin treat the Anabaptists? Balke, in a brief preface to the second edition of *Calvijn en de doperse Radikalen,* cites the following evaluation from an unpublished study in the Mennonite Historical Library at Goshen College, Indiana: "In Calvin's writings he deals with the Anabaptists in an exceptionally fair manner for his times. In the chief point of disagreement, the nature of the church, his criticisms go to the heart of the matter. So, though he certainly wastes no love on the Anabaptists, one must conclude that he is fair and adequate in his writings against them."[92]

Other authors are more favorable to the Anabaptists. Hans J. Hillerbrand in his "Anabaptist View of the State"[93] attempts to correct Lutheran and Zwinglian misconceptions. Hillerbrand does not mention Calvin, but he rejects the supposition that the Anabaptist position represents some "incidental byproduct of a Biblical naiveté which is not aware of the complexities of social life."[94] He also denies that the *Articles* implies that the ban is an attempt at perfectionism.[95]

Hillerbrand lists four reasons for the Anabaptists' rejection of office holding: (1) "There is in the Scripture no evidence for a true Christian's participation in government"; (2) "The example of Christ himself speaks against participation"; (3) "The command of Christ is plain in its rejection of participation in government office," the *locus classicus* being Matthew 20:25–27; and (4) "Anabaptist arguments against participation in government focused on the radical distinction between the church of Christ and the world."[96]

As for the state, Hillerbrand notes that the Anabaptists have always recognized that it is ordained of God to punish evildoers and to protect the law-abiding. Hence "the notion of rebellion or revolution must therefore have been utterly foreign to the Anabaptist mind."[97] With respect to the state substantial discrepancies appear between the Anabaptists and the Reformers only in the area of the limitations of government and religious liberty. Hillerbrand acknowledges, however, that "Anabaptist

92. Lois Beachy, "John Calvin's Writings against the Anabaptists," Thes. Goshen College 1956, pp. 38–39.

93. Hans J. Hillerbrand, "The Anabaptist View of the State," *Mennonite Quarterly Review* 32 (1958): 83–110.

94. Ibid., p. 108.

95. Ibid., p. 99.

96. Ibid., pp. 95–97.

97. Ibid., p. 87.

thinking does not attempt a synthesis" of its rejection of office holding with its recognition of the state's divine institution. Hence, he admits that "a basic paradox remains unanswered in Anabaptist thinking"—the very paradox which Calvin probes.

Hillerbrand further explains that the Anabaptist view of the state is based on both a "New Testament monism" and a sharp dualism between the kingdom of Christ and the "world." But then these are inseparable characteristics of the "Anabaptist Vision."[98]

Part Two: Rebuttal of the Melchiorites

Calvin's second major division focuses on the Melchiorite "celestial flesh" theory of Christ's incarnation. Melchior Hofmann's views were transmitted to Dutch Anabaptism by Obbe Philips (ca. 1500–1568)[99] and rearticulated by Menno Simons (1496–1561) in his *Brief and Clear Confession* (1544).[100] It is highly unlikely that Calvin knew of Menno's views in 1544, for only in 1545 did Calvin become apprised of Menno's Christology. Albert Hardenberg of Bremen in that year sent Calvin a copy of John à Lasco's tract against Menno's work.[101] Later Calvin would also learn of Menno's views through correspondence with Martin Micron and John à Lasco himself.[102] Calvin's *Institutes* of 1559 contains a section directed against Menno's views. (References to Menno's work which may illuminate Calvin's objections to the Melchiorite position have been included in the footnotes to Chapter 5 of the *Brief Instruction.*)

One additionally notes in this second division Calvin's puzzlement as to why the *Articles* fail to mention the celestial-flesh theory. It is obvious Calvin is unaware of the distinction between the Swiss Brethren and the Netherlandish and Melchiorite Anabaptists whom he had come to know firsthand in Geneva and Strassburg, as the celestial-flesh theory is not a tenet of the Swiss Brethren.

98. Ibid., pp. 100–101, 109.

99. See "Philips, Obbe," *Mennonite Encyclopedia,* vol. 4, pp. 9–11.

100. See *The Complete Writings of Menno Simons,* trans. Leonard Verduin, ed. John C. Wenger (Scottdale, Pa.: Herald, 1956), pp. 427–440.

101. Hardenberg to Calvin, March 24, 1545—*CO* 12, cols. 49ff.

102. à Lasco to Calvin, March 13, 1554—*CO* 15, cols. 82f.; Micron to Calvin, February 28, 1558—*CO* 17, col. 68. See also Balke, *Calvijn,* pp. 205–211.

Part Three: A New Version of the ***Psychopannychia***

Calvin's final division is a rather free and less technical version in French of his earlier *Psychopannychia.* Calvin apparently added it to his refutations in response to Farel's request.[103] Although it is less technical than the earlier version, it is nonetheless a thoughtfully presented work in which Calvin (1) explores the variety of ways the word *soul* is used in Scripture, (2) demonstrates that souls "have a proper substance," and (3) argues that souls are awake after death, that "souls sense and recognize their condition and state."

As previously indicated, the Mennonite historian Christian Neff denies that "the sleep of the soul" was ever a doctrine espoused by Anabaptists or Mennonites anywhere.[104] Perhaps this is true of Sattler's group and of the German-speaking Evangelical Anabaptists, but reference to this doctrine in *Les Chroniques de Metz,* its appearance at Cornaux, and Farel's conviction that Calvin's translation of the *Psychopannychia* would aid in the struggle at Neuchâtel suggest that historians should continue to study this problem.

Much can be said of this section. In addition to its orderly structure it is marked by a unique clarity, simplicity, and singleness of purpose. Calvin's somewhat philosophical approach is also of interest. He seems concerned with both demonstrating that his two a priori premises (i.e., that souls have a proper substance and are sentient after death) are biblically rooted and exploring the Scriptures to deduce from them a theological position.

Heinrich Quistorp has accused Calvin of developing a "doctrine of the soul which is more philosophical than theological and which does not accord with Biblical anthropology."[105] He charges Calvin with too hastily identifying the mortal body with sinful flesh,[106] with using "spirit" and "soul" too loosely and interchangeably,[107] disesteeming the body altogether,[108] literally

103. Farel to Calvin, February 23, 1544—Herminjard, *Correspondances,* vol. 9, pp. 174f., no. 1332.

104. See Neff, "Sleep of the Soul," *Mennonite Encyclopedia,* vol. 4, p. 543.

105. Heinrich Quistorp, *Calvin's Doctrine of the Last Things,* trans. Harold Knight (London: Lutterworth, 1955), p. 73.

106. Ibid., p. 57.

107. Ibid., p. 58.

108. Ibid., p. 60.

making the soul into a substance independent of the body with a life and being of its own,[109] and hence giving it immortal status, a conclusion Quistorp suggests is not biblical.[110]

As for the state of the soul after death, Quistorp finds Calvin's view ultimately contradictory.[111] For though the soul will be at rest, yet it will experience a form of "progressive glorification," enjoying both a peace of conscience and an awareness of God.[112] And while the soul "waits," it "anticipates" reunion with its body and its "glory" with Christ.[113] Quistorp commends this latter view, however, noting that the "glory" of the Christian will not be disclosed apart from the "glory" of Christ.[114]

Quistorp observes Calvin's dependence on the early Fathers for his principal views and regrets that in this case the Reformer did not subject them to as thorough a scrutiny as he did in other matters.[115] Quistorp also comments on Calvin's "horror of fanatical excesses" and thinks this horror made him too cautious in his eschatology.[116] As a result, Calvin tends to minimize the imminent, spiritualize the apocalyptic, and subordinate the eschatological to the ethical.[117] Although Quistorp acknowledges that he prefers Luther's position to Calvin's,[118] this bias does not detract from the force of his criticisms.

In Calvin's defense, however, it can be argued that his concept of the "soul" is rooted in his understanding of the "image of God"; because God is "immortal," man's "soul" is certainly more than a "transient phenomenon."[119] It can also be said that Calvin balances any overemphasis on the "immortality of the soul"—his Platonic heritage—with a strong emphasis on the resurrection—his biblical position.[120] Perhaps Calvin was seeking a synthesis of

109. Ibid., pp. 62, 68.
110. Ibid., p. 73.
111. Ibid., pp. 81–82.
112. Ibid., pp. 84ff.
113. Ibid., p. 90.
114. Ibid.
115. Ibid., p. 91.
116. Ibid., pp. 109, 113, 123.
117. Ibid., pp. 110, 123, 125.
118. Ibid., pp. 97ff., 101.
119. *CO* 7, col. 112.
120. Ibid., col. 114.

the best philosophical (Platonic), theological (patristic), and biblical positions he had mastered as a young humanist (keep in mind that this piece was first drafted in 1534).

Calvin concludes his treatise with a disparaging remark about a "certain Michael" and his martyrdom, in which he echoes Farel's harsh view of Sattler's death.[121] This seems to strengthen the idea that Calvin did not know who Michael Sattler was, although he had come to know a great deal about Anabaptist positions.

121. See Farel's letter to Calvin, February 23, 1544—Herminjard, *Correspondances,* vol. 9, pp. 173f., no. 1332.

Preface

John Calvin to the Ministers[1] *of the Churches in the Canton of Neuchâtel*

If anyone wonders, my dear brothers and companions in the work of the Lord, why I am bothering[2] to reply to a book worthy of neither attention or comment, seeing I am capable of employing myself, one would think, in better and more productive ways, it should be sufficient, as my excuse, to explain[3] that I have done so at the request and insistence of several good faithful men,[4] who sent me the book from some distance,[5] with the request[6] that it would be extremely beneficial for the welfare of many poor souls if I should do so. For I certainly think[7] that such ought to satisfy those who want a reasonable explanation as to why I have acceded to both the judgment and wishes of those whom I know to be zealous for the glory of God and the edification of His people.

Still, I have another reason, as an answer, with regard to those who might want to think that it is folly for me to occupy myself with anything as meager and frivolous as this booklet, which appears to have been composed by ignorant persons,[8] and that

1. Note in *CO* 7, col. 49: "ministris et pastoribus."

2. *m'amuse* = *occupe à des choses vaines.*

3. *d'alléguer.*

4. Notably Farel and his colleagues at Neuchâtel. See Farel's letter to Calvin, February 23, 1544—Herminjard, *Correspondances,* vol. 9, pp. 172ff., no. 1332.

5. Neuchâtel.

6. *tesmoignage.*

7. *pense bien.*

8. Cf. Zwingli's charge that the central Anabaptist leaders are "thoroughly ignorant," "unskilled," "endowed . . . with untaught audacity" (*Refutation,* p. 126;

is, that we do not have any greater privilege than the prophets of God had and that our pain is no more precious than theirs. For we know that Ezekiel (13:17) was constrained to speak and to write not only against ignorant seducers and persons of no reputation, but also against women who wanted to become prophetesses. Seeing that the prophet did not spare himself disputes against women, and indeed was commanded so to do by our Lord, inasmuch as by their lies they were leading the people into superstition and error and were impeding the course of truth, it would be presumptuous of us not to be willing to undertake the same.

It is true that this book, which I have been asked and exhorted to condemn, contains nothing beneficial for persons of learning and understanding, seeing that, in addition to being inept and haphazardly written, it sufficiently discredits itself.[9] But inasmuch as it does have the capacity[10] to deceive and misguide the simple, who lack the judgment to discern, our wish is to help them and to warn them against the ruses[11] of Satan, that they may not be seduced by imprudence. "We are debtors one to another," says Saint Paul (Rom. 1:14). Therefore we must be of service to all, as much as we possibly can, whenever necessity requires it. I confess, therefore, that my sole intention is to point out briefly to all the poor faithful, who are uncultured and without letters, the nature and poisonous character of the doctrine of the Anabaptists, and to arm them with the Word of God against the same, in order that they might not be entrapped by it, or if there might be any who are already enveloped in their snares, to guide them back to the right road.

Therefore I entreat all who have the desire to continue in the pure knowledge of Jesus Christ and in the obedience of His gospel to have the patience to read attentively this present

---

Corpus Reformatorum 93, col. 23). F. H. Littell corrects this view: "Although the best-educated leadership was martyred during the first years, the early leaders—Grebel, Hubmaier, Denck, Hetzer—were men of marked accomplishment in the university world, a world inspired by the new Humanistic studies" (*Origins*, p. 61). Calvin himself later acknowledges in the closing pages of this treatise that the framers of the *Seven Articles* represent "the most intelligent and sober" scholars among them.

9. *se redargue = se blâme.*

10. *a quelque couleur.*

11. *cauteles = ruses.*

booklet, as if it were dedicated to them from me, and to take the trouble to give serious thought[12] to the reasons that I shall cite for them, in order to stop at the truth when it has been declared.

The reasons that have prompted me to address this present tract to you are twofold. First, I do so in order that it might serve as a public testimony to the union that I have and desire always to have with you, and that all might know how we are united in doctrine as in affection of heart. Secondly, I do so in order that the reading of it might better be recommended to all to whom you have the obligation of bringing the word of Jesus Christ, to the extent that the churches, which the Prince of Pastors has commissioned to you as ministers, might continue in pure doctrine and be preserved from all perverse opinions that are contrary to the truth of the holy gospel.

It is true that you, my dear brothers, might easily have discharged me of this task. And even now our brother, Master William Farel,[13] according to the grace he has received from the Lord, which he has put to continual use for a long time now, has fought against all the enemies of truth and resisted all false doctrines in order to maintain the reign of Jesus Christ. Even he has ably fulfilled in part what you require of me, as I have seen from the acts of a conference held at the good town.[14] In fact, with regard to the articles that are treated therein, no one could ask for a clearer explanation[15] for resolving his conscience than what is provided there. But because those to whom I desire and hold myself to be obedient make me believe that it is necessary for me to accept this charge, I acquiesce in their request, without offering further excuses.

May the Lord ever hold you, and His churches to which He has commissioned you, in His holy protection. May He always guide you by His Holy Spirit that by means of your ministry you might serve Him to His honor as well as to the salvation of His poor people.

From Geneva. The first of June, 1544.

12. *bien poiser = bien examiner.*

13. Calvin's former associate at Geneva, now at Neuchâtel.

14. A reference to Farel's colloquy with the Anabaptists at La Neuveville (Bonneville), held sometime in April or May of 1544. Note in *CO* 7, col. 52: "Bonneville (Neuenstadt) is a borough of the canton of Bern located on the left bank of the Lake of Bienne."

15. *declaration = explication.*

Introduction

Brief Instruction for Arming All the Good Faithful Against the Errors of the Common Sect of the Anabaptists

To write against all the false opinions and errors of the Anabaptists would involve me in too long a matter and would result in an abyss from which I would never come out. For these vermin differ from all other heretical sects in that they not only err in certain points, but they give rise to a whole sea of insane views. So much so that one will scarcely find an Anabaptist who is not tainted with fantasy. Therefore, to examine minutely, or even recount, all the corrupt doctrines of the sect could never be done. But in the end, all belong to two principal sects.[1]

The first,[2] although it is full of many perverse and pernicious errors, falls within the bounds of a greater simplicity. For at least this sect receives the holy Scripture, as do we. And if we dispute with its members, we can perceive in what we differ from them and the meaning they give to their conceptions. In sum, we can see where we agree with them and where controversy remains.

The second[3] is a labyrinth, without parallel, of so many

1. See Stauffer's comparison of Zwingli's *Refutation* with Calvin's *Brief Instruction*. Stauffer notes that whereas Zwingli includes the radical Spiritualists of St. Gall as well as Hans Denck (ca. 1500–1527), Ludwig Hetzer (ca. 1500–1529), and Jakob Kautz (1500–?) among the Anabaptists of Sattler's group, Calvin is more selective and discerns two distinct groups ("Zwingli et Calvin," pp. 129f.).

2. This is Michael Sattler's group, the Swiss Anabaptists or, in Williams's typology, "Evangelical Anabaptists."

3. A reference to the Libertines (Quintin and Pocquet), perhaps the Spiritualists of St. Gall, and even "Revolutionary Anabaptists."

absurd views that it is a marvel how creatures who bear the human figure can be so void of sense and reason as to be so duped and fall victim to such brutish fantasies. This sect is called the Libertines.[4] And they so imitate the Spirituals that they no more esteem the holy Word of God than they do fables, except when it suits them and when they can change[5] it by force to serve their diabolic opinions. Besides, they mumble a jargon, somewhat in the way that wandering mendicants[6] do, which no one can interpret nor they themselves understand, unless they intend by such a device to cover up the turpitude of their doctrine. Because their intentions are to confuse any difference between good and evil, so to mix the Deity and the devil[7] that one cannot discern between the two, and to make men appear not only stupid before God and their consciences but also as an affront before the world. Thus, that is why they hide in their caverns of obscure and uncertain words, lest we should discover their villainy and hold them in horror and execration. As in fact our human nature does find repugnant such monstrosities as they maintain.

Therefore, in sum, to write against the errors of the Anabaptists, the shortest and most expedient way is to adhere to this division and to single out in one tract the errors of those who are not entirely mad and desperate and in a second treatise to uncover the venomous malice of those wretches who under the guise of spirituality want to turn men into brute beasts.

Now it is quite true that those who belong to the first sect are not in such accord with each other that one can easily produce a collection[8] of their errors for the purpose of condemning them

4. See n. 3 above.

5. *depraver* = *altérer.*

6. *ilz ont un gergon, comme gueux de l'hostiere.* Cotgrave lists the following for *gueux d'hostiere:* "such as beg from door to door." The *Corpus Reformatorum* editors provide this footnote: "They by the way have a peculiar way of preaching (whom because of their custom we call in French *Guei Hostiariae*)," *CO* 7, col. 53, n. 1. See the *Corpus Reformatorum* editors' elaboration on this term in *CO* 7, col. 168, n. 2, where they explain that the group originated in Bohemia. It is possible that the term is a reference to the Hutterite "wanderers" of Moravia. See F. H. Littell, *Origins,* pp. 119ff. See also "Hutter, Jakob," *Mennonite Encyclo pedia,* vol. 2, pp. 851–854.

7. *Dieu avec le Diable.* The use of *gergon* and *gueux* (see n. 6 above) along with *Dieu* and *Diable* reveals Calvin at his alliterative, if not sarcastic, best.

8. *recueil* = *rassemblement* or *réunion.*

in any order. But because the principal doctors, and as it were the patriarchs of the whole synagogue, after having patched up [their differences], have made a final statement in which they have enclosed a summary of what they maintain in opposition to us as well as the papists—a summary in *Seven Articles*[9] to which all Anabaptists commonly adhere—and also because they have found a means for publishing this lovely[10] resolution which they have taken together for the purpose of sowing their poison everywhere and infecting the poor people, I shall content myself for the present, confident such is sufficient, with a remonstrance of the falsities contained in the greater part of this *Seven Articles*, in order that they cannot complain that I lay against them all the fault of several parts and thereby unjustly defame the entire sect. That done, if I have some spare time, I shall write another little treatise against the second group of which I spoke, namely, the Libertines.[11]

But as I have said, it will suffice for the present to demonstrate to all lovers of truth that what these poor people maintain with common accord as the invincible foundation of their faith is a mortal error[12] as deadly as the plague. That is my advice[13] to all who want to be obedient to the truth.

For there are a few of this beggarly gang, and principally those who wish to imitate the doctors, who, being preoccupied with pride and presumption, are unable to make out anything that anyone says to them. Or rather through obstinacy and malice, they deliberately close their eyes in order not to see the light, though it is presented to them in complete clarity. So much so that one strives in vain[14] to proceed with them by reason to

9. For the first time Calvin identifies the Anabaptist document he intends to refute: *The Schleitheim Confession*, or the *Seven Articles*. He does not, however, identify the document or the articles as a title; he simply refers to them as "seven articles."

10. *belle.*

11. See the second half of this present volume. The *Corpus Reformatorum* editors supply the following footnote: "Here one reads on the margin of the 1545 edition these printed words: *Such was done.* The chronological order of these three publications is found, therefore, to be established in an authentic manner. The first edition of the *Treatise Against the Libertines* is placed between the two editions of the *Treatise Against the Anabaptists*" (*CO* 7, col. 55, n. 1).

12. *abusion = erreur.*

13. *ie dy.*

14. *battre l'eaue = s'efforce en vain.*

get them to turn about, except that some small profit is gained when the good recognize their desperate impudence and extricate themselves and flee from them as from poison.

Now inasmuch as there is no fairer guise for seducing poor Christians, who are zealous to follow God, than to quote[15] God's Word, the Anabaptists, against whom we are currently writing, always preface their remarks by this pretext.[16] And certainly when anyone says to us that it is God who speaks, all creatures ought to be moved, out of reverence for His name, to listen in humility to what is said. When we understand that it is truly the Word of God that we are hearing, then a rejoinder is out of the question, as well as opening our mouth, in order to dispute to the contrary. We do not say as the papists that it is necessary to subsume the holy Scripture under the authority of men. For we consider that subterfuge an execrable blasphemy. But we grant that everything that appears to have come from God and derives from His holy Word ought to be received by us all, humbly and without any controversy or difficulty.

Furthermore, we do not believe that any other doctrine should be recognized as true and certain unless it comes from this fountain of all truth. Therefore, whether Anabaptists or others say to us that what they declare they have received from God and taken from His mouth, let us give this glory to God and modestly understand and listen to see if such is the case.

But as it is our duty to listen carefully to what is said to us until we have understood it, so also we must be prudent and discern between the truth and falsehood and judge whether what is alleged to be the Word of God is so or falsely taught. For we are commanded to test the spirits to know if they are of God (I John 4:1). And in fact, we see how necessary this is, knowing that even the devil has armed himself with the Word of God and has used it as a sword to assail our Lord Jesus (Matt. 4:6). And we know from experience that he daily makes use of this means through his instruments to overturn[17] the truth in order to lead poor souls into perdition.

With regard to these poor fantastic ones who thus pride themselves that God's Word is on their side, facts reveal the

15. *pretendre.*
16. *ont tousiours ceste preface en la bouche.*
17. *depraver = dètourner du vrai sens.*

actual case. For a long time now we have labored continually [to support] that the holy Word should be returned to a place of preeminence, and we have undertaken a battle against all the world to achieve this. But they, what have they done to advance this, or in what way have they helped?[18] Rather, to the contrary, they have impeded and troubled[19] us, to such an extent that one cannot say wherein they have profited, unless it lies in deferring to that Word once it had been advanced by us. Moreover, on several principal points of Christianity, they agree closely[20] with the papists, holding a view directly repugnant to all the holy Scripture—as with free will, predestination, and the cause of our salvation. It is, therefore, with deception that they abuse this pretext, making the simple believe that they wish to be governed totally according to the Scripture. For they do not hold to it whatsoever, but only to the fantasy of their brain.

Now let us come to the first article of the seven, contained in their absurd beautiful resolution, which they hold as revelation descended from heaven.

18. Note in *CO* 7, col. 56, n. 2: "have they helped us, 1566 [edition]."
19. *destourbez = déranger.*
20. *ilz s'accordent tresbien.*

1

The First Article
On Baptism[1]

Baptism ought to be given to those who have been instructed in repentance, who believe that their sins have been blotted out by Jesus Christ, and who want to walk in His resurrection. Consequently it ought to be administered to those who request it for themselves, not for infants, as is done in the pope's kingdom.[2]

Refutation[3]

That is what they say. But I reply, first of all, that infant baptism is not a recent introduction, nor are its origins traceable to the papal church. For I say that it has always been a holy ordinance

1. Note in *CO* 7, col. 56: "In the French editions of 1566 and afterwards, one reads: *Article I. On Baptism.*" See Calvin's discussion of infant baptism in the *Institutes* 4.16.1–32. As John T. McNeill points out, a considerable segment of the chapter (sects. 17–23) is devoted to refuting Hubmaier's *Concerning the Christian Baptism of Believers.* (For the English translation see William R. Estep, Jr., *Anabaptist Beginnings: 1523–1533, A Source Book,* pp. 65–98.) The chapter also contains references to *The Schleitheim Confession* and the views of Melchior Hofmann and Conrad Grebel. See the *Institutes,* vol. 21 of the Library of Christian Classics, pp. 1324–1359, nn. 1–2, 22, 30–36, 38, 40, 44, 48. For further sources in English see Williams and Mergal, *Anabaptist Writers,* pp. 73–85, 114–135. Almost all of Calvin's chapter on infant baptism appeared as early as the 1539 edition. Calvin at the close of this article refers to his *Institutes* (4.16).

2. Cf. *The Schleitheim Confession,* article 1—Yoder, *Sattler,* p. 36.

3. Note in *CO* 7, col. 57: "This rubric: *Refutation,* is not found in the 1544 and 1545 editions." Compare Zwingli's reply to this article in *Refutation,* pp. 178–80; *Corpus Reformatorum* 93, cols. 108–111. Zwingli charges that the denial of baptism to infants and the emphasis on believer's baptism is a form of "justification by works," an elevation of "free will," and a rejection of the Old Testament as authoritative canon. See also Stauffer, "Zwingli et Calvin," p. 131.

observed[4] in the Christian church. There is no doctor, however ancient, who does not attest that it has always been observed since the time of the apostles.

I wanted to touch on this point in passing for the sole reason of informing the simple that it is an impudent slander for these fanatics to make others believe that this ancient practice is a recently forged superstition and to feign that it derives from the pope. For the whole church held to infant baptism long before one ever knew about the papacy or had ever heard of the pope.

Besides, I do not ask antiquity to legitimate[5] anything for us unless it is founded on the Word of God. I know that it is not human custom that gives authority to the sacrament, nor does its efficacy depend on how men regulate it. Let us come, therefore, to the true rule of God, of which we have spoken, that is to say, His Word, which alone ought to hold here.

Their view is that one ought to administer baptism only to those who request it, to those who have made a profession of faith and repented. And thus infant baptism is the invention[6] of men, opposed to the Word of God.

In order to prove this they cite the passage from Saint Matthew's last chapter (28:19), where Jesus Christ says to His apostles, "Go and teach all nations, baptizing them in the name of the Father, and of the Son, and of the Holy Spirit."[7] To which they add this sentence from the sixteenth chapter of Saint Mark (v. 16): "Whoever believes and is baptized will be saved."[8] That to them seems an invincible foundation.

In response I say that baptism is mentioned only incidentally in these texts. For it is put there as an accessory to the preaching of the gospel. Our Lord Jesus sends His apostles out to preach to

4. *gardée.*

5. *approuver = légitimer.*

6. *est controuvé = est imaginé, inventé.*

7. See the *Institutes* 4.16.27 where Calvin earlier (in the 1539 edition) cited this same passage and objection, possibly countering Grebel as well as Hubmaier. See the *Institutes,* vol. 21, LCC, p. 1350, no. 48. See Grebel's letter to Joachim Vadianus, September 3, 1524, in Estep, *Anabaptist Beginnings,* p. 28. Hubmaier especially emphasizes Matthew 28:19 and Mark 16:16. See *Christian Baptism,* in *Anabaptist Beginnings,* pp. 72–76, 78, 81–83, 87. Hubmaier argues that before a Christian can be baptized he must be instructed and that baptism cannot replace that instruction. He argues (p. 87) that the apostolic order was, "First, Word; Second, Hearing; Third, Faith; Fourth, Baptism; Fifth, Works."

8. *Institutes* 4.16.27.

and to teach the world; then He adds baptism as a confirmation of their teaching.[9] Now it is necessary to note that by this means instruction[10] must precede this sacrament, which is added to it for the purpose of sealing it. And we accept this. But one should understand how.

Now these poor fanatics go astray in not considering the means.[11] For whenever a man, outside the Christian church, whether he is a Turk, Jew, or any kind of pagan, becomes a Christian, it is not a question of beginning with his baptism, but before he is baptized, he needs to be instructed.[12] And such was the approach of the early church. For those who converted to Christianity received, for a long time, their preaching apart, which was called catechizing. Then, after they had witnessed to their faith and repented, they were baptized.

Reason dictates as much.[13] For seeing that man is not only brought into the fellowship of the church by baptism, but also has his attestation sealed there, God acknowledging him as one of His children, there can be no doubt about instruction[14] preceding it. For by it man is taught that he needs to convert to God with faith and repentance.

We see that our Lord acted the same way toward Abraham with regard to circumcision. For before He conferred this sign on him, He received him into His covenant and instructed him in His Word.

But we must now note that when a man is received of God into the fellowship of the faithful, the promise of salvation which is given to him is not for him alone but also for his children. For it is said to him: "I am thy God, and the God of thy children after thee" (Gen. 17:7).[15] Therefore the man who has not been received into the covenant of God from his childhood is as a stranger to

9. *la doctrine.*

10. See the *Institutes* 4.16.2.

11. That is, in not considering how baptism ought to be administered.

12. See the *Institutes* 4.16.27 where Calvin rejects the supposition that children cannot receive baptism until they are instructed. Grebel had argued this point; see the *Institutes,* vol. 21, LCC, p. 1350, n. 48; also Grebel's letter to Thomas Müntzer, Sept. 5, 1524, in *Anabaptist Beginnings,* p. 36. See Hubmaier's argument against pedobaptism (*Christian Baptism,* in *Anabaptist Beginnings,* pp. 71, 73–76). Also see n. 7 above.

13. *la raison le veut ainsi.*

14. *la doctrine.*

15. See the *Institutes* 4.16.3, 12, 24, where Calvin elaborates on this text.

the church until such time as he is led into faith and repentance by the doctrine of salvation. But at that same time[16] his posterity[17] is also made part of the family of the church. And for this reason infants of believers are baptized by virtue of this covenant, made with their fathers in their name and to their benefit. Herein, thus, lies the mistake of the poor Anabaptists. For since this doctrine[18] must precede the sacrament, we do not resist it.

But the whole matter, as we have said, is to consider how [this ought to be done] and by what means. For when it is a question of baptizing a man of age, who has not been a Christian, then before such can be done, he must be taught what baptism means. But with respect to his children, they are baptized under the doctrine which he has received, which holds that God is not only his personal Savior but also the Savior of his children.

Still, in order to understand it more clearly: when a man has been outside the fellowship of believers and is converted to our Lord, the doctrine under which he is baptized is addressed to him. Therefore he is expected to understand and comprehend it before he receives the sacrament.

The doctrine, on the basis of which the children of Christians are baptized, is not addressed to them but to their parents and to all the church. Thus it is not required of them to understand the sacrament before they receive the sign.

Consequently, when one resorts to the argument, "Our Lord commanded His apostles to preach before they baptized and said that whoever believes and is baptized shall be saved," it thus follows that no one can be admitted to the sacrament of baptism who does not already believe.[19] But such is a very bad conclusion. For it is a well-known fact that our Lord speaks in these passages only of persons who are capable of being taught and who at the time are not members of the Christian church. If we disregard this consideration, then we will misinterpret[20] many texts and be confused in expounding them.

It is written that whoever does not work shall not eat (II Thess.

16. *quant et quant = en même temps.*
17. *sa semence = postérité.*
18. *la doctrine.* The doctrine here is that the promise of salvation given to parents also includes their children.
19. See nn. 7, 8, 12 above.
20. *confondrons.*

3:10).[21] But no one would be so cruel as to condemn infants to starvation. For anyone can clearly see that the apostle did not have them in mind but was speaking solely of those who are strong and have the capacity to work.

Seeing then that in these passages[22] our Lord makes special mention of those who can be taught, and who at the time have not become His disciples, it is entirely misleading and a perversion to apply them to the children of Christians who lack the capacity to understand,[23] and yet are included in the covenant God made with their fathers by which they became part of the family[24] of the church.

These poor fanatics cite the usage and practice of the apostles.[25] It is written in Acts 2:37 that after hearing the sermon of Saint Peter, four thousand men of Jerusalem, being touched in their hearts, asked what they should do. And Peter answered them, "Repent and believe in the gospel." Again, when the eunuch asked to be baptized, Philip replied that he could, provided he believed with all his heart (Acts 8:37). From this they conclude that the apostles required faith and repentance from men before they could be baptized.[26]

I grant this of men who must be received anew into the fellowship of the Christian church, but of children who belong to the church[27] before they depart their mother's womb, a different reason applies. For their fathers and forefathers received the promise upon which their baptism is founded.

Thus it was necessary for the inhabitants of Jerusalem, who were outside the Christian church and who had consented to the death of our Lord, to have true repentance before receiving testimony through baptism that the Lord Jesus accepted them into the number of the faithful. It was necessary that the eunuch,

21. See the *Institutes* 4.16.29 where Calvin uses this text in the same way.

22. See the *Institutes* 4.16.28 where Calvin elaborates on Mark 16:16 and the problem at hand.

23. *ouyr.* See Hubmaier, *Christian Baptism,* in *Anabaptist Beginnings,* pp. 75–77 and passim.

24. *domestiques.*

25. A reference to an unquoted portion of *The Schleitheim Confession,* article 1—Yoder, *Sattler,* p. 36. Yoder identifies the apostolic witness to which the *Confession* referred as Matthew 21:19; Mark 16:16; Acts 2:38; 16:31–33; 19:4 (p. 50, n. 46).

26. See Calvin's similar argument in the *Institutes* 4.16.23.

27. *qui en sont.*

through true faith, become part of the flock of Christ before he was capable of carrying His mark.

But since this promise is made to every faithful believer: "I am the God of your descendants"[28] (Gen. 17:7), his children have another privilege: that God recognizes them as His own, because of their fathers. And lest one think I am making this up in my mind, our Lord demonstrated it for us in the example of Isaac (Gen. 21:12).

It is true as we have said that before giving the sign of circumcision to Abraham, God instructed him in the doctrine of faith and repentance. But once He received him into His church, He decreed that his descendants were participants of the same benefit. And thus Isaac and all the other successors were circumcised at infancy.

Thus God is the author of this difference, upon which depends all the difficulty of this question.

But because they will not accept this similitude that we acknowledge[29] between circumcision and baptism,[30] it will be expedient, before proceeding further, to demonstrate that the two are the same. When anyone wants to talk about a sacrament, it should be observed that all the substance and property should be assessed from the doctrine of which the sacrament is a confirmation. Let us, therefore, note that the doctrine is principal; the sacrament is accessory. Let us now compare baptism with circumcision.[31]

Baptism entails repentance, or the renewing of life, with the promise of the remission of our sins. Circumcision entails the same, no more, no less. That this is true, regarding repentance, mention is often made of it, whether in Moses or the prophets, wherever the "circumcision of hearts" is spoken of. For this is what the New Testament calls "mortifying the old man" (Rom. 6:6; Eph. 4:22). In sum, circumcision carries the same spiritual worth as repentance. With regard to the second part, that is, the remission of sins, one could not ask for a clearer proof[32] than the text in Saint Paul where he says that circumcision was given

28. *lignée.* See Calvin's elaboration on this text in the *Institutes* 4.16.3, 12, 24.

29. *amenons = citons.*

30. See Hubmaier, *Christian Baptism,* in *Anabaptist Beginnings,* pp. 81f. See also the *Institutes* 4.16.10–16 where Calvin debates this point with the Anabaptists.

31. See Calvin's development of this comparison in the *Institutes* 4.16.10–16.

32. *approbation = preuve.*

to Abraham in order to confirm him in the free grace[33] which he had obtained by faith (Rom. 4:11).

Now, therefore, if anyone argues that it is contrary to reason to baptize infants who are without faith or repentance, seeing that baptism is the sacrament of regeneration and spiritual cleansing which we have in Jesus Christ, I reply that the same thing could be said about circumcision. And nevertheless, God did not fail to command little children to be circumcised. Consequently, one argues against God to maintain that this position contravenes reason, or that a sacrament, which is a testimony of repentance and salvation, may not be administered to infants.

What shall we say then? Certainly, if we hold as good what God has done, we have a precedent[34] that it is not necessary that the truth, which is signified in a sacrament, always precede, but it is sufficient sometimes for it to follow, at least in part. For the renewing of life was clearly signified by circumcision, and similarly justification[35] which we obtain by faith. Neither repentance nor faith was in any infant. Nonetheless, children were not excluded from the sacrament. Thus you see how a sign can precede the truth it signifies. If that was considered lawful in former times and conforms to reason, then why is it now considered repugnant?

But someone may reply that it is not enough to allege that the similarity exists; rather, one must show that the same is required today.[36] I grant that and have no intention of insisting on the baptism of infants unless I can show that such is the will of God. But let us retain, in the meanwhile, what I have already proven, that to want the truth to come always before the sign is to dispute against God.

As to the rest, we must prove that it is according to the Word of God that we baptize little children. This will be easy for each to understand, without going into a long process, if we are acquainted with the grace that our Lord Jesus made available to us with His coming. Up to that time, God promised the Jews that He would be the God of their children, and in witness to that He marked them with the sacrament of His covenant. But now, as

33. *iustice gratuite.*
34. *doctrine.*
35. *la iustice.*
36. See the *Institutes* 4.16.14.

Saint Paul says (Rom. 15:8–9),[37] the Lord Jesus has come to ratify the promises made to the Jews and to pour out upon all the world the mercy of God. He also notes the same[38] in another passage (Eph. 2:14),[39] where Christ has broken down the dividing wall of separation, eliminating any difference between the two, in order that all of us together might have the same privilege of being children of God.

Therefore, whoever wants to make the grace of God less toward us and our children than it was toward the Jewish people inflicts a great injustice on Jesus Christ and blasphemes Him.

But someone might object that we do not decrease the grace of God toward ourselves by not receiving children for baptism, provided that we do not deny that God is as merciful toward them as toward the children of the Jews. I agree. For we have to understand the grace of God principally through the means by which God declares it to us, both by His Word and by His sacraments.

Therefore, seeing that baptism is commanded of us today for the purpose of sealing in our bodies the promise of salvation, just as in ancient times circumcision was required of the Jewish people, to deny to the children of Christians this confirmation would be to defraud their parents of a unique[40] consolation. For believers have always had this confirmation: a visible sign by which our Lord shows that He accepts their children into the fellowship of His church.

I am quite familiar with the ruse that the Anabaptists invent here,[41] taking allegorically the name "children" to mean those who are "children of malice" and not "children in age."[42] Conse-

37. See the *Institutes* 4.16.14.

38. *voire* = *et même.*

39. See the full context of this passage. Calvin might have had in mind Ephesians 2:12 where specific mention is made of "strangers to the covenants of promise." Although Paul has in mind the separation between Gentiles and Jews, Calvin, possibly leaning upon Ephesians 2:12, broadens this distinction to incorporate believers and their children. Thus there is no partition between them with respect to the "promises" of grace. See *Institutes* 4.16.15.

40. *singuliere.*

41. *qu'ont icy.*

42. A possible reference to Melchior Hofmann's view. See the *Institutes,* vol. 21, LCC, p. 1334, n. 22; S. Cramer and F. Pijper, *Bibliotheca Reformatoria Neerlandica,* 10 vols. (The Hague: Martinus Nijhoff, 1903–1914), vol. 5, p. 294.

quently, they mock us for being so simple as to take this reference literally.[43] But what subtlety is it, I ask you, to want to turn upside down these perfectly clear and plain[44] promises, where it is written that God is merciful upon the seed of the faithful even after their death?[45]

Moreover, what better and more certain exposition of this matter can we have than the Holy Spirit? For He has interpreted through the apostles what was formerly declared by the prophets. Now Saint Peter testifies to the Jews that they are children of the promises, that is to say, heirs, inasmuch as they are descendants of Abraham's race (Acts 2:39; 3:25).[46] And Saint Paul, although he deliberately fights against the foolish presumptions of the Jews which they retained in their carnal parentage, nevertheless does not deny that Abraham's race was specially sanctified because of and in virtue of the covenant which God made with him (Rom. 3:2; 9:4).

It is certainly true that when children of believers reach the age of discernment they will have alienated themselves from God and destroyed utterly the truth of baptism. But this is not to say that our Lord has not elected them and separated them from others in order to grant them His salvation. Otherwise, it would be in vain for Saint Paul to say that a child of a believing father or mother is sanctified, who would be impure if he were born of and descended from unbelievers (I Cor. 7:14).[47]

Seeing then that the Holy Spirit, author and source of all sanctification, testifies that the children of Christians are holy, is it our business to exclude them from such a benefit? Thus, if the *truth*[48] of baptism is in them, how can we dare deprive them of the *sign*, which is less significant and inferior?

But the Anabaptists reply that the custom and practice of the apostles was to the contrary.[49] For it is written that Saint Paul and Silas preached the Word of the Lord to the jailer, or guard

43. Calvin has in mind the *literalis sensus* of a text, a principle of biblical interpretation to which he strongly adhered.

44. *faciles.*

45. See Exodus 20:6.

46. Cf. the *Institutes* 4.16.15 where Calvin cites the same passages.

47. Ibid.

48. *"Truth"* and *"sign"* are italicized for emphasis.

49. See nn. 25 and 26 above.

of the prison, and to his servants before they were baptized (Acts 16:31f.).[50]

I have already provided a solution to this charge, pointing out that with respect to a man who is outside the church, instruction[51] indeed ought to precede the sacrament. But as soon as God has received him into the fellowship of believers, then the promise of life is made both to him and to his children.

But they think they have a passage that is precisely in their favor in Acts 19:2ff.,[52] where it is written that Saint Paul, having discovered certain disciples who had not yet received the Holy Spirit, "rebaptized"[53] them. Now it is certain that Saint Luke, in this text, is speaking of the visible gifts[54] of the Holy Spirit. For otherwise, what he says would not be in agreement with the fact that those of whom he speaks, who were Jews, reply that they did not even know that the Holy Spirit was given.[55]

Now these disciples could not have been unaware that God sanctifies His servants by means of His Spirit, for all the prophets often speak of this. But what they did not know was whether these gifts, of which Saint Paul interrogated them, were given to the Christian church. Seeing therefore that they are called "disciples," they could not have been so ignorant as to be totally unacquainted with God and Jesus Christ, as it were a simple Christian of the common people. But their default is that they had not received the visible gifts that God pours out on His servants. These, then, were conferred upon them by the laying on of hands by Saint Paul.

Now there is nothing new about the term *baptism* being understood in this way, as we have an example, where it is said that the apostles remembered the words of the Lord, that John had baptized with water, but they would be baptized with the

50. See Hubmaier, *Christian Baptism*, in *Anabaptist Beginnings*, p. 88; Hubmaier cites the same text in his argument for believer's baptism.

51. *la doctrine.*

52. See the *Institutes* 4.15.6, 7, 8, 18, where Calvin discusses this text.

53. Calvin denies that Paul rebaptized the Ephesians in Acts 19:2ff. Cf. Hubmaier, *Christian Baptism*, in *Anabaptist Beginnings*, pp. 67, 77, 82. In that Hubmaier does not acknowledge infant baptism as a valid baptism, he rejects the charge that Anabaptists "rebaptize" anyone. See Torsten Bergsten, *Balthasar Hubmaier: Anabaptist Theologian and Martyr*, trans. I. J. Barnes and Wm. R. Estep (Valley Forge: Judson, 1978), pp. 276ff.

54. *graces.*

55. Note in *CO* 7, col. 63: "if there is a Holy Spirit."

Spirit (Acts 11:16).[56] It is also a frequent practice in Scripture to explain a word or a passage by another. Thus it is written [in Acts 19:5–6] that Saint Paul baptized them in the name of Christ, and then, in order to explain what this means, it is added that he placed his hands on them and the Holy Spirit came upon them. This is nothing other than the same thing being explained in two ways, in accordance with the practice of Scripture, as we have said!

Nonetheless, let us see what these good people want to, or can, infer in their efforts to get us to grant them what they demand. They cannot accept anything other than that Saint Paul rebaptized these disciples, owing to their ignorance. But if it is necessary for baptism to be repeated on these grounds, then why weren't the *apostles*[57] rebaptized, who three years after their baptism were so filled with errors and misleading[58] opinions as to think that the kingdom of Jesus Christ was earthly, understanding nothing of His death and resurrection and many other similar things? Such ignorance[59] certainly ought to have required a second baptism, if it was necessary to rebaptize an ignorant man. And as for *ourselves*, we would constantly require a lake or river in readiness,[60] if it were a matter of receiving baptism anew every time our Lord should purge us of error.

Besides, it is stated that Saint Paul baptized those in question before he laid his hands on them. If what these poor fanatics say is true, then that would constitute an ill-advised procedure. For according to their delusions, the Holy Spirit must first be given to the disciples and then consequently the sign. But what need is there to dispute this matter further, seeing we understand[61] it most clearly?

Thus they do not have any other calumny with which to criticize the baptism of infants except that it is nowhere mentioned

56. See the *Institutes* 4.15.18; Hubmaier, *Christian Baptism*, in *Anabaptist Beginnings*, p. 84.

57. Italics for emphasis. The apostles are here being compared with ordinary Christians in a subsequent sentence.

58. *lourdes.*

59. *rudesse.* This is one of Calvin's favorite terms for describing humankind. It means "ignorance." But it is an appalling kind of ignorance, a backwardness and blindness that grips humankind.

60. *a la queue;* literally, "at our back."

61. *avons.*

that the apostles made use of it. I reply that nowhere at all do we ever read that they administered the Lord's Supper to a single woman. Therefore why does the one problem cause them more difficulty than the other? They dare not say that women are incapable of receiving the Lord's Supper. Nevertheless, we do not read that they ever received it from the hands of the apostles. On what basis then can we hold with certainty that women may receive it? By considering the institution, nature, and substance of the sacrament! For in so doing, we see that it is as fitting for them as it is for men.

Now we have pointed out the same with respect to baptism, that it is both fitting and belongs to infants, inasmuch as our Lord regards[62] them as servants of His church. What more can we ask? It is certainly superfluous to inquire of the custom, where the right is perfectly and clearly made plain.

With respect to this matter, I say, the sole pleasure of God must suffice us. As for this point, I hope, to God's pleasure, to have fully satisfied those who want to be on the side of truth. Nevertheless, if anyone wants a more ample explanation, he can see how I treated the subject in the *Christian Institutes*,[63] where all the arguments are refuted in detail.

62. *tient.* Calvin seems to be alluding to Matthew 19:13–15, the blessing of the children.

63. *Institutes* 4.16.1–32.

2

The Second Article
On the Ban[1]

The practice of the ban ought to be used against all who have made a profession of faith and who have been baptized, but who nevertheless have fallen into some error inadvertently without intention. They should be exhorted and warned twice privately. The third time they should be publicly banished before all the congregation so that we may together, in the same spirit, break the bread and drink from the cup.[2]

Refutation[3]

We do not deny that the ban is a sound and holy order, not only useful but also necessary in the church. Moreover, it is from us that these poor ingrates have taken what they know, except, by their ignorance or presumption, they have corrupted the doctrine which we on our part teach with purity. But briefly to settle[4] this article, I shall note wherein we are in accord and wherein they differ from us.

As I have already said, for our part, we constantly teach that the ban, which has been ordained by Jesus Christ, ought to be used; and we maintain that it is a necessary means for preserving the church.[5] In addition, we earnestly attempt and seek to see,

1. Note in *CO* 7, col. 65: "After 1566: *Article II. On the Ban.*" See Calvin's chapter on church discipline in the *Institutes* 4.12.

2. Cf. *The Schleitheim Confession*, article 2—Yoder, *Sattler*, pp. 36–37.

3. Note in *CO* 7, col. 65: "This rubric was introduced in Beza's edition." Compare Zwingli's reply to this article in *Refutation*, pp. 180–182; *Corpus Reformatorum* 93, cols. 111–113. See also Stauffer, "Zwingli et Calvin," pp. 133f.

4. *vuider* = *vider*. The word can mean "to empty."

5. *Institutes* 4.12.1.

insofar as possible, that it is restored and practiced as it ought to be,[6] pointing out that it is a grave error and an equally[7] reprehensible vice for it not to be done. Therein, consequently, the Anabaptists are not different from us.

If we did condemn the ban, or make believe that it was a superfluous and useless thing, or indeed taught that it had no place whatever in the church, then they might have reason to murmur against us. But in all that we are in sound[8] accord.

The debate is over this: they think that wherever this order is not properly constituted,[9] or not duly exercised, no church exists, and it is unlawful for a Christian to receive the Lord's Supper there.[10] Thus they separate themselves from the churches in which the doctrine of God is purely preached, taking this pretext:[11] that they do not care to participate in the pollution committed therein, because those who ought to be excommunicated have not been banished.

We, on the contrary, confess that it certainly is an imperfection and an unfortunate stain[12] in a church where this order is absent. Nevertheless, we do not hold it to be the church, nor persist in its necessity for communion, nor do we hold that it is lawful for people to separate themselves from the church.

Now because it is insufficient simply to assert that, let us see if a good approbation for our doctrine doesn't exist in Scripture. For I willingly submit to this condition: that no one ought to believe anything I might say unless it is founded on Scripture.

Thus the first question is to know if we ought to accept[13] as the Christian church a fellowship whose practice of the ban is not that which the Lord Jesus ordained. Some who default in this were at Corinth during the time Saint Paul was writing them, as he points it out and complains about it. Nonetheless, though they did, he honored them by calling their congregation a Christian church.

6. *Institutes* 4.12.
7. *fort.*
8. *bon.*
9. Literally, "in its estate."
10. See Stauffer's observation ("Zwingli et Calvin," p. 134, n.26) that Calvin, contrary to Bucer and the Anabaptists, refused to make "discipline" a "third mark" of the church.
11. *couleur* = *prétexte.*
12. *mauvaise tache.*
13. *tenir.*

There were diverse sects and parties among them; ambition and avarice reigned over them. They were in the process of devouring each other. A crime which was deemed execrable among pagans was not only tolerated by them but almost approved. Moreover, in addition to such a corruption of morals, they were also plagued with errors of doctrine. Nevertheless, Saint Paul, speaking of himself as the mouth and organ of the Holy Spirit, entitles his letter, "To the Christian church at Corinth" (I Cor. 1:2; II Cor. 1:1).

What will become now of those among us who take it upon themselves to be more severe in their judgments than God? Those who dare do so indeed display their rashness, but they change nothing of what God said on that occasion.[14]

What shall we say of the Galatians? We know of the confusion and disorder that befell them. But that did not stop Saint Paul from recognizing them as the church (Gal. 1:2). Indeed we must strive,[15] to the best of our ability, to reach that perfection which ought to be in the body of Christ. But nevertheless we must not have confidence[16] in any other condition in the church than that which has been promised[17] us by the infallible truth.

Therefore, let us not deceive[18] ourselves by imagining that a perfect church exists in this world, since our Lord Jesus Christ has declared that the kingdom[19] will be like a field in which the good grain is so mixed with weeds that it is often not visible (Matt. 13:24).[20] Again, the kingdom will be like a net in which different kinds of fish are caught (Matt. 13:47). These parables teach us that although we might want an infallible purity in the church and take great pains to achieve it, nevertheless, we will never see the church so pure as not to contain many pollutions.

For what is written about the Lord Jesus having shed His blood to cleanse the church in order that it might be free of spot or wrinkle (Eph. 5:26) does not mean that at the present the church will be free of all stain. But rather she must grow and

14. *une foys.*
15. *estudier = s'appliquer.*
16. *attendre = se fier a.*
17. *predict.*
18. *abusons = séduçons.*
19. Literally, "it."
20. The *CO* editors have corrected this reference which originally read "Matthew 3:12" (*CO* 7, col. 66).

profit, from day to day, moving toward this goal which she will never attain in this world.

Moreover, the church is tainted by vice in two ways. First,[21] not a member of the church is so pure or perfect as not to be surrounded by many imperfections. Thus, all the faithful, as long as they live[22] in this world, always carry about some impurities resident in their flesh, as all Scripture testifies to this and especially Saint Paul in the seventh chapter of Romans (vv. 7ff.). Concerning these impurities, even if we had the best-disciplined church in the world, nevertheless we could not evade the fact that we would daily need our Lord's cleansing of us in delivering us from our sins by His grace.

The second way in which the church is soiled is that it always contains among the good flock evil hypocrites who infect the fellowship with their filthiness. In addition, the church also contains the contemptuous, persons of a profligate and scandalous life, and even those who keep themselves in line[23] out of fear[24] of being brought before men, but who, nevertheless, display that they neither fear nor revere God.

This pollution ought to be eliminated by the discipline of the ban, and the church ought to diligently work, to the best of its ability, to do so. But we find many churches that are unwilling to exercise their duty and reject such filth. Other churches diligently go to great lengths in their efforts, but they never arrive at a point where there still aren't a large number of unpunished evildoers present. For the malice of hypocrites is often hidden or, at least, is not so well discovered as to permit one to pronounce sentence against it.

Therefore, in sum, let us hold to what our Lord says, that until the end of the world, it is necessary to tolerate many bad weeds, for fear that if we should pull them all up we might lose the good grain in the process (Matt. 13:25, 29).

What more do we want? Our Lord, in order to test[25] His own, has willed to subject His church to this poverty, so that it has always contained a mixture of good and bad. Therefore let us pass on.

21. Literally, "for."
22. *conversent* = *habitent.*
23. *se contregarederont* = *se ménageront.*
24. *paour* = *peur.*
25. *esprouver* = *prouver.*

In fact, we have good reason to do so. For we owe this honor to the Lord's holy Word and to His holy sacraments: that wherever we see this Word preached, and, following the rule[26] that it gives us, God therein purely worshiped without superstition, and the sacraments administered, we conclude without difficulty that there the church exists. Otherwise, what would you have? That the wickedness of hypocrites, or the contemptuous of God, should be able to destroy the dignity and virtue of the Word of our Lord and His sacraments?

Now I readily[27] acknowledge that discipline also belongs to the substance of the church—if you want to establish it in good order—and when discipline[28] is absent, as when the ban is not practiced at all, then the true form of the church is to that extent disfigured. But this is not to say that the church is wholly destroyed and the edifice no longer stands, for it retains the teaching[29] on which the church must be founded.

Furthermore, I say that, in regard to their proposal, if we should not have any other consideration than men and their morals, we would frequently open ourselves to error by rejecting a fellowship and not esteeming it fit as the church, owing to its imperfections. For it would be possible in a single blow to cause injury to many good and holy people, of which the number is hidden among the evil ones as good grain is under straw. Besides, we have to think about those who have vices and who are displeased with them and who, with true repentance, desire to be free of them, in order to serve God more completely.

Moreover, it is too rigorous to reject a person for one fault. In addition, our nature is so inclined toward malignity and temerity that it creates suspicion and sits in judgment before a matter can be fully[30] and rightly grasped[31] by us. Therefore we must that much more carefully guard against yielding to that part of our nature.

But, as I have said, it would be incorrect to base consideration solely on men. For the majesty of the Word of God and His sacraments ought to be so highly esteemed by us that wherever

26. *la reigle.*
27. *bien.*
28. *bonne police.* Literally, "good order."
29. *la doctrine.*
30. Literally, "well."
31. *congneue.*

we see that majesty[32] we may know with certainty that the church exists, notwithstanding the vices and errors that characterize[33] the common life of men.

In summary, whenever we have to decide what constitutes the church, the judgment of God deserves to be preferred over ours. But the Anabaptists cannot acquiesce in the judgment of God, as we have shown.

The second question on this article is, when the practice of the ban[34] is not regulated[35] in a church, or exercised as it should be, by this default are we to separate ourselves from it, and is it lawful for us to receive the Lord's Supper in it? The Anabaptists say that wherever the undisciplined[36] are not excluded from the communion of the sacrament, the Christian corrupts himself by communing there.

We, to the contrary, say that a Christian ought certainly to be sad whenever he sees the Lord's Supper being corrupted by the reception of the malicious and indignant. To the best of his ability, he ought to work to see that such does not happen. Nevertheless, if it does happen, it is not lawful for him to withdraw from communion and deprive himself of the Supper. Rather he ought always continue to worship God with the others, listen to the Word, and receive the Lord's Supper as long as he lives in that place.

Let the Anabaptists produce their author to prove what they say.[37] As for us, we hold to nothing other than what is in accordance with our Lord Jesus and all the prophets and apostles.

We see the vices which the prophets attack in the church in Judah, or rather the abominations against which they cry. These were not confined to one human species or to one estate. Rather they say that from the government, whether spiritual or temporal, to the common people, everyone was so corrupt that at great pain was there a single whole[38] person (Isa. 1:6). Those are their words.

32. *la.*
33. Literally, "that are able to be in."
34. *l'ordre d'excommuniment.*
35. *dressé = dirigé.*
36. *les mauvais.*
37. Michael Sattler was the author of *The Schleitheim Confession.* But he paid for it with his life in May 1527. It is possible that Calvin did not know the extent to which Sattler was its author.
38. *sain.*

Nevertheless, did they stop[39] assembling with the people, thus perverted and malicious, in order to worship God, offer sacrifices, or hear the teaching of the law? Did they set up an altar of their own or build a separate temple in order to have a pure church? If a true believer[40] is corrupted by participating with the malicious when he makes his prayers and receives both the teachings[41] and the sacraments of our Lord, then all the prophets were corrupt and have become as captains in order to lead us all, by their example, into perdition.

Let us turn to our Lord Jesus and to His apostles. First of all, we know what the condition of the church in Jerusalem was at that time. Nevertheless, our Lord Jesus willed to be circumcised along with the others. Then on the day of purification He willed to be taken to the temple in order to be presented to God, as was the custom (Luke 2:21f.).

If anyone charges that He was received by the hands of a holy person, namely Simeon, I reply that that all was done in the name of the church, which was full of much refuse and many abominations. If someone replies that He was an infant and therefore not acting on His own, I reply that He was truly an infant in human nature, which He took from us, but nonetheless He was governed by His divine providence, which never permitted Him to be contaminated by any act that contradicts[42] the purity of God's children. But being perfect man, preaching, and, what is more, exercising His office, He pursued this path until His death.

If it is offensive to God to enter into a congregation, from which all the wicked have not been banned, in order to pray to God and make a confession of His faith, what are we to make of our Lord, and of the example He sets for us, when He goes to the temple of Jerusalem to sacrifice with the scribes and Pharisees and a people as depraved as they were? I well expect that they will reply at once that Jesus Christ only went up to the temple with the intention of observing the vices that were committed there and not for the purpose of participating with the others in their sacrifices and other confessions of their faith.

39. *laissé = cessé.*
40. *l'homme fidèle.*
41. *la doctrine.*
42. *contrevenir = être contredictoire.*

But that this answer is false is easy to demonstrate. It is not without cause that Saint Paul writes that He was subject to the law (I always understand Jesus Christ) in order to redeem those who were under the law (Gal. 4:4). Now he speaks specifically of the ceremonial law. Therefore when He went up to the temple, and especially to the solemn feasts—though He went there for the purpose of having a better means to advance the gospel and to correct the wickedness of sinners—nevertheless, His actions demonstrate that He was an observer of the law in doing what was commanded: to come to the temple to worship and sacrifice.

Our Lord[43] confirms this by His own mouth when He spoke to the Samaritan woman. For speaking in the person of all the Jews, He said, "We know what we worship; you do not know what you worship, for salvation is from the Jews" (John 4:22). Certainly He does not set Himself apart with respect to worshiping God, which also includes the sacrifices, but He numbers Himself among the ranks of the common. The explanation which He adds provides still further confirmation, that is, "that salvation is from the Jews." For the only thing He means by these words is that God accepted the worship that was being made to Him in Jerusalem only because of the covenant of salvation which He had made with its people.

Therefore we see how a man, participating with wicked people in the sacraments ordained by God, was not contaminated by their company. For, on His part, He had a pure and clean conscience.

The apostles acted in the same way, following the example of their Master. But lest we become too verbose, let us be content with Saint Paul. I could claim that wherever he went he never had any trouble entering the synagogue of the Jews in order to pray to God and teach the Scriptures. Similarly, I could claim that he never made any scruples about presenting himself at the temple in order to worship God there and make use of the lawful and permitted ceremonies, in common with the others—notwithstanding the disparaging wickedness of the priests and scribes who were there. But I won't, not because this is not relevant, but because we have even clearer proofs[44] that are less subject to attack. That is, he complains that all those who ought

43. The text simply reads, "he."
44. *probations = épreuves, preuves.*

to be his helpers seek their own gain instead of the honor of Jesus Christ and the advancement of His church (Phil. 2:21). Nevertheless, we do not read that he separated himself from their company for fear of being corrupted.

Again, in reproving the shocking vices which were among the Corinthians and Galatians, he did not say to those who were pure and free of them that they should no longer have communion with the others until everyone could be purged, but he was content to exhort them to correct the faults he had reproved, each in its own place, without speaking of any such separation as these fanatics[45] want to introduce (I Cor. 5:1ff.; Gal. 5:4ff.).

And why do we need to dispute this? For the same apostle in another text (I Cor. 11:28), treating how each ought to be disposed toward rightly receiving the Lord's Supper, does not command everyone to examine the faults of his neighbors, but says accordingly, "Let every man search *himself*,[46] and then eat of the bread and drink of the cup. For whoever comes in an unworthy manner will receive his condemnation."

In these words there are two matters to note. The first is, to eat the bread of the Lord in an unworthy manner does not mean having communion with those who are unworthy of it, but not preparing oneself properly by examining if one has faith and repentance. The second is, that when we come to the Lord's Supper, we ought not begin by examining others, but each should examine himself.

In fact, when all that is carefully considered, all who have the ample leisure to inquire about others most often forget to think about their own situation. There is a man, still living, who was detained by this error, and who was afraid to receive the Lord's Supper with us, and because of the imperfections of some deprived himself of the fellowship of the church. Nevertheless, he had two servants in his house whose lives were debauched and scandalous. Being advised of this, I pointed out to him, insofar as he was able to hear me at the time, that shouldn't he indeed think about purging his house of that over which he had charge if he thought he was being contaminated by the sins of those who were committed to him in his control?

As a result, he recognized his folly and accepted it as a

45. *ces phantastiques.*

46. Italics for emphasis.

chastisement which God had sent him in order to make fun of his presumption. And thus he was reconciled both to me and to the church, realizing that the principal thing is to think about oneself and one's family, then afterwards about others, not for the purpose of withdrawing ourselves from the church by despising those who aren't what they should be, but in order to correct and redirect them if we can, or in order to banish them from the Lord's Supper, otherwise commending them to God that he might bring order therein.

One could reply that in the same letter Saint Paul vigorously reproves the Corinthians (I Cor. 5:2) for not using the ban as a means of punishing the vices that are in their congregation and for even defending their living with[47] adulterers, drunkards, impostors, idolaters, and the like. To that I reply that it is certainly a highly reprehensible vice for a church not to correct sins. Besides, I say our Lord will punish an entire people for this single fault. And therefore let no church, still not exercising the discipline of the ban, flatter itself by thinking that it is a small or light sin not to use the ban when necessary. Rather let everyone attempt, in his own place, to use and establish it. Similarly, let every man in particular employ it and support it with all his power.

But this is not to say that an individual is justified in withdrawing from the church whenever things are contrary to his will. For we must note that this office[48] does not belong to the power of a member but must be exercised by the consent of all the people. Moreover, Saint Paul does not address himself specifically to individuals to fault them, but faults the entire group.

In summary, with regard to the communion of the church, we ought to take pains to see that all the members—however rotten or infected with contagious maladies—that is to say, all who pursue a scandalous life, are rescued[49] from it. But let us take thought of what we can do.[50] And when we have done what was in our power and duty,[51] if we cannot achieve what we had hoped to and what would have been desirable, let us commend the rest to God that He might put His own hand to it, as it is His

47. *converser avec = vivre avec.*

48. *police.*

49. *retranches.* Literally, "retrenched," "cut off."

50. Literally, "what is in us."

51. *office.*

work. Meanwhile, though we are rightly saddened[52] not to see the church of God in its perfect state, nevertheless, let us endure the imperfections that we are unable to correct.

As for Saint Paul's argument that we ought not drink or eat with those who live a scandalous life (I Cor. 5:11), that applies to private conduct,[53] not to public communion. But someone might say that if it is not lawful for a Christian man to associate with the wicked and take his corporal repast with him, then even less is it permissible to eat the Lord's bread in his company.

To that I reply that associating privately with the wicked and enjoying familiarity with them is a matter within our liberty and power. Therefore we must each, as much as possible, abstain from it. But to receive the Lord's Supper is not something based on our decision.[54] And consequently the reason is diverse.

Therefore, let us note, if the church tolerates and endures an unworthy man, let anyone who knows such a person abstain from his private company and let him do it as often as possible, providing that he does not engage in schism or separate himself from the church with respect to public communion.

As to the method[55] of applying the ban, as much has been said as needs to be said, except that in passing I want to warn all lovers of truth of a point contained in the Anabaptists' article mentioned above, that they might see how worthy the rest of it is. Which is, that they claim that a man who has inadvertently erred without deliberate malice, having been admonished twice in secret, ought to be chastened in public or excommunicated.

I can forgive them for such an error. For our Lord does not want the church to proceed as far as excommunication, even when the sinner has scorned two private admonitions, but wants, even on the third time before he is rejected, for him to be publicly admonished.

They err yet another time, for they do not consider at all that our Lord in that passage does not even speak of secret sins. For

52. *marris = attristés, peinés, irrités.*

53. *conversation = conduite, manière de vivre.*

54. *disposition = decision.* This whole passage is reminiscent of the Stoic Epictetus's distinction between "things in our power and things not in our power." See *Arrian's Discourses of Epictetus* in *The Stoic and Epicurean Philosophers,* ed. Whitney J. Oates (New York: The Modern Library, 1940), p. 224. This passage may indicate Calvin's familiarity with or some indebtedness to Epictetus.

55. *matière.*

with respect to those who are notorious and a scandal to people, there is another means of dealing with them than relying on secret remonstrance. Thus here are two mistakes that clearly reveal what great theologians[56] these Anabaptists are and their spirit for reforming everything, seeing they do not know how to say three words without confusing everything.

But still I can pardon all that in order to come to a point of the greatest consequence. For in saying that whoever sins out of ignorance and not by forethought ought to be rejected, they denote, as in fact they teach and maintain openly, that if a man sins willingly, he should never obtain forgiveness. For, according to their notion, all voluntary sin is sin against the Holy Spirit, which is unpardonable.

I reply that this view is a detestable blasphemy against the grace of God and a pernicious delusion that casts all poor souls into despair.[57] For I have seen what has happened to some who have been seduced momentarily by this wretched sect.[58]

It is true that we must indeed remind ourselves and point out to others that it is no small thing to offend God knowingly, or to commit any act against our conscience that would provoke His anger[59] against us. Therefore whoever would use these terms to urge us, having come to know God, to sin against our conscience, saying it is an easily forgivable fault and that our Lord does not consider it so grave a matter as to torment us very much, such a one ought to be rejected as a Satan who would like to lead us by such flatteries into contempt[60] for God.

Rather, let us always realize[61] that it is no small crime to contravene the holy will of God by rebellion and contumacy, deliberately violating His justice, for it represents an outrageous

56. *docteurs.*

57. In French this passage rings with controlled alliteration. To express indignity with reserve, yet with power and style, was part of the Humanist tradition Calvin had studied and respected. See Quirinus Breen, *John Calvin: A Study in French Humanism* (Grand Rapids: Eerdmans, 1931), and Francis Higman, *The Style of John Calvin in His French Polemical Treatises* (Cambridge: Oxford, 1967).

58. A possible reference to his work in Strassburg of reconverting Anabaptists. See Calvin's letter to Farel, February 6, 1540—Herminjard, *Correspondances,* vol. 6, pp. 165ff., no. 846. See Williams, *Radical Reformation,* pp. 590f.

59. *ire = colère.*

60. *contemnement = dédain, mépris.*

61. *meditons.*

abuse of His grace toward us. Besides, there is a great danger that the man who so behaves[62] will not be amenable to reproof and will become hardened in malice and never able to be changed.[63]

Let us also be humbled[64] by the threats which the Scriptures make concerning such ingratitude. But when all that is said and done, must it not cast into despair those who err following such advice? For where does it lead us? With great effort you will hardly find one in ten who can boast that he has not sinned[65] willingly after coming to know God. Does it not ruin the whole church to want to cast them all into despair?

They say it benumbs their consciences and inspires them to do evil. I say, rather, that those who are benumbed are those who think they sin only out of ignorance and who see themselves as being so pure and innocent as never to have had an evil will or evil intention.

I beg of you to consider the different ways the devil tempts us. Why should we be surprised? For who is so virtuous as not to have erred at some time, though he was warned by God and his conscience bore testimony of the same in an effort to restore him to the right path?

They claim that all sin against the Holy Spirit is unpardonable. I concur. But it is going too far to say that all willful sin is against the Holy Spirit. For whoever resists the Holy Spirit impugns overtly the truth of God and attempts through agitation,[66] insofar as possible, to overthrow it. Thus a man who knowingly sins, but who nonetheless does not want to come into conflict with God, does not blaspheme His Word.

But we can have a quick and easy solution to this problem if we will accept the decision of God, that is to say, if we will acquiesce in what He has said about it, as reason should dictate. For since He reserves to Himself the sole authority to forgive sins, it is also His right to determine which sins are forgivable and which are not.

62. Literally, "overflows himself."

63. *se convertir* = *changer d'idée.*

64. *reduisons* = *humilions.* A note in *CO* 7, col. 74, suggests the Latin text, *revocemus in memoriam,* might be closer here: "let us keep in mind," or "let us call to memory," etc.

65. *fally.*

66. *despit* = *irritation.*

Now from the beginning He ordained that among the people of Israel there should be two types of daily sacrifices: one type for willful sins and one for those committed out of ignorance, adding the promise of forgiveness to both the first and the second (Lev. 4f.). What can these poor fanatics say about that?

Our Lord declares that He will remit the willful sins of the faithful (for the sacrifices were made for those who were already members of the church). But they want to bind the hands of God and prevent Him from acting with such lovingkindness.

If they reply that that occurred under the old law but other reasons apply in our time, such sophistry is too frivolous. For we know that the infinite bounty of God was not restrained by the coming of our Lord Jesus, but rather increased.

Besides, we know that the ancient sacrifices were only figures[67] of what was to be accomplished in Jesus Christ. Thus when the remission of willful sins is incorporated in the ancient sacrifices, and it is written that the sins of the members of the household of faith will be remitted, this is a clear and unquestionable witness that believers obtain through Jesus Christ remission, not only of their inadvertent sins, but also of their offenses knowingly committed.

In fact, we have so many examples of this that it is a great impudence to hold the matter in doubt. If we take the Old Testament, the patriarchs, when conspiring to kill their brother, were not ignorant of the fact that this was wrong (Gen. 37:18). Reuben did not contaminate his father's bed out of ignorance[68] (Gen. 35:22). Judah was sufficiently aware that adultery[69] was a displeasing thing to God, and yet that did not prevent him from committing it (Gen. 38:16ff.). David, who daily punished the evil deeds of his subjects, was not able to commit his act of adultery out of simple inadvertence (II Sam. 11:4). The mercy that God showered upon them all, is it spent or dead that He cannot act as mercifully today?

But we hardly have to rely on the Old Testament for our examples. For there are just as many in the New. Did not Saint

67. See the *Institutes* 2.7.1–2 and other related texts.

68. *simplesse* = *innocence.*

69. *paillardise.* This can mean "adultery," or sexual immoderation of any sort; "whoring around" is not too strong an expression for conveying Calvin's meaning here.

Peter, before denying our Lord Jesus, hear this sentence: "Whoever denies Me before men, I will deny him before God My Father" (Matt. 10:33)? Thus he could not pretend he had acted out of ignorance. And yet the Lord Jesus had mercy on him.

Saint Paul complains of some who were living riotously in Thessalonica, but he did not abandon hope for them, on condition that they could be corrected and led to repentance (II Thess. 3:11, 15). Those who were given over to licentiousness and impurity in the church of Corinth, and who so fully indulged their vices that they did not want to hear a single remonstrance, were indeed guilty of having sinned deliberately.[70] Nevertheless, the same apostle does not cease to exhort them to control themselves, always reserving for them the hope of finding the grace of God. Do we not read that Saint Peter acted similarly toward Simon Magus (Acts 8:22)?

What more do we want? Our Lord opens the treasures of His grace to those who are overcome by their concupiscences, who though they know evil are overcome by the infirmity of their flesh. What man would close the door to these poor sinners and not permit them to receive the grace God offers them? Therefore we see that there is a mortal poison hidden in these words of the Anabaptists when they only define[71] pardonable sins as those committed inadvertently.

To make an end to this article, it is necessary for all Christians to be aware of its consequences. For though one rightly judges that it is too extreme a position not to accept[72] some default in a church, nevertheless, at first, one does not see how pernicious this opinion is until one considers its consequences.

In the early church there were two heretical sects that caused grave trouble. One was called in Greek the *Cathari,* that is to say, "the pure"; the other sect was the Donatists, named after their first author and leader.[73] These, whether of the first or second, held to the same fantasy as do these poor dreamers today, looking for a church in which one could find no fault. Therefore they separated themselves from all of Christianity in order not to be in any way soiled by the imperfections of others. But what

70. *de mauvaise volunté.*

71. *font.*

72. *supporter.*

73. For a complete elaboration of Calvin's views on the Cathari and the Donatists, see the *Institutes* 4.1.13; 4.8.12; 4.12.11; 4.15.16.

came of it? Our Lord confounded them all by their own presumptuous enterprise.

Therefore let that serve us as a warning that whenever, under the pretext of a zeal for perfection, we cannot tolerate any imperfection, either in the body or the members of the church, then the devil inflames us with pride and seduces us through hypocrisy to leave the flock of Jesus Christ, knowing well that he has won everything when he has withdrawn us from the church. For seeing that there is neither forgiveness of sins nor salvation elsewhere (Acts 4:12), though we might have an appearance of sanctity greater than angels enjoy, if by such a presumption we should separate ourselves from the Christian fellowship, we would become devils.

Their *third article*[74] is on the reception of the Lord's Supper, in which they say nothing with which we are not in accord with them, as we preach the same every day. That is, that no one dare come to this holy table who is not truly of the body of Jesus Christ, worshiping one God along with all the believers, and serving Him in a good and lawful vocation.

But when they declare in the *fourth article*[75] that men must separate themselves from all the pollutions of the world in order to associate with God, they begin to go astray[76] altogether. Though in the beginning they had a good cause: as in condemning the papal superstitions and prohibiting all Christians from participating in them. But in the tail the venom lies,[77] as the proverb says. For in the end they conclude that the use of all arms is a diabolical thing.

74. See *The Schleitheim Confession,* article 3—Yoder, *Sattler,* p. 37. Cf. Zwingli's reply to this article in *Refutation,* pp. 183–188; *Corpus Reformatorum* 93, cols. 114–120. Zwingli strongly defends infant baptism and accuses the Anabaptists of being schismatics.

75. See *The Schleitheim Confession,* article 4—Yoder, *Sattler,* pp. 37f. Cf. Zwingli's reply to this article in *Refutation,* pp. 188–193; *Corpus Reformatorum* 93, cols. 120–126. See also Stauffer, "Zwingli et Calvin," pp. 136ff. Stauffer notes that Zwingli's criticism is quite incisive, as Zwingli accuses the Anabaptists of failing to understand the true meaning of "separation." For "separation" does not mean simply withdrawing from the world; instead, it requires a careful searching of one's heart in order to kill the world in oneself, an act that should be done in the context of faith with other sinners.

76. *depraver = détourner du vrai sens.*

77. *Mais en la queue gist le venim.*

Now it is true that the usage of the sword[78] in particular must not be entrusted to just anyone for resisting evil. For the arms of Christians are prayer and gentleness in order to pass their days[79] in patience and conquer evil by doing good, in accordance with the teaching of the gospel (Luke 21:19; Rom. 12:21). Thus the duty of each of us is to suffer patiently when someone offends us rather than to use force and violence.

But to condemn the public sword which God ordained for our protection is a blasphemy against God Himself. The Spirit of God Himself proclaims through Saint Paul (Rom. 13:4) that the magistrate is a minister of God for our benefit and on our behalf, for the purpose of restraining and preventing the violence of the wicked. And for that reason the sword is placed in his hands in order to punish crimes.[80]

Since God has ordained him to this end, who are we to impede him? Similarly, since God grants us such a safeguard, why is it not lawful to use it?

Furthermore, it is clear that the intention of these poor fanatics is to condemn all munitions, fortresses, shoulder arms, and all similar things, which are necessary for the defense of a country, as well as prevent their subjects from being obedient to their princes and superiors when they want to serve them in times of necessity.[81]

Now to reprove what our Lord has never reproved is too ambitious for mortal man to do. Let us rather maintain that it is a usurpation of the authority of God to condemn as evil what our Lord permits us to do. And at no point do the Scriptures prohibit princes the use of arms in order to defend their countries against those who would wrongly molest them.

78. See the *Institutes* 4.20.3–7. See Littell's discussion of the Anabaptist rejection of the use of the sword in *Origins*, pp. 101–106. For an excellent summary of the issue, see H. S. Bender, "State, Anabaptist-Mennonite Attitude Toward," *Mennonite Encyclopedia*, vol. 4, pp. 611–618. For a detailed study, see James M. Stayer, *Anabaptists and the Sword* (Lawrence, Kan.: Coronado, 1972). See also H. J. Hillerbrand, "The Anabaptist View of the State," pp. 83–110.

79. *posseder leurs vies.*

80. *les malefices = crimes, mauvaises actions.*

81. See Bender, "State, Anabaptist-Mennonite Attitude Toward." Zwingli interprets the Anabaptist rejection of the sword in the worst possible light. He accuses the Anabaptists of wanting to subvert the sword so that their members can indulge in the violent excesses associated with the Spiritualism of St. Gall. See *Refutation*, p. 198; *Corpus Reformatorum* 93, col. 133.

It is indeed true that the prophets speak of the kingdom of Jesus Christ, saying that swords and spears will be turned into instruments of labor for cultivating the earth (Isa. 2:4; Mic. 4:3). But by such forms of speech they mean nothing other than that all war and enmity between believers will be destroyed. And may it please God that the gospel will be of such a benefit to the world that this will be practiced by all! But seeing that the faith and love of God do not govern for the most part in such a way that ambition and avarice are not often superior, when someone unjustly invades a country and troubles it with war, rather than doing evil by resisting unjust violence, the prince, who is ordained of God for the protection and defense of his country, is bound to do it by the requirements of his office.

It is certainly true that a Christian prince ought to pursue every means of peace, being ready to pay a dear price for it at a loss to himself. He should never come to the sword until he has tried every means of avoiding the necessity. But when he has done everything he can and has drawn back as far as he can, if he has no other means to defend his country which is committed to him, his last refuge is to make use of the sword which God has put in his hands.

In fact, the same reason that permits one to unsheathe the sword for punishing evildoers who disturb the public good[82] also permits one to repulse those who unjustly attempt to assail a country. In this case too, the Christian man, if according to the order of his country is called to serve his prince, not only does not offend God in taking up arms, but also fulfills a holy vocation, which cannot be reproved without blaspheming God.

In fact, we see that when the soldiers came to John the Baptist to be instructed, he did not command them to throw down their arms, nor did he denounce their vocation, but only admonished them to be content with their wages, not to steal and harass anyone, and to abstain from all evil (Luke 3:14). Saint Peter baptized Cornelius who was a centurion, that is to say, a captain of a hundred men (Acts 10:47ff.), yet he did not command him to leave his post as if it were something evil. What is more, having received the Holy Spirit visibly, he still did not leave his command of arms.[83]

82. *ordre.*

83. See Augustine's letter to Count Boniface (A.D. 418) in which he commends

The *fifth article*[84] is on pastors, a subject about which they have changed their mind some. For in the beginning they were of the false opinion[85] that God did not approve of a pastor being called[86] to a certain place, but they wanted them to run about from one place to another, imitating[87] the apostles like apes and not as true imitators.[88] But I think they did this for a good reason that they had: that the ministers who taught them faithfully might leave the place empty so they could spread their poison everywhere.

But now, insofar as they recognize their error, or give their pastors[89] more privilege than they originally wanted to accord others, we are in sound agreement with them that no church can hold itself together without ministers and that every congregation ought to have an ordained minister. This of course provided they acknowledge, wherever one finds a duly constituted minister who faithfully exercises his office, that whoever wants to become a Christian must adhere to him and make use of his ministry with the rest of the flock.

Now what do they do? Because we are not willing to accept their errors, though we preach the Word of Jesus Christ purely, we are ravishing wolves to them and are held in such abomination that they think they are mortally offending God to hear one

---

the use of force and arms by citing a similar but more complete list of texts (letter 189, in *Nicene and Post-Nicene Fathers*, ed. Philip Schaff, first series [1886–1888; reprint ed., Grand Rapids: Eerdmans, 1979], vol. 1, p. 553).

84. See *The Schleitheim Confession*, article 5—Yoder, *Sattler*, pp. 38f. Cf. Zwingli's reply to this article in *Refutation*, pp. 193–196; *Corpus Reformatorum* 93, cols. 126–129.

85. *resverie.*

86. *deputé = choisi, fixé, destiné à.*

87. *contrefaisans = imitant.*

88. One must recall that the Anabaptist leaders were frequently expelled and driven from town to town. Calvin's criticism is not as heartless, however, as Zwingli's, as Zwingli mocks the Anabaptists for meeting in secrecy, which they were compelled to do (*Refutation*, p. 191; *Corpus Reformatorum* 93, col. 124). Calvin might have had in mind the "Missionary Synod" of 1527, at which Anabaptists, meeting at Augsburg, divided Europe up into missionary zones. See Littell, *Origins*, pp. 121f.

89. *se donnent.* Literally, "give themselves."

of our sermons. At that they appoint ministers in a hurry, thereby creating separation in the church, destroying the people, and setting one group against another, to the extent that the name of God cannot be invoked at all in unity and concord as it ought to be.

3

The Sixth Article

On the Magistrate[1]

We hold that the sword is an ordinance of God, outside the perfection of Christ. Hence the princes and authorities of the world are ordained to punish the wicked and to put them to death. But in the perfection of Christ, the ban is the heaviest penalty, without corporal death.[2]

Refutation[3]

Now one will note that they have moderated their position in order to correct what they had said initially,[4] for they saw that owing to its absurdity they were being rejected by everyone. For the way they honored principalities and lordships was to hold them as forms of brigandage.[5] But seeing this position was not

1. Note in *CO* 7, col. 80: "*Article VI. On the Magistrate.* In the 1566 and following editions." For Calvin's own view on civil government, see the *Institutes* 4.20.1–32. See also Balthasar Hubmaier, *On the Sword,* in *Anabaptist Beginnings,* pp. 1, 8, 125. Hubmaier is an exception among the Evangelical Anabaptists because his view is closer to the Reformers than to the Anabaptists.

2. See *The Schleitheim Confession,* article 6—Yoder, *Sattler,* pp. 39ff. For further references to the Anabaptist view of the use of the sword, see Calvin's refutation of article 4 on p. 72, n. 78.

3. Note in *CO* 7, col. 80: "This rubric is not found at all in the editions of 1544 and 1545." Cf. Zwingli's reply to this article in *Refutation,* pp. 196–206; *Corpus Reformatorum* 93, cols. 129–141.

4. See *The Schleitheim Confession,* "The Cover Letter"—Yoder, *Sattler,* p. 42: "These are the articles which some brothers previously had understood wrongly and in a way not conformed to the true meaning."

5. A possible reference to Spiritualist excesses at St. Gall. See Williams, *Radical Reformation,* pp. 127–134. H. S. Bender argues that any "'left-wing' element in the Reformation which advocated or practiced overthrow of the

accepted, they decided to retract themselves ever so carefully, using the convenient ruse that temporal power is indeed an ordinance of God, but outside the perfection of Christ. Now by this they mean that it is an illicit calling,[6] one that is forbidden of all Christians, as they go on to explain.[7]

Thus we have to consider whether Christianity and the office of justice or temporal power are incompatible things. So much so that if a man chooses one he must reject the other.

First of all, I ask, if this calling to fulfill the office of the sword or of temporal power is repugnant to the vocation of believers, then how is it that the judges in the Old Testament, especially good kings like David, Hezekiah, and Josiah,[8] and even a few prophets like Daniel, made use of it? To say that it was a faulty imperfection in them is hardly a reason, for the Holy Spirit testifies in behalf of the judges that God raised[9] them up to deliver His people. Above all, this is true of Moses who, having an express commandment, would gladly have withdrawn himself if possible. But in order for him to be obedient to God it was necessary that he receive this charge. As for David, his reign is not only approved by God, but praised and decorated with very honorable titles. The same must be said of his successors for identical reasons. Thus the only subterfuge left to these enemies of all order is to claim that our Lord requires a greater perfection[10] in the Christian church than He did of the Jewish people.

Now that is true with respect to the ceremonies. But that there exists a different rule of life with respect to the moral law—as it is called—than the people of old had is a false opinion.[11] Those who think so have based this on Saint Matthew's

---

state . . . must be considered non-Anabaptist or deviationist. . . ." He asserts that from earliest times Anabaptists viewed the state as essential for a "decent human society" (*Mennonite Encyclopedia*, vol. 4, p. 612).

6. *estat.*

7. *exposent* = *expliquent.*

8. Hubmaier makes a similar point, naming the same three kings (*On the Sword*, in *Anabaptist Beginnings*, p. 117).

9. *suscitez* = *a fait parus.*

10. Hubmaier argues similarly that "many brothers say, 'A Christian may not bear the sword, since the kingdom of Christ is not of this world'" (*On the Sword*, in *Anabaptist Beginnings*, p. 109).

11. Cf. the *Institutes* 2.9.3–5 where Calvin rejects the exaggerated opposition of law and gospel.

fifth chapter,[12] where it seems, at first glance, that our Lord Jesus has added something to what He had already commanded the people. But when we carefully consider what the law of Moses contains and compare the other with it, we realize that the intention of our Lord Jesus was not to add anything to it, but solely to restore the true meaning of the law in its entirety, which the rabbis had reversed[13] by their false glosses.

Therefore let us hold this position: that with regard to true spiritual justice, that is to say, with regard to a faithful man walking in good conscience and being whole before God in both his vocation and in all his works, there exists a plain and complete guideline[14] for it in the law of Moses, to which we need simply cling if we want to follow the right path. Thus whoever adds to or takes anything from it exceeds the limits. Therefore our position is sure and infallible.

We worship the same God that the fathers of old did. We have the same law and rule that they had, showing us how to govern ourselves in order to walk rightly before God. It thus follows that a vocation that was considered holy and lawful then cannot be forbidden Christians today, for a vocation is the principal part of human life and the part that means the most to God. From which it follows that we should not deny ourselves the vocation of civil justice, nor drive it outside the Christian church.[15] For our Lord has ordained it and approved it as good for the people of Israel. And He has appointed His most excellent servants to it and even His prophets.

They will reply, possibly, that the civil government of the people of Israel was a figure of the spiritual kingdom of Jesus Christ and lasted only until His coming. I will admit to them that, in part, it was a figure, but I deny that it was nothing more than this, and not without reason. For in itself it was a political government, which is a requirement among all people.

That such is the case, it is written of the Levitical priesthood that it had to come to an end and be abolished at the coming of our Lord Jesus (Heb. 7:12ff.). Where is it written that the same is

12. Matthew 5:40. Hubmaier denies that this text forbids Christians to bear the sword (*On the Sword,* in *Anabaptist Beginnings,* p. 112).

13. *depravée = altérée.*

14. *declaration.*

15. Cf. Hubmaier's similar view (*On the Sword,* in *Anabaptist Beginnings,* pp. 110f., 113, 117, 120–122).

true of the external order? It is true that the scepter and government were to come from the tribe of Judah and the house of David, but that the government was to cease is manifestly contrary to Scripture.

But lest we have any doubts about it, we have a still more evident and direct proof. For when the prophets speak of the kingdom of Jesus Christ, it is written that kings will come to worship and pay homage to Him. It is not said that they will abdicate their positions in order to become Christians, but rather, being appointed with royal dignity, they will be subject to Jesus Christ as to their sovereign lord. Following this, David, exhorting them to do their duty, does not command them to throw down their diadems or their scepters, but solely to kiss the Son, that is to say, to pay homage to Him in order to be subject to Him in His domination over others (Ps. 2:12).

Without a doubt[16] he is speaking of the kingdom of our Lord Jesus. He admonishes all kings and authorities to be wise and to take heed to themselves. What is this wisdom? What is the lesson he gives them? To abdicate it all? Hardly! But to fear God and give honor to His Son.

Furthermore, Isaiah prophesies that the kings will become the foster fathers of the Christian church and that queens will nurse it with their breasts (Isa. 49:23). I beg of you, how do you reconcile the fact that kings will be protectors of the Christian church if their vocation is inconsistent with Christianity? If our Lord only bestowed on them that place among His people that He also gave His former prophets, that would suffice to prove our point. But now that He assigns them a place so honorable in the midst of His people as to grant them the honor, I say, of ordaining them "protectors of His church," what impudence is it to exclude them from it altogether? Thus we conclude that princes who serve God can be Christians as well, inasmuch as our Lord has given them such a place of preeminence in Christianity.

In fact, it would be quite an irony if a vocation so magnified and exalted by God should prevent a man from being a servant of God. Saint Paul exhorts each Christian to continue in the vocation to which he has been called (I Cor. 7:20). Shepherds

16. *une foys;* the Latin reads, *certum est* (*CO* 7, col. 82, n. 1).

and plowmen,[17] manual laborers, and all similar workers ought to consider their calling holy and let nothing obstruct them with respect to Christian perfection.

Let us consider now which calling is more approved of God, a shepherd's or a governor's? And not simply approved, but prized as worthy and excellent among the others? I will not cite many references[18] that might be pertinent, only because of brevity. Also, one should be enough for all. Should we want the highest praise of a calling, one that even the mouth of God calls "divine" (Ps. 82:6)? If then the vocation of princes is called "divine," who will dare say that it is unworthy of a believer?

But there is more.[19] For our Lord bestowed this favor on princes—to call them gods—not because of anything in themselves,[20] but out of consideration for the dignity they bear. Our Lord Jesus explains that it is for this reason that God has commissioned them and given them such a charge (John 10:34). In our view our Lord could not give a more express endorsement of the worthiness of this calling than when He bestows His name on the man who is appointed to exercise it here, as if He were calling him His lieutenant, who represents Him personally. That is why I conclude that whoever despises this calling so honored of God blasphemes against God's heavenly majesty.

They will answer that it isn't despising it to make it inferior to Christian perfection.[21] But I reply that they could not speak of it with greater contumely. For in saying that it is in no way compatible with Christianity, they reject it as profane.

I care nothing for their fine pretexts[22] by which they hide their blasphemy in saying that it is "an ordinance of God."[23] For the sum of it is this: whether it is a holy office and can be performed by believers, or, indeed, if a man in coming to it is corrupted by it? For they say that whoever sits on the seat of justice is unworthy to be called a Christian, because the office of the sword has no place at all in Christianity.[24]

17. The Latin reads, *opiliones et bubulci* (*CO* 7, col. 83, n. 1).
18. I.e., biblical references.
19. *d'avantage* = *de plus.*
20. *de leurs personnes.*
21. See Hans J. Hillerbrand's four criteria for the Anabaptist rejection of office holding on p. 31, n. 96.
22. *couleurs* = *prétextes.*
23. Cited from the epigraph on p. 76.
24. See nn. 1, 10, 21 above.

If we had nothing but what Saint Paul says, that would be enough to satisfy all who can acquiesce in reason. He proclaims that princes are ministers of God and that the sword has been put in their hand by God in order to protect the good and punish the wicked (Rom. 13:1f.).[25]

At this, these frantic people[26] carp that it may be true that they are ordained of God, but it is not lawful for a believer to involve himself with them. It's as if they should say, "I admit that this task is commanded of God, but none can do it in good conscience, and whoever does renounces God." I beg of you, what man who has a single ounce of brains would speak like that?

But let them reply to this comment! Since they do not doubt that all callings that serve the common good[27] of human beings are lawful and holy, why do they exclude from this number the calling of princes, which surpasses all the others? For example, they do not deny that a Christian can be a tailor or a cobbler. And yet these vocations are not expressly mentioned in the Scriptures. Why then don't they permit a Christian to be a minister of justice, seeing that this calling is so amply approved with praise by the mouth of God?

God declares that princes and all authorities are His ministers and that He has appointed them to be guardians of the good and the innocent and to punish the wicked. And when they do, they execute His work that He has committed into their hands. Who then has forced these foolish men to add that magistrates in serving God are debarred from the fellowship of Christians? This is not even done to the hangman of dogs, by their own admission.

I shall cite one more passage and then end. Saint Paul, seeing that in his time the majority of princes were mortal enemies of the gospel and that such might rouse the indignation of believers not to grant them a high affection, orders Timothy that one must not cease to offer solemn prayers for them in the church,

25. Hubmaier uses this text as a basis for his similar viewpoint (*On the Sword,* in *Anabaptist Beginnings,* pp. 113, 122).

26. *povres phrenetiques.* Literally, "poor frantic [people]."

27. *utilité.*

justifying it on the grounds that God wants all men to be saved and to come to the knowledge of truth (I Tim. 2:2).[28]

He does not mean that God wills to lead to salvation, and consequently to the knowledge of His gospel, all men of the earth, from the very first to the very last, but he means all conditions and states[29] of men. For it seemed to him that the office of princes, of which he spoke, had become rejected and accursed, inasmuch as they all persecuted the gospel. Now if this were so, it would have been superfluous and a folly to pray for them.

Now let us gather from the apostles' words what can be clearly gleaned and deduced. If God wills to lead princes to the knowledge of truth, by what authority do Anabaptists repulse them? If anyone says to me that princes can be converted to God, but must quit their office, that is a blatant lie! For Saint Paul does not say that they have to renounce their political power[30] in order to become Christians. And even the words he uses in no way support such an interpretation.[31] For if it were necessary for a prince to abdicate his office[32] in order to become a Christian, it would follow that his calling would remain outside the grace of God as unworthy and damned.

But they are confident that they have invincible objections for excommunicating the calling of princes from the church and from all hope of salvation in citing several passages, badly misunderstood, which they impudently turn in their favor. First of all, they cite that our Lord Jesus did not order that the woman who was caught in adultery be stoned to death, as the law of God requires. Rather He had mercy on her, saying, "Go and sin no more" (John 8:11).[33]

Before replying, I ask but one question. They say that the ban has replaced the temporal sword in the Christian church,[34] so much so that in place of punishing a crime by death as was

28. Hubmaier again uses the same text to support a view similar to Paul's (*On the Sword,* in *Anabaptist Beginnings,* pp. 117, 124).

29. *estatz.*

30. *principauté.*

31. Literally, "evasion."

32. *dignité.*

33. See *The Schleitheim Confession,* article 6—Yoder, *Sattler,* p. 40.

34. Hubmaier does not agree with the Anabaptist view here (*On the Sword,* in *Anabaptist Beginnings,* pp. 111f.).

formerly done, today we must punish the delinquent by depriving him of the fellowship of believers. Thus I ask them, how do they excuse Jesus Christ for what He has done? For He did not observe their rule. For He neither condemned the woman by banishing her from the fellowship of believers nor condemned her to death. Thereby we already see what poor scatterbrains they are, speaking without reason.

Now I come to the true solution that is quite easy. It is to note that these poor fools in this passage follow that exposition with which the papal priests feather their nests. For since marriage was prohibited them, they wanted as a recompense a license to commit adultery. Thus they borrowed the wives of their neighbors. Now in order for it not to appear that adultery was such a great sin, they said that we should be under the law of grace with respect to it. And hardly recognizing the grace of Jesus Christ in anything, they said adulterers should go unpunished.

These poor people, as I have said, follow them. And thus they experience what Jesus Christ said, that "if a blind man leads another, both fall into the pit" (Matt. 15:14; Luke 6:39).

Now it is certain that our Lord did not want to change anything about the government[35] or the civil order, but without reviling it in any way, He made His office, for which He came into the world, that of forgiving sins. For He was not sent by God His Father in order to perform the office of an earthly judge, but to ransom the world by His death and to testify, by the preaching of the gospel, to the grace of this redemption and similarly to all the benefits which we receive through Him.

For as we see, He promised to receive the thief in His paradise (Luke 23:43); nonetheless, the thief had to pay the price of his crime. Thus He gave the same absolution to both the woman and the thief. But earthly justice punished the thief. The woman went unpunished, because the judges withdrew in shame.

In sum, the action which our Lord Jesus took toward the adulteress is nothing other than what His servants and ministers of His Word take today toward all malefactors. For they only try to exhort them to repent and to turn around on the right road. Then they comfort their consciences by presenting them with the grace of our Lord Jesus and by assuring them of the remission of sins. They do not attempt to punish them. Such does not

35. *police.*

belong to them. But they do not stand in the way of justice doing what it must.

In summary, let us understand the office of our Lord Jesus, and we will surmount any difficulties. His office is to forgive sins and to address His Word to the consciences of sinners. To mete out corporal punishments is not His task, but He leaves these to those to whose authority it belongs and to whom the charge has been commissioned, according to what He says in another text: "Render to Caesar the things that are Caesar's" (Matt. 22:21).

From the same ignorance proceeds the second allegation they make. "Jesus Christ," they say, "did not want to be the divider between the two brothers (Luke 12:14).[36] Thus it follows that a Christian must not meddle in civil disputes in order to adjudicate them."[37]

First of all, Saint Paul permits Christians to do what Jesus Christ refused in this passage: that is to reconcile[38] amiably the differences that happen unexpectedly between believers over worldly goods. For after reprimanding the Corinthians for seeking litigation before pagan judges, and in that way blaspheming the name of God, he admonishes them how much better it would be if they would settle[39] their controversies by arbitration, choosing judges from among the believers to decide their cases (I Cor. 6:1ff.).[40] And [Paul] even makes this argument [that Christians should settle their differences themselves] stronger by observing that we shall judge the angels, a strong reason indeed that we are capable of judging worldly things.

If, according to the example of Jesus Christ, we must shun all arbitration and judgments, then Saint Paul is wrong to indicate that we can. Now it is certain that the Holy Spirit speaks through his mouth. Thus one sees how these giddy people blaspheme God in wanting to condemn what He approves.

36. Hubmaier cites this text to deny the Anabaptist allegation (*On the Sword,* in *Anabaptist Beginnings,* p. 115).

37. A quotation from *The Schleitheim Confession,* article 6—Yoder, *Sattler,* p. 40. Hubmaier also denies this Anabaptist charge (*On the Sword,* in *Anabaptist Beginnings,* pp. 112f.). For the right of Christians to seek litigation, see the *Institutes* 4.20.17–21.

38. *appoincter = réconcilier.*

39. *vuydassent.*

40. Hubmaier uses this text to argue similarly (*On the Sword,* in *Anabaptist Beginnings,* p. 115).

Besides, if it is not lawful for a Christian man to enter into litigation with anyone in order to settle quarrels regarding possessions, inheritance, and other matters, then I ask these good theologians,[41] what will become of the world? For it is not possible for men to exist together, making bargains with one another as human necessity requires it, without experiencing from time to time doubts that require a mediator to work with them, whether a judge or an arbitrator.

If they say that doesn't happen among Christians, they are daydreaming. For even two men of good conscience, owing to the infirmity that is in our nature, can fall out over some difference.[42] Since we are blind to our own faults, each thinks of himself as being right. If Christian men may not resort to arbitration in order to handle their controversies, then what confusion results in the end!

Thus it is easy to see that these miserable fanatics have no other goal than to put everything into disorder, to undo the commonwealth of property in such a way that whoever has the power to take anything is welcome to it. Though they firmly deny this with vigor! But let all trials and arbitration be taken from the world, according to their wish, and what will happen following their "private admonishments" except wholesale robbery? Or else, they will be content to have persuaded all authorities and ministers of justice to abandon their place to them that they may succeed them and put themselves therein as in an empty possession.

What then? Will they say that our Lord Jesus should have refused to do anything good and holy? Let us listen to His reply and this question will be solved. "Who has made Me," He says, "a judge or a divider between you?" He does not say that it was something unlawful,[43] but He claims only that He was not ordained to that end. In fact, it would have obscured His office for which He had come into the world, if He had occupied Himself with such things.

However, if we truly want to profit from this example in order to follow it well, let us hold to the rule that Saint Paul gives us:

41. *docteurs.*

42. Cf. Hubmaier's argument (*On the Sword,* in *Anabaptist Beginnings,* p. 109).

43. Hubmaier and Calvin concur on this point (ibid., p. 115).

that each consider to what he is called and, since we are one body in our Lord, that the arm not infringe on the eye nor the hand the foot (I Cor. 12:21). And to conclude in a few words, I ask if it isn't a lawful thing to arbitrate[44] between Christians, or if everything indeed must be confused? For if it is permissible to divide inheritances, whoever participates in this act does nothing worthy of reprehension, provided he is appointed to do so.

These enemies of government[45] come up with still another argument. Jesus Christ withdrew into the mountain and hid Himself when the people wanted to make Him king (John 6:15).[46] Thus it follows that if a Christian should be elected to a position of justice, he must never accept it, but reject it following the example of the Master.

I am almost ashamed to recount such trivial things. But since I know that the simple and ignorant[47] are seduced by them, I am constrained to point out how they may avoid them.

Everyone knows the silly fantasy which the Jews had about the Messiah: that is, how they thought He would have a kingdom flourishing in this world, that they might live in this world in ease and comfort and triumph over others. So much so that even the apostles, until after His resurrection, held this notion in their heads, as Saint Luke points out in the first chapter of Acts (v. 6).

That is what motivated the people to want to make Jesus Christ king by force, in order that by this means they might be free of subjection to the Romans. Therefore it is no surprise that our Lord hid Himself, since that wish derived from a wicked and perverse error and would have had a most pernicious consequence.

It is clear that His kingdom is not carnal, nor of this world,[48] but spiritual, and consists in things that do not belong to the earth. Now what kingdom should one give Him? If He had submitted to the folly of the people, would He not have confirmed the error that had been so deeply rooted so long? Would He not also thereby have buried His grace and His virtue, since one would have only thought of Him as being carnal?

44. *faire partages.*

45. *police.*

46. See *The Schleitheim Confession,* article 6—Yoder, *Sattler,* p. 40.

47. *rudes.*

48. Hubmaier and Calvin again concur (*On the Sword,* in *Anabaptist Beginnings,* p. 109).

Besides, He would have been made king by sedition and by those to whom it [the right to bestow kingship] did not belong. For since Judea was under the subjection of the Roman Empire, the people did not have the liberty to elect a new king when it pleased them. Thus for these reasons Jesus Christ refused to be made king and not because He considered the calling wicked or repugnant to the Christian life.

Furthermore, it is written (Prov. 8:15) that it is by Him that kings reign, that He is the one who gives grace to ministers[49] of justice in order to make laws and statutes and to govern the people in equity. What more do we want? Jesus Christ Himself[50] is not a king, but He is the protector of all kingdoms, as He has founded and instituted them.

But these fanatics reply that He has commanded us also to do the same when He said to His apostles, "The kings of the world lord it over their people, but it shall not be so with you" (Luke 22:25f.).[51] I reply that the office of the apostles and that of worldly rulers is not at all the same and least of all a matter of exercising domination. Jesus Christ only wanted to make a comparison between the two. For the matter grew out of the apostles' already being in contention among themselves as to which of them was the greatest and should rule over the others in the kingdom of Jesus Christ. To eliminate such an ambition, He taught[52] them that His kingdom is spiritual and that it does not consist in worldly pride, pomp, or lordly power, but that all the pre-eminence that His ministers and officers have is to serve.

Seeing then that this passage does not speak about whether kings can become Christians, but only says that the apostles and ministers of the church may not be as kings who lord it over others, it is pure nonsense[53] to infer from it that Jesus Christ has denied us all authority. It's as much as if someone should say, "It is not lawful for a king to fulfill the office of a minister to which he is not called. Thus the calling of the ministry is an evil and unlawful thing." I beg of you, does the distinction and difference

49. *gens;* literally, "people."

50. *en sa personne.*

51. See *The Schleitheim Confession,* article 6—Yoder, *Sattler,* p. 40. Hubmaier denies that this text invalidates the temporal sword (*On the Sword,* in *Anabaptist Beginnings,* p. 121).

52. *remonstre = remontre, enseigne.*

53. *une grande bestise.*

between the two vocations require us to condemn the one because the other is honored and praised?

Thus let kings keep within their limits[54] and let spiritual pastors similarly be content to perform their office without usurping what doesn't pertain to them, and all will go well. And our Lord Jesus will approve of both. Thus it is a poor exposition on the part of these fanatics to say that the power of the sword is prohibited in this passage.

They equally cite, in order to amass a great pile of references, what Saint Paul says: "that those whom God foreknew, He has preordained to be conformed to the image[55] of His Son" (Rom. 8:29).[56] I grant them that following the exhortation that Saint Paul makes there he summons us to bear the mortification of Jesus Christ in our bodies and to endure the tribulations and miseries by which God wills to test us. But does it follow from this that a believer may not govern a people who have been committed to him? They say yes, because Jesus Christ suffered and did not lord it over others.

As regards the first, that He suffered, I say so also did David, in whose person Christ's passion and sufferings were prefigured. And yet this is not to say that he did not govern. Thus they add on their own this second part from the text of Saint Peter,[57] maliciously falsifying it in order to deceive poor simple people. For they pretend in their booklet[58] that Saint Peter thus speaks, but that is not the case.

So there you have David, who was a king, administering the power of the sword, and nonetheless he was not thereby spared having to suffer in order to be conformed to the image of Jesus Christ, indeed to the point that he represented Him. Moreover, when Saint Philip had to baptize the eunuch who was one of the governors of the kingdom of Ethiopia, he did not impose on him the condition that he could govern no more, but simply asked him if he believed with all his heart in Jesus Christ (Acts 8:37), and left him in his vocation as he was.

54. See Calvin's discussion of the limits of civil government and magistrates in the *Institutes* 4.20.1–13.

55. The Latin reads, *imagini.*

56. See *The Schleitheim Confession,* article 6—Yoder, *Sattler,* p. 40.

57. Calvin has in mind Sattler's reference to Peter, where the Anabaptist cites I Peter 2:21 (ibid.).

58. The *Seven Articles,* or *The Schleitheim Confession.*

In fact, if it is contradictory for a Christian man to govern, what is true for one man should also be true for a people. But Saint Paul granted Christians superiority and rule over their serfs, who were at that time like slaves, and did not command them to surrender this right but only to use it moderately (Eph. 6:9; Col. 4:1), treating their serfs with affection and humanity. What is more, he even appealed to Philemon, whom he calls his companion, to keep his serf under his authority,[59] only he recommended him to treat him humanely (Philem. 1:16f.).

Thus we see, though it was expressly said that Jesus Christ did not govern, how silly it is to argue, "Jesus Christ suffered but did not govern, therefore all domination is reproved." For it is as if someone should say, "Jesus Christ had no place to rest His head, as He testifies (Luke 9:58). Thus it is wrong[60] for a Christian to own either a house, or a garden, or to possess any inheritance." Now as anyone can see, that is completely unreasonable.

In the end, as a drunk after belching loudly throws up the foul broth that lies heavy on his stomach, so these wretches, having reviled this holy calling which our Lord so esteemed, vomit finally at the top of their voice far more disturbing blasphemies.

"The government of magistrates," they say, "is of the flesh, while that of Christians is of the Spirit."[61] It sounds to me like advice I hear from Pope Siricius,[62] blaspheming against holy marriage. For he uses the same terms. But that is nothing in comparison with what follows. "The habitation of magistrates," they say, "is permanent in this world, that of Christians is in heaven."[63] And similar things.[64]

59. *en sa personne.*

60. *mal faict.*

61. A quotation from *The Schleitheim Confession,* article 6—Yoder, *Sattler,* p. 40.

62. *Syrice.* See the *Institutes,* vol. 21 of the Library of Christian Classics, p. 1178, n. 24; and 4.9.14.

63. *The Schleitheim Confession,* from which Calvin is quoting, reads, "Their houses and dwelling remain in this world, that of the Christians is in heaven" (article 6—Yoder, *Sattler,* p. 40).

64. Some similar things: "Their citizenship is in this world, that of Christians is in heaven. The weapons of their battle and warfare are carnal and only against the flesh, but the weapons of Christians are spiritual, against the fortification of the devil. The worldly are armed with steel and iron, but Christians are armed with the armor of God, with truth, righteousness, peace, faith, salvation, and with the Word of God" (ibid., pp. 40f.).

I beg of you, in the name of God—you true faithful ones—and I admonish you to consider carefully what Saint Peter and Saint Jude have said about the corrupters who already in their time were perverting the faith of the simple, and make a comparison of their words with those of the Anabaptists which I have just quoted. I say to you nothing but what each of you will find, that on this point the one group differs in nothing from the other. But because you do not have the books in hand, I will add here the passages.

The first says accordingly, "They will be proud and haughty, despising authorities, and not ashamed to blaspheme against the glorious ones, similar to dumb brutes, reviling matters they cannot understand" (II Peter 2:10, 12). And Saint Jude (8ff.): "They reject," he says, "authorities and blaspheme against the glorious ones. But when the archangel Michael, contending with the devil, disputed over the body of Moses, he was not so bold to pronounce an abusive judgment against him, but said, 'Satan, may God rebuke you!' But these men slander[65] everything they do not understand, and whatever they know by instinct, as dumb brutes do, brings[66] them to grief."

Those are the words of the apostles that apply so appropriately to our Anabaptists of today that it seems they were expressly written for them.

As for their statement that "the habitation of princes is permanent in the world," how often does David contradict them, solemnly affirming[67] that his meditation was totally an effort to reach and aspire to spiritual life? It is likewise certain that the other good kings sought to do the same.

God commands Daniel to perform his office of earthly government in the court of the Persian king (Dan. 12:9, 13), while he awaits those things which have been revealed to him, down to the day of the resurrection. And Moses, the prince of prophets, did not cease to have the course of his thoughts[68] in heaven in hope and desire, though here below he had charge of the civil government of the people.

I thus put in opposition to the Anabaptists Moses, David,

65. *detractent* = *médisent.*

66. *se corrompent* = *se brisent.*

67. *protestant* = *affirmant solennellement.*

68. *sa conversation* = *les cours de ses pensées.*

Hezekiah, Josiah, Joseph, Daniel, and all the kings and judges of Israel, to see if they can support their cause by asking whether these kings were banished from the kingdom of God for having had charge of the sword in this world? If they say that all the anxieties of princes are those of this world, then Isaiah certainly contradicts[69] them, promising that earthly kings will serve in the heavenly and spiritual kingdom of Jesus Christ (Isa. 60:3).

Saint Paul also says the same, exhorting us to offer prayers for those who hold positions of authority in order that we might lead a peaceful life under them, in the fear of God and in holiness (I Tim. 2:2).[70] Therein he shows that the chief end of magistrates is not to maintain the peace of their subjects according to the flesh, but rather to ensure that God is served and honored in their countries and that each person leads a good and honest life.[71]

Thus we see with respect to this matter how false and perverse the Anabaptists' allegations are, by which they condemn the vocation of magistrates, which God has so highly approved. We even see how the devil speaks through their mouths in order to lead princes astray and to hinder them from doing their duty. For instead of one being obligated to exhort them to apply themselves and to take pain to see that the name of God is exalted, and that He reigns over them so much so that they are only His vassals and officers, these people want to believe that that is of no importance to them and that they should in no way meddle therein or be concerned for the honor of God.

As for the end to which they lay claim, I only have two words to say: that in it they reveal themselves to be the enemies of God and of the human race. For they make war against God in wanting to revile what He has exalted. And we could not imagine a better way of trying to ruin the world and ushering in brigandage everywhere than in seeking to abolish the civil government or the power of the sword,[72] which indeed is thrown down if it is not lawful for a Christian man to exercise it.

69. *repugne = contredit.*

70. See n. 28 above.

71. Cf. the *Institutes* 4.20.9.

72. Zwingli also interpreted the Anabaptist rejection of the sword in a very poor light. See *Refutation*, p. 198; *Corpus Reformatorum* 93, cols. 132f.

4

The Seventh Article
On the Oath[1]

We are in agreement concerning the oath that it is a confirmation that ought to be made only in the name of God, and in truth, not in falsehood, according to the commandment of the law. But for Christians, all swearing[2] is forbidden by our Lord Jesus Christ (Matt. 5:34).[3]

Refutation[4]

It seems at first glance that there is nothing wrong in this article. We know[5] how the world today overflows[6] with swearing.[7] There is not a single good heart who is not offended to see the name of God so cheapened. Such makes every oath, whatever it might be, odious. Moreover, in these words[8] of our Lord Jesus which

1. Note in *CO* 7, col. 92: "In the 1566 and following editions: *Article VII. On the Oath.*"

2. *serment* = *serments. Serment* in the singular is ordinarily translated as "oath" or "promise," in the plural as "swearing"; however, throughout this article *serments* is sometimes translated as "oaths," owing to the context.

3. See *The Schleitheim Confession,* article 7—Yoder, *Sattler,* pp. 41f. See also the *Institutes* 2.8.22–27. Cf. Neff, Bender, and Klassen's article "Oath," *Mennonite Encyclopedia,* vol. 4, pp. 2–8, in which they cite early Anabaptists who rejected the oath and discuss the history of the oath's use among Mennonites.

4. Note in *CO* 7, col. 93: "Again, this rubric is missing in the editions of 1544 and 1545." Cf. Zwingli's reply to this article in *Refutation,* pp. 206–219; *Corpus Reformatorum* 93, cols. 142–155.

5. Literally, "we see."

6. *desbordé* = *se laissé aller avec excès.*

7. *iuremens* = *serments.*

8. Calvin is referring to Matthew 5:34–37.

they cite, there are specious grounds[9] for arguing that all swearing in general is forbidden. Or so it seems, if one doesn't pay close attention to the meaning.

Now with regard to the first [paragraph, concerning the superfluity of swearing], it is true that such a dissolution and enormously despised license exists in the world today, concerning the matter of swearing,[10] that we ought to be greatly displeased. Indeed it would be much better not to swear at all than to swear so lightly and thoughtlessly at every turn. Nevertheless we have to note that the way to repair and correct an abuse is not to mix and confuse it with its proper use, thereby indifferently condemning both together.

There is today an excessive pomp and superfluity among some in their drinking and eating, especially at their banquets. Drunkenness, which is a highly indecent and ugly vice, reigns at the present in many people. If in order to correct these abuses someone were to condemn totally the use of wine and all good meats, would this not amount to blaspheming God and thus reprimanding and reproving the good things which He has destined for our consumption?

So much and more is it true of the oath. The Lord has ordained it for confirming and ratifying the truth when it is necessary to do so. Such a manner of swearing redounds[11] to His honor doubly. For by this means charity is sustained between men, and the truth, for which God has a singular concern,[12] is maintained. And inasmuch as one utilizes the oath as a sole witness to the truth, one renders Him, in doing so, one of the highest praises He requires.

In fact, He denotes in the law that a true and legitimate oath is a form of honor which is rendered to Him by His people (Deut. 6:13; 10:20). For even as He commands us to worship Him and to call upon Him alone, so He also commands us to swear by His name. And the prophets, crying out against idolatry, often mention that the people swore by false[13] gods; while on the other hand, when wanting to signify the restoration of the worship of

9. *il y a quelque apparence.*
10. *serment.*
11. *revient.* Literally, "returns."
12. *qu'il a en singuliere recommendation.*
13. *estranges.* Literally, "foreign" or "strange."

God in its entirety, they say men will swear by His name (Jer. 5:7; Hos. 4:15; Amos 8:14; Ps. 63:11; Isa. 45:23).

Here then is the right way in which to treat the oath. First of all, it is necessary to demonstrate its twofold usage: that is to say, for testifying to past and already[14] accomplished events, and for obligating us in the future to fulfill what one can lawfully require of us. Next, it is necessary to explain again that swearing means to call upon God as a witness, and therefore it constrains us to show therein with what reverence we esteem His name. From this it follows that man ought never open his mouth to swear except in fear of God and in singular honor and humility. Thus, by this means, all those forms of blasphemy in which the name of God and Jesus Christ is taken contemptuously are rightfully[15] reproved.

Furthermore, it is necessary to point out the many ways in which the name of God is taken in vain, and to rue,[16] in the first place, lies and false accusations as detestable blasphemies, seeing that by them the truth of God is turned[17] into a lie, and that all His glory is overturned, and that one can almost force Him to deny[18] Himself. Next[19] we have to show what contempt for God it is to take His sacred name so thoughtlessly,[20] as if for pleasure, or for the purpose of coloring up[21] our language, or filling it up with superfluous rubble, or in anger, or for laughter and merriment; and we must reprove this vice that has become so widespread and so deeply rooted in the world today that we see how common a custom it has become. Finally, we must censure[22] the superstitions by which the name of God has been polluted when people have sworn by[23] the names of the saints and indifferently mixed them with His.

If this were done, the oath would no longer carry any profanation of the name of God but would greatly serve His honor.

14. *[de] ia = dèja.*
15. *tresbien.*
16. *detester = maudire.*
17. *convertie = tournée.*
18. *denouncer = renier.*
19. *consequemment = ensuite.*
20. *a la volée.*
21. *farder = peindre, colorer.*
22. *taxer = censurer, accuser, blâmer.*
23. *prins.* Literally, "taken."

For if such were its purpose or end, then who would dare say that it was a vile or evil thing?

In summation, let the world be warned that God considers nothing as great as the glory of His name and works to maintain it in its entirety and punishes those who sully or diminish[24] it. Therefore, let no one take His name except out of great reverence in order solely to make it serve such an end that God is glorified in it.

But the Anabaptists throw a fit[25] and hastily condemn all oaths[26] without exception, without discerning whether some are good or evil. And for that reason[27] it appears that their saying is in no way founded on reason. Let us turn, therefore, to the authority, that is to say, to see whether they have any support from the Word of God.

They depend[28] heavily on the words of our Lord Jesus where He forbids any swearing at all (Matt. 5:34).[29] And from that they conclude that it is not lawful to swear, whether true or false.[30]

In response, first of all, I ask them whether they think Jesus Christ wanted to add to the law of God His Father, or whether He simply wanted to interpret it? In reply they say that He taught "the perfection of the Law."[31]

But I insist further[32] and ask if this perfection hadn't already been understood earlier? For if they reply no, then I say that is an obvious lie. Moses, after publishing the law, solemnly affirmed[33] to the people that he had shown them the way of life and the way of death (Deut. 30:19). Then, recapitulating it all in a brief summary, he says that his teaching leads to this end: "that man should love God with all his heart and with all his mind and with all his soul and with all his strength" (Deut. 6:5). And still in another passage: "And now, Israel, what is it that God requires of

24. *amoindrie* = *amoindrir.*
25. *se iectans aux champs.*
26. *serment.* One could translate this as "swearing."
27. *pourtant* = *pour cette raison.*
28. *font bien un grand boudiers* = *s'appuyent bien sur.*
29. See *The Schleitheim Confession,* article 7—Yoder, *Sattler,* p. 41.
30. Ibid. The sentence Calvin has in mind is, "Christ . . . forbids . . . all swearing, whether true or false."
31. Ibid.
32. *plus outre* = *plus loin.*
33. *protesta* = *affirma solennellement.*

you, but to cling to Him with all your heart?" (Deut. 10:12) and so forth.

These passages indeed sufficiently prove that the teaching of the law contains a rule for right living,[34] for leading man to a complete perfection. Thus, beyond a doubt, God has declared in the law His good will. He has, I say, once and for all delivered judgment[35] on good and evil, on what is pleasing to Him or displeasing.[36]

Consequently, our Lord Jesus, speaking on the perfect life, always referred those whom He taught back to the law (Matt. 19:17 and elsewhere). And Saint Paul in the twelfth chapter of Romans (v. 19) refers us to the same source in order to help us better understand our duty.

Therefore to say that Moses only half taught the people of Israel to honor and serve God is a blasphemy forged first of all by the papists and now renewed by these poor fanatics, who accept[37] as heavenly revelations all the fables they ever heard their grandmothers recount.

If one replies to this that nevertheless Jesus Christ is called "the perfection of the law," and that it is written that we are no longer under a childish doctrine,[38] as were the people of old (Heb. 5:13f.), I reply that this word "perfection" does not refer to the doctrine but to the grace of the Holy Spirit, through whom what is contained in the law is written and imprinted on our heart, in order that our Lord might speak, not only to our ears, but also to our will, and that not only might we hear what He commands us, but do it.

There is also a second reason: which is that our Lord Jesus has Himself fulfilled all righteousness in Himself[39] and has completely observed the law in order that the obedience He has rendered to God His Father might be imputed to us.

As for Saint Paul's calling the law "a childish doctrine" (Gal. 4:1f.), that only refers to the ceremonies and figures. And in this same sense it is written that the law cannot lead His disciples to

34. *bien vivre.*

35. *prononcé.*

36. See the *Institutes* 4.20.15 where Calvin emphasizes the enduring authority of the law.

37. Literally, "take."

38. *doctrine puerile.*

39. *accomply toute iustice en sa personne.*

perfection (Heb. 7:19). Thus all the more are the end, accomplishment, and truth of the law in Jesus Christ.

Furthermore, regarding its teaching on life, what was true from the beginning is still true now and is common to us along with the people of Israel. For it does not vary at all; rather, just as the will and righteousness of God are immutable, so also the law, which is a true and unquestionable[40] declaration of the same, will endure to the end as it was from the beginning.[41]

If one concedes that Jesus Christ simply interpreted the commandment of God His Father concerning the oath, and added nothing to it—as it is necessary to admit—then we have won the point we wanted to make. For the law does not forbid the taking of the name of God *whatever,* but forbids the taking of it *in vain,*[42] signifying that there are legitimate and permissible ways in which it can be taken and used.

Nevertheless, it is necessary to expound the words of our Lord Jesus, because it does seem at first that He intends to prohibit all swearing. Now, in order to understand it correctly,[43] it is necessary to understand the occasion which prompted Him to speak as He did.

The scribes and the Pharisees—as it appears throughout the fifth chapter of Saint Matthew—had by their misleading glosses so corrupted the people that anyone was free to contradict in different ways the commandments of God, provided he had some evasive means of covering himself. Thus in general one did not think at all that it was wrong to swear in vain and thoughtlessly by heaven or by earth, provided one did not swear directly by the name of God.

Now our Lord Jesus shows that it is a foolish deception and sophistry to want to justify[44] oneself before God in this way, seeing that under the terms "heaven" and "earth" His name is indirectly included. Thus when He forbids swearing at all, these words, "at all," refer to one's form of speaking or to the words which are used. This can easily be confirmed by what He adds

40. *certaine.*
41. See n. 36 above.
42. Italics for emphasis.
43. *en avoir bonne et seure intelligence.*
44. *purger = purifier, nettoyer.*

next: "neither by heaven, for it is the throne of God, nor by the earth, for it is His footstool."[45]

Now the Anabaptists falsely[46] apply this to the grounds or to the cause, as if it were forbidden to swear at all, whatever the reason might be. This is contrary to the Lord's intention and contrary to the meaning which He Himself gives in His own[47] procedure and deduction from words.

However, they want to make us believe that we misinterpret[48] this passage, making it say that it is wrong to swear by heaven or by the earth, but it is permitted to swear by God.[49] Or at least, they charge us with that before simple idiots who have neither seen nor heard anything of ours in order to judge for themselves. And then having emitted this slander they moan, saying, "O what blind fools who cannot see that God is greater than His throne!"[50]

But whom are they addressing except themselves, seeing that they, and not others, have invented this in their fantastic brains? And because it follows in the words of our Lord that none ought to swear by his head, inasmuch as none of us knows how to make a hair of his head white or black,[51] they say that this is the reason all oaths are forbidden, for we do not know how to perform what we promise.[52]

But I say, to the contrary, that if animals could talk, they would speak more wisely. For in the first place there is an obvious contradiction in what they babble. For in particular, oaths serve a purpose when we promise to do something in the future. Thus it follows that an oath, by which I shall affirm something that has already been done, cannot be bad.

Of necessity, I beg of you, are they not completely insane to

45. Matthew 5:34–35.

46. *perversement* = *faussement.*

47. *la.*

48. *glosons.* Literally, "we gloss."

49. See *The Schleitheim Confession,* article 7—Yoder, *Sattler,* p. 42: "Others say that swearing cannot be forbidden by God in the New Testament when it was commanded in the Old, but that it is forbidden only to swear by heaven, earth, Jerusalem, and our head."

50. Ibid. Not quoted word for word.

51. See Matthew 5:36.

52. See *The Schleitheim Confession,* article 7—Yoder, *Sattler,* p. 42.

argue as they do? [For they argue] that since we cannot perform what we promise, therefore all oaths are forbidden.[53]

Our reply to that is prompt, for there is a type of oath in which it is not a question at all of obligating oneself to do anything, but solely of bearing testimony to the truth concerning a past action. In fact, it is the type of swearing most used.

Secondly, the meaning is far different from what they imagine. For our Lord Jesus proceeds to show, as He did from the beginning, that if anyone swears by his head, he is equally taking the name of God indirectly; the same if he swears by heaven, the earth, or by Jerusalem. For in the same way that He said that heaven is God's throne, the earth His footstool, and Jerusalem His holy city, He consequently proves that man's head is a part of God's sovereignty, since He alone uses it as He wills.

It is as if He were saying, "If anyone swears by his head, and thinks that he is swearing by something that belongs to himself, without his oath committing an offense[54] against God, he is deceived. For God so reigns there that man can do nothing. Thus he always takes the name of God."

We see how our Lord carried out His meaning. But these harebrained people want to take it over[55] for themselves and turn it into a cock-and-bull story.

The conclusion is that our yes should be yes and our no, no, and anything more than this comes from evil. These words are easy to understand, except these swine overturn them with their snouts, so much so that they completely confound them. For they say that they mean no more than if Christ had said that our speech[56] should be yes and no and that it is wrong to add anything further.[57]

Now our Lord Jesus twice states each of these two words in order to indicate that we should be firm and faithful in our

53. Calvin's paraphrase of this argument is slightly misleading; perhaps the fault is due to the French text on which Calvin depended. In *The Schleitheim Confession* Sattler argues that since God can keep His Word and His promises, it is permissible for God to swear that He will fulfill them; but since it is quite another thing for men to keep their promises, "therefore we should not swear" (article 7—Yoder, *Sattler,* pp. 41f.).

54. *attouche à = port atteinte à.*

55. *transporter = entraîner.*

56. *propoz.*

57. See *The Schleitheim Confession,* article 7—Yoder, *Sattler,* p. 42.

speech. It's as if He were saying, "Do not change so as to have to retract your words each time. And let your speech be free of lying and hypocrisy. But let your yes be yes and your no be no." In fact, Saint James, wanting to teach the same lesson,[58] says word for word the same: "Let your yes be yes and your no be no" (James 5:12), by which he means that believers ought to have a firm constancy[59] in their words.

If there were such a loyalty and firmness in us, all oaths would be superfluous. For this simplicity of words, to affirm and deny, would suffice, without having to swear. Consequently the truth must not reign where oaths are frequently used. Therefore, our Lord was not without cause to declare that such proceeds from evil. For to tell the truth, the reason why we are led to swear is that since the whole world is so full of lies, cunning, sham, and disloyalty, there is no one who dares trust even his own brother. Thus one evil leads to another.

But in all that our Lord Jesus in no way condemns[60] lawful oaths that were permitted in the law; rather,[61] He only repairs and corrects this license which the people, being badly taught by corrupt teachers,[62] had given themselves. For, in the first place, they did not think that their swearing was an indirect taking of God's name, nor did they have an aversion for lies; thus they looked upon all vain and thoughtless oaths as nothing.

Seeing I have sufficiently overturned all the foundations on which the Anabaptists depend, by which they want to condemn all swearing without any distinctions or exceptions, it now remains to show through sound reasons[63] and the testimony of the Scriptures how a Christian may lawfully swear without offending God. Now I solemnly reaffirm here what I said earlier, that I have no intention of giving full license to the world to let it abuse the name of God by indulging in thoughtless and rash oaths.

I know that it is a vice that is only too common, and therefore it is necessary to urge its repression rather than its augmentation. I also know that it is no small sin to take God's name in vain

58. *doctrine.*
59. *tenure.*
60. *n'attouche nullement.*
61. *ains = mais, plutôt.*
62. *docteurs.*
63. *bonnes raisons.*

and that so much the more ought we to strive, by every means, to prevent such an evil.

But alas! To condemn what is good in order to check abuse is not a good means of procedure. For this reason,[64] when I say that it is lawful in some instances for a Christian man to swear, let each be warned that I am speaking of a correct usage, which is characterized[65] by a fear and reverence of the name of God, and let no one take advantage of my words to rush out in order to engage in vain, superfluous, or otherwise vicious oaths.

Now in order to define more clearly[66] what I mean by saying that a Christian man may swear without offense, first of all I mean when it is a matter of rendering testimony to the truth. Secondly, if it is an affair that warrants it, for which consideration ought to be given for the honor of God and the love of our neighbor. That is to say, when it might be expedient and profitable to swear, as much for the honor of God as for preserving charity among ourselves. Thirdly, if necessity requires it; that is to say, whenever it is necessary to use such a confirmation. Fourthly, if the intention[67] and aim[68] of the one swearing is such. And finally, if it proceeds in fear, being concerned to sanctify the name of God. In those cases, and not otherwise, I say swearing is permitted of Christians. If any *bon vivant*[69] abuses this, he does so to his condemnation.

In order to confirm what I say, I cite the commandment of God to which I hold.[70] That is that He has ordained and willed for us to swear by His name, whenever we have a legitimate cause.[71] From this I conclude that to swear is neither a simple thing nor in itself evil. For it cannot be that anything evil could ever please God. Furthermore, since it is a kind of homage which the faithful render God—as He often shows in the prophets—to say that it is a vice and sin is too blatantly opposed to the truth. For at the same time there is a reason, which is that it is often

64. *parquoy = pour cette raison.*
65. *conioinct avec.*
66. *apertement = clairement.*
67. *deliberation = intention.*
68. *la fin.*
69. *gaudisseur = bon vivant, railleur.*
70. Calvin does not cite a specific text. He may have had in mind Leviticus 19:12, Numbers 30:2, or Deuteronomy 23:21.
71. The texts cited in n. 70 support Calvin's point here.

expedient for the truth, which otherwise is doubtful, to be confirmed. And an oath is the only means for doing this.

What the Anabaptists cite,[72] with respect to correcting this commandment, is an obvious blasphemy. For it would follow that Jesus Christ had retracted what had earlier been established by God His Father. This cannot in any way be tolerated, as we have seen.

In fact, the apostle, speaking on the oath—although he spoke of it only incidentally while treating another subject—does not say that its usage has been abrogated, but calls it the final confirmation in human disputes (Heb. 6:16). I beg of you, when the apostle, speaking to Christians, declares that the oath exists for the purpose of putting an end to all controversies, does he not sufficiently indicate that it is an order approved of God, which has a place in the Christian church?

What temerity it is, then, to revolt[73] against it and to reject this remedy which he gives as a damnable vice!

Accompanying this teaching are many examples—as many involving God as all His servants. Men, says the apostle in the passage just cited, swear in the name of God, inasmuch as He is above them; God swears by Himself, inasmuch as He does not have a superior but is sovereign over all.[74]

As for God, the Anabaptists reply that He can indeed swear, seeing that He can accomplish whatever He says, and thus is beyond any danger of perjuring Himself. For He is faithful and wants to fulfill what He promises.[75] But it is a different matter with mortal man, who often cannot fulfill what he promises, though he wants to, and therefore it is rash of him to swear, obligating himself to what is above his power.[76]

When they have thrown this solution up in the air, they think that that is it, and that they have closed our mouths. But my reply is prompt. For they cannot say the same of all the patriarchs, prophets, holy kings, and ancient fathers, who indeed also swore following the example of God. For there is Abraham, the

72. Calvin seems to be referring to the Anabaptists' use of Matthew 5:34. See *The Schleitheim Confession,* article 7—Yoder, *Sattler,* p. 41.

73. *se rebecquer = se révolter.*

74. See Hebrews 6:13.

75. Calvin follows Sattler's own argument very accurately here. Cf. *The Schleitheim Confession,* article 7—Yoder, *Sattler,* p. 41.

76. Ibid.

father of all believers, who swore. And Isaac, and Jacob, and David, Hezekiah, and Josiah, who all did the same (Gen. 14:22; 21:23; 31:53; I Kings 1:17, 29; II Chron. 34:31).

What difference is there between them and us? At least, it appears that their response above is pure sophistry. And it is even easy to see how, as animals, they betray themselves on the first word.

If to escape they claim that these examples are taken from the Old Testament[77] and at present in the Christian church we are held[78] by tighter[79] reins—although that error has already been refuted—nevertheless they profit nothing by this. For we can easily produce the apostles for them, who used oaths, even in their writings, when it was necessary.

Saint Peter and Saint Paul, they say, did not swear in order to promise anything, but only to testify[80] to the promise made by God.[81] We can easily see here how those who resolve[82] to contradict the truth clearly entangle themselves in a thousand absurdities and nonetheless are unashamed of their impudence.

To begin with, in giving such a response, they concede to us that some oaths are lawful, that is to say, when one testifies to past events. For it follows from their words that the oath is only wrong when we promise something in the future.

Still are they not ashamed to lie so openly, wanting to make believe that there is nothing to what the eye sees? Saint Paul swears to the Corinthians that, in order to spare them, he did not come to them, since had he it would have been necessary to treat them harshly[83] (II Cor. 1:23f.). He vows[84] to the Romans that he would be content to be rejected by Christ if it would save

77. Ibid. See William Klassen's article "Old Testament," *Mennonite Encyclopedia*, vol. 4, pp. 49–52. Klassen discusses the Anabaptist view of the Old Testament, discusses the unfair attacks of the Reformers on the Anabaptists for their supposed rejection of the Old Testament, and describes the major Anabaptist views on the Old Testament (those of Hans Denck, Ludwig Hetzer, Hans Leupold, Leonhard Schiemer, Pilgram Marbeck, and Menno Simons). See Klassen's bibliography on p. 52 of the article.

78. *nous avons.*

79. *roide* = *raide.* Can mean "inflexible."

80. *asseurer* = *rassurer.*

81. See *The Schleitheim Confession*, article 7—Yoder, *Sattler*, p. 42.

82. *se deliberent* = *se décident.*

83. *asprement* = *âprement.*

84. *iure.* Literally, "swears."

the Jewish people (Rom. 9:3). To confirm the love he has for the Philippians, he takes again God as his witness[85] (Phil. 1:8). Again he testifies[86] to the Corinthians that his life[87] among them was in good conscience (II Cor. 1:12). Still again, to the Thessalonians, he testifies that he did not live among them by avarice or for gain, and he calls God as a witness to his saintly behavior (I Thess. 2:5, 10).

These poor fools[88] say that the apostles never swore to affirm their own actions, but only to testify to the covenant of God.[89] I beg of you, what does such an impudence deserve? Are they even[90] worthy of our opening our mouth to speak to them?

Still it is necessary to clear up this difficulty which they put forward, that is, that a man should not promise anything based on an oath, seeing he cannot fulfill it. To that I reply that when a subject swears to his prince to perform what his duty requires, it is his responsibility to obey and to be faithful. It is not in confidence of his strength, or by virtue of his pride, as if he were despising God and mocking[91] Him, but rather in invoking God's aid that he responds with his will that such will or ought to be.

In any event, it is an insane fancy to reprove oaths while permitting simple promises. For if there is temerity in the one, there will be temerity in the other. Therefore, if it is lawful for us to make promises, it is necessary to explain why we cannot guarantee[92] our promises with an oath when necessity requires it.

But with respect to oaths being sanctified[93] and lawful, we have several examples of such in the Scriptures, three of which are very notable. It is written in the Book of Chronicles that Asa, king of Judah, being warned by Azariah, a priest and prophet, called all the people to Jerusalem and there made them vow to serve God forever (II Chron. 15:14). The same is recited by Josiah, when the Book of the Law was recovered, that in order to renew

85. In the text simply *iure.*
86. *iure.*
87. *qu'il a conversé.*
88. *phrenetiques.*
89. See *The Schleitheim Confession,* article 7—Yoder, *Sattler,* p. 42.
90. *pour le moins.*
91. *luy faisant la figue = luy moquant.*
92. *acertener = rendre certain.*
93. *sainct.*

the covenant made with Moses, he called upon the people, making them promise forever to remain obedient to God (II Chron. 34:32). The third example involves Ezra and Nehemiah and that instance when the people, having returned from Babylon, swore to follow, from that time on, God and His Word (Neh. 10:29).

Now when everything is taken into consideration, the same was done at the first publication of the law. But because, I say, I am having to deal with harebrained and obstinate people, I only wanted to cite those passages where the oath is notably made mention of.

So there we have the entire church of Israel making a solemn oath to God, promising the most difficult thing there is: to cling faithfully to Him. It was done several times. That the act was good there can be no doubt. For it was witnessed and even praised by the Holy Spirit.

I shall not attempt at length to explain[94] how men can be thus obligated to God to do what isn't in them, except that it is fitting for us to remember what I have touched on in passing, that believers should always presuppose that God will never defraud[95] them of the grace which He has promised them, and on this they may justify[96] their oaths. But since it is the case that God approves of this kind of oath and that by His ordinance His church has used it many times, I ask of our heedless crowd,[97] by what authority do they dare reprove it?

Or rather, without having a good time at their expense—seeing that so much time is lost—I pray and exhort all servants of God to consider what audacity it is for these poor ignoramuses to make such authoritative decisions and to want to compel the world to accept them as irrevocable judgments, beyond contradiction.

As for myself, I am confident that with respect to this matter of the oath, as well as the preceding matters, I have fully satisfied those who have ears and understanding and who want to consent to[98] the known truth.[99]

94. *ie ne m'arreste pas beaucoup à exposer.*

95. *defaudra = frustra.*

96. *fondent.*

97. Literally, "of our heedless ones," or "of our giddy ones," or "of our dullards."

98. *acquiesur à = se complaire, se reposer.*

99. *la verité congneue.*

5

On the Incarnation[1]

I have dispensed[2] with the seven articles contained in the booklet[3] which the patriarchs of the Anabaptists have circulated[4] as their final resolution of what they hold apart from others. Therefore there should remain nothing more than to conclude and to bring this present tract to an end, were it not that they have passed on two articles as equally great in consequence as any of the others which need to be examined. For in general all the Anabaptists hold to them. Even, I say, those who composed this splendid[5] resolution taught them at the time.[6]

The one is that they do not hold that Jesus Christ was true man, but rather, with respect to His body, make Him into a phantom.[7] The other is that they think that souls being separated from their bodies sleep until the day of judgment, without consciousness or understanding,[8] or rather that man's soul

1. The last two sections of this treatise are untitled in the *Calvini Opera.*

2. *despeché = exposé, traité.*

3. *livre,* i.e. the *Seven Articles* or *The Schleitheim Confession.*

4. Literally, "have made."

5. *belle.*

6. It is highly improbable that Michael Sattler taught the view of incarnation that Calvin rejects in this section. The position Calvin attacks is attributed to Melchior Hofmann (1495–1543); it was transmitted to Dutch Anabaptism by Obbe Philips (ca. 1500–1568) and rearticulated by Menno Simons (1496–1561). For a discussion of the Melchiorite position, see Williams, *Radical Reformation,* pp. 325–337. Menno's work was not called to Calvin's attention until 1545, but footnotes will cite Menno's *Brief and Clear Confession* (1544) where such references may illuminate Calvin's objections. See n. 40 below for further references to Hofmann. Also see p. 32.

7. *phantosme.* A reference to Hofmann's celestial-flesh theory. See n. 40 below.

8. *sans rien sentir ni cognoistre.*

alone constitutes his life,[9] which swoons[10] in dying until it is resuscitated.[11]

Anyone can see the consequences that these two errors entail.

That they have not mentioned a word of this, I do not know if it has been by way of a ruse[12]—seeing that they are so odious—or whether with good reason they knew their doctrine would be rendered damnable by it. Whatever the case, since I have undertaken to arm all the faithful against their false teachings,[13] it is not good for me to close my eyes[14] to these two gravely[15] persistent and spiteful views, since they are so common among them.

What some among them have held concerning [the holding of] property in common,[16] or that a man may have several wives, even compelling some to take more who were content with one, and a thousand other absurdities,[17] I refrain[18] from mentioning. For even they, being confounded in their madness, have for the most part retracted these.[19] But of the two points I have cited, there is another reason, since these persist among them.

9. *n'est que sa vie.*

10. *deffaut.*

11. Or, "raised again." This second article involves the psychopannychist views which Calvin had earlier rejected in his *Psychopannychia.* See pp. 19–24. Also see Williams, *Radical Reformation,* pp. 581–592.

12. *cautell = ruse.* Since Calvin did not distinguish between the Anabaptists he knew in Orléans, the Melchiorites, and Sattler's Swiss Brethren, he was puzzled by the silence of the *Seven Articles* on the celestial-flesh theory and the sleep of the soul.

13. *opinions.*

14. *dissimule = ferme les yeux sur.*

15. *tant.*

16. *des communauté des biens.* Literally, "community of goods." The Münsterites and the Hutterites held this view. See Ulrich Stadler's *Cherished Instructions on Sin, Excommunication, and the Community of Goods,* in Williams and Mergal, *Anabaptist Writers,* pp. 274–284; Stadler's work appeared about 1537. See also Calvin's *Against the Libertines,* chap. 21, nn. 3, 4, 5, where he rejects the Libertine-Anabaptist doctrine of the "community of goods."

17. Calvin is apparently referring to the views of the Münsterites, Davidians, and Batenburgers, who advocated polygamy. See Williams and Mergal, *Anabaptist Writers,* p. 29. Calvin might also have had the radical Anabaptists of St. Gall in mind. See Williams, *Radical Reformation,* pp. 127–134. Cf. Calvin's *Against the Libertines,* chap. 20, in which he attacks the concept of "spiritual marriage."

18. *ie me deporte = je m'astiens.*

19. Sattler writes in the preface to *The Schleitheim Confession,* "A very great offense has been introduced by some false brothers among us, whereby several have turned away from the faith, thinking to practice and observe the freedom of the Spirit and of Christ. But such have fallen short of the truth and (to their own

As for the first, concerning the body or the human nature of our Lord Jesus Christ, we must note that there were two ancient heresies that conform to, or approach, what they say about it. For the Manichees[20] fantasized that Jesus Christ brought[21] a heavenly body into the womb of the Virgin His mother. The Marcionites[22] had a little different delusion, that He did not have a truly substantial body, but only one that appeared or seemed to be a body—what we call a phantom.[23] The end of both has been to deny that Jesus Christ was descended from human seed.[24]

Therefore we see that the Anabaptists, in this way, only stir up errors that the devil has kept alive for one thousand four hundred years and that were refuted[25] by the Word of God. Nevertheless, as I have affirmed from the beginning, I do not want this to prejudice their case in any way unless I can refute[26] them first of all by means of the pure Word of God, as if men had never said anything about it.

What I shall say about it is solely as a warning so that each person may know the origin from which proceeds what the Anabaptists put forward at the present, as if it had been revealed to them almost from heaven. And I do it to warn[27] them as well. For even the greatest theologians[28] who have belonged to their

---

condemnation) are given over to the lasciviousness and license of the flesh. They have esteemed that faith and love may do and permit everything, and that nothing can harm nor condemn them, since they are 'believers'" ("The Cover Letter," in *The Schleitheim Confession*—Yoder, *Sattler*, pp. 35–36).

20. The Manichees, who posited a dualism of light and dark, were founded by the Persian Gnostic Mani (A.D. 216–276).

21. *apporter = rapporter, produire.*

22. See Calvin's *Institutes* 2.13.1–3 where he singles out the Marcionites and refutes their views.

23. *phantosme.* Marcion of Pontus (A.D. 150) denied the materiality of the body of Christ. See Menno Simons, *The Incarnation of Christ,* in *Complete Writings of Menno Simons,* trans. Leonard Verduin, ed. John C. Wenger (Scottdale, Pa.: Herald, 1956), pp. 427–432. Calvin labels the Anabaptists the "new Marcionites" (*Institutes* 2.13.3).

24. *semence humaine.*

25. *confonduz.*

26. *convaincuz = refutes.*

27. *advertir = avertir.*

28. *docteurs.* Littell dismisses this charge (*Origins*, p. 61) by pointing out that Hans Denck (ca. 1500–1527), Conrad Grebel (ca. 1498–1526), and Balthasar Hubmaier (1480?–1528) were all university trained; Hubmaier even held a Doctor of Theology degree from Ingolstadt.

sect have been so ignorant of history and all antiquity that I do not think a single one of them has ever known what Marcion's name signifies.

It is thus good that they, as well as the others, be informed that the first author of this opinion, with which they besmear[29] the world today, was rejected and anathematized along with it, not by a few members, but universally by the entire Christian church, shortly after, that is to say, about forty years after, the death of the apostles. For Eusebius[30] and Saint Jerome[31] report how Polycarp, who was a disciple of and familiar with Saint John the apostle, upon encountering Marcion at Rome, called him "the first-born[32] of Satan." I will not mention the other errors with which he troubled the church. For when this one has been carefully examined, one will understand, as I hope, that one would have to go to great trouble to find a more damnable error.

First I will show by many and very convincing[33] testimonies of the Scriptures that our Lord Jesus truly took on[34] our flesh and human nature when He was revealed to us by God His Father in this world. And I will demonstrate it so clearly that even a little child will realize what a grave[35] impudence it is for the Anabaptists to deny it any longer. However, it will not be necessary to bring to bear all the passages that might serve this purpose. Thus, to avoid prolixity,[36] I shall choose those which in my view are the most fitting.

We know that from the beginning of the world our Lord promised Eve that her *seed*[37] would be victorious over the serpent (Gen. 3:15). Let us see if this has been accomplished in us, or if it has ever been accomplished in a mortal man, except

29. *brouillent = barbouillent.*

30. Eusebius, *Church History,* in *Nicene and Post-Nicene Fathers,* ed. Philip Schaff, second series (1890–1900; reprint ed., Grand Rapids: Eerdmans, 1979), vol. 1, p. 187.

31. Jerome, *Lives of Illustrious Men,* in *Nicene and Post-Nicene Fathers,* second series, vol. 6, p. 367.

32. *filz aisné = fils l'ainé.*

33. *trescertains.*

34. *a prins.*

35. *trop grande.*

36. "longwindedness."

37. "Seed" in this instance and in subsequent paragraphs is italicized, as this word was one of the key terms in dispute.

by the means of Jesus Christ, who has vanquished and overcome Satan for us.

Now because this promise was still so obscure, it was later greatly clarified, for both Abraham (Gen. 12:3) and Jacob (Gen. 28:14), when it was said to them that in their *seed* all the nations of the earth would be blessed. Now this seed, as Saint Paul interprets it (Gal. 3:16)—and reason demonstrates—is Jesus Christ. Thus this promise cannot be verified in any other way unless Jesus Christ is descended from Abraham's race.

The same holds true for what was said to David: "I will set upon your throne the fruit of your loins, to reign for ever" (Ps. 132:11; 89:28ff.). And also in the same sense when it is confirmed by the prophet Isaiah (Isa. 11:1) that "a shoot shall come forth from the root of Jesse." We know that that can only refer to the same Redeemer who had been promised to Abraham. Thus it was necessary that He should be from the line of David, according to the generation of the flesh, or the promise would have been without effect.[38]

For this reason[39] Saint Matthew, wanting to trace His genealogy, begins it by calling Him the "Son of David, Son of Abraham" (Matt. 1:1), in order to specify more expressly that this is He who had been promised. In fact, this was a form of speech commonly used among the Jewish people, to speak of Him as we see the evangelists doing (Matt. 9:27; 12:23; 15:22; 20:30; 21:9, 15; 22:42, etc.).

To all this the Anabaptists offer a solution which alone shows sufficiently what animals they are and how audacious their impudence is. He is called, they say, the "Son of David," not because He has taken anything from the Virgin Mary or was made man from her substance, but only because she carried Him in her body, as water passes through a tube.[40]

38. *frustratoire = sans effet, vain.*

39. *pourtant = pour cette raison.*

40. This view is attributed to Melchior Hofmann (see n. 6 above). For sources of Hofmann see Cramer, *Bibliotheca Reformatoria Neerlandica,* vol. 5; W. I. Leendertz, *Melchior Hofmann* (Haarlem, 1883); Friedrich Otto zur Linden, *Melchior Hofmann: ein Prophet der Wiedertäufer* (Haarlem, 1885); and Hans Schoeps, *Vom himmlischen Fleisch Christ* (Tübingen, 1951). See also "Hofmann, Melchior," *Mennonite Encyclopedia,* vol. 2, pp. 778–785. See the *Institutes* 2.12.1–3; 2.13.1; 2.14.1–6. These passages (appearing in the Strassburg edition of 1539) suggest that Calvin came to know of the Melchiorites during his sojourn at

This might be so, if the word *seed* were not present.[41] However, in truth, all men of good judgment would see that this is a subterfuge. They would regard it as a pretext and with suspicion.[42] But inasmuch as it is so often reiterated that He is of the *seed* of Abraham, does it not remain a sophistry to deny that He was true man?

In fact, when Isaiah prophesies His coming, he does not simply say that He will be "born of a virgin," but he says first of all that He will be "conceived" (Isa. 7:14). This "conception" means that He had to be formed from her *seed*, as anyone who understands the meaning of the word realizes.

Besides, Saint Paul presses them further when he says that "He was made from the seed of David according to the flesh and was nonetheless declared the Son of God by His power" (Rom. 1:3f.). Thus on the one hand you have Jesus Christ pronounced the "Son of God," then it is added that, according to His human nature, He is "descended from David's lineage." Thus does it not follow that a man must be mad to close his eyes and stop his ears to this, in order to persist and maintain to the contrary that Jesus Christ possesses nothing from the nature of men with respect to the substance of His body?

Similarly, in another place, the same apostle, speaking on the dignity and nobility of the Jews, says among other things that they are the successors and the offspring of the fathers, from whom Christ descended, "according to the flesh" (Rom. 9:5). I pass over many other passages: as when it is said that God "was manifested in the flesh" (I Tim. 3:16), as well as that He "suffered" in humility "in the flesh" (I Peter 4:1). So also the fact that Saint John says that "the Word became[43] flesh" (John 1:14), and above all that he himself so often attributes [to Christ] the title "Son of man," and other passages, because they are superfluous in the light of the two notable passages that I have cited.

Strassburg. John Bomeromenus and Herman of Gerbehaye, Anabaptists whom Calvin converted to Protestantism, may have shared Melchiorite views. See Calvin's letters to Farel, February 6 and 27, 1540—Herminjard, *Correspondances*, vol. 6, p. 165, no. 846; and p. 189, no. 854. See also Menno's *Incarnation*, in *Complete Writings*, p. 432: "[Christ] did not become flesh of Mary, but in Mary. . . ."

41. *exprimé*. Literally, "expressed."
42. Literally, "Nonetheless there might be a little more pretext or suspicion."
43. Literally, "was made," or "has been made."

I am content, thus, to cite[44] these texts, along with those that prove my point, that declare at the same time how necessary it is for us to believe that our Lord Jesus was clothed with and truly took a nature in common with ours when He was made man.

The apostle in the Epistle to the Hebrews (2:16) uses a good argument to amplify the love Christ has for us, which is that He did not assume[45] the nature of angels, but ours. If we accept the fantasy of these miserable Anabaptists, this grace and inestimable bounty of the Lord Jesus would be obliterated from our memory, and we would no longer realize that He has honored us more than He has angels.

In addition, He says that by the means of the communication which He has with us, in His flesh and His blood, He is called our brother and enjoys true brotherhood with us (Heb. 2:11). From that we have to conclude that the greatest benefit that we can have would be taken from us if Jesus Christ had not communicated with us in flesh and in blood. For how could we be children of God without being His brothers?

Now the apostle says that we obtain such a benefit because He is united with us in the same nature and not another. Then he adds further that it was expedient that He should be similar to His brothers in order to be a "faithful and merciful high priest" (Heb. 2:17). From this he deduces a singular consolation: that "we do not have an advocate who is unable to sympathize with our weaknesses, since He Himself has been tempted, being made similar to us, except without sin" (Heb. 4:15). Seeing then that in this similitude, which he introduces between us and Jesus Christ, he only makes this single exception of sin, it follows that in the rest He is like us—it being understood that he is speaking primarily of human nature.

Thus in these passages we see not only how our Lord Jesus is truly our brother in union with a same humanity, but also the benefit it therein gives us, of which the Anabaptists strip and deprive us, since they attribute to Him (I know not what) a heavenly body that has nothing in common with ours.

Similarly, that entire argument that Saint Paul uses[46] with the Corinthians, in order to found our universal resurrection on that

44. *amener* = *citer.*

45. *prins.*

46. *mene* = *cite.*

of Christ's, would no longer hold up[47] if He did not have a nature common to ours (I Cor. 15:12ff.). "Since Christ is resuscitated," he says, "we shall be resuscitated." And if there had been no resurrection for us, Christ would not have been resuscitated [i.e., raised].

That would be promptly contradicted if one could claim that Jesus Christ brought a heavenly body with Himself into His mother's womb.[48] For it would hardly be marvelous if a substance that has come from heaven should be free of corruption. Nor would it follow that our bodies, which are terrestrial and only composed of corrupt material, should rise again.

Therefore in order to have a solid[49] foundation under this argument,[50] it is required that our Lord Jesus should participate in a same nature with us. For therein lies the only certain hope of resurrection that we can have, that this corruptible flesh which we presently carry about has already been raised[51] in Jesus Christ, has taken possession of heaven, and is immortal there.

By this means, I say, we possess a firm[52] and sure foundation for reassuring ourselves. Otherwise not.

And in another passage the same apostle, wanting to show how the Lord Jesus is our mediator, specifically says that He is "man" (I Tim. 2:5). Besides, He knew that we would never have been induced to turn to Him if we had not been first of all persuaded that He was our neighbor and had to do with us.

Therein, accordingly, lies our confidence that helps us cling to Jesus Christ and seek Him as mediator, because He is united with us and participates in the same nature with us. This is what the prophet Isaiah means when he says that He was made "Immanuel" (Isa. 7:14), that is to say, "God with us." For that cannot be apart from a true resemblance and union of nature.

There are still other incontrovertible reasons in support of this which, although they are not expressed in the Scriptures, are nonetheless certain, since they are founded on them. For

47. *consisteroit = resterait ferme.*

48. Again, Hofmann's view. See Menno's *Incarnation,* in *Complete Writings,* pp. 430f.

49. *bon.*

50. *en toute ceste deduction.* Calvin is referring to Paul's argument.

51. *est desia ressuscitee.*

52. *bonne.*

that it was necessary that He who should be our mediator had to be true God and true man, belongs to the mediator's office, which exists to reconcile men with God and to abolish the mortal enmity that formerly existed between them. Now there was no hope that this could be done, unless the majesty of God descended to us, uniting itself with the weakness of our nature.

Equally it was the mediator's task to make us children of God and heirs of His kingdom, instead of being heirs of death and damnation. Therein, accordingly, lies the foundation for our assurance[53] that we are children of God, seeing that the natural Son of God took on body of our body and flesh of our flesh in order to be made one with us.

Furthermore, the matter was necessary for our redemption: that the disobedience which was committed in our nature might also be repaired in the same. For this reason[54] our Lord Jesus became true man, presenting Himself as in the person of Adam, whose name He also assumed (Rom. 5:14; I Cor. 15:47), in order to pay the price of sin in the flesh in which it was committed.

Therefore those who strip Jesus Christ of His human nature effectively[55] obscure His goodness. Plus they also do us a great wrong by destroying the true means[56] which we possess for having a right and full assurance in Him.

Now lest it appear that I am only closing my eyes to those texts that might be useful to them, I shall produce all those that they might be able to cite in order to disguise[57] their fantasy.

Saint Paul writes in one place (Phil. 2:7) "that Jesus Christ emptied Himself, taking the form of a servant, being made similar to men, and in appearance showed Himself [as] man." From that Marcion concluded that His body was a phantom. The Anabaptists today use it to show that His body was not like ours.[58]

53. *fiance = assurance.*

54. *par quoy = pour cette raison.*

55. *bien.*

56. *obiect.*

57. *donner couleur.*

58. See nn. 40 and 48 above. The Melchiorite view to which Calvin objects is exemplified in these passages of Menno's *Incarnation:* "This same woman conceived in her womb the afore-mentioned seed, which is God's Word, not from her body nor of her body, but of God, by the power of the Holy Ghost, through faith." "The Word . . . was not Abraham's natural flesh and blood." "For Christ

Our response is easy enough. For in that passage Saint Paul does not deal with the substance of Jesus Christ's body, but he solely teaches[59] that although He is capable of revealing Himself in His glorious majesty as God, He became[60] as a simple man in complete insignificance.

[Thus] Paul exhorts the Philippians in humility. To achieve this, he cites Christ as an example for them, saying that "though He was in the form of God," that is to say, in the glory of God, "He nevertheless emptied[61] Himself." Then he adds how He revealed Himself in the form of man and became[62] as man.

What can these words mean other than that under the veil of His flesh, in which He appeared small and contemptible, He hid the glory of His divinity in such a way that one could only recognize in Him His fragile condition, which He showed outside. Thus there is no difficulty with respect to solving this passage.

But there is another one that appears to contain some leeway.[63] It is in the fifteenth chapter of First Corinthians (v. 47), where Saint Paul says that "the first Adam was of the earth, made from dust; the second is heavenly, having come from heaven." From that the Anabaptists, following the example of their predecessors, the Manichees, conclude that Jesus Christ had a heavenly body and was neither formed nor created from human seed, that is, from the substance of the Virgin His mother.[64]

The solution to this argument lies in considering why Saint Paul states[65] and holds the two ideas together, not in cutting out or holding back a word that would change[66] the meaning. Thus Saint Paul, in the process of showing the origin of death and the origin of the resurrection, that is, the first from Adam, the second

---

Jesus, as to His origin, is no earthly man, that is, a fruit of the flesh and blood of Adam" (*Complete Writings*, pp. 433, 437).

59. *remonstre = remontre.*

60. *s'est porte = s'est comporte.* Literally, "he demeaned himself," or "he conducted himself."

61. *s'est aneanty.*

62. *s'est porte.*

63. *d'apparence.*

64. See nn. 40 and 58 above.

65. *demene = dit, raconte.*

66. *depraver = alterer.*

from Jesus Christ, says, among other things, that "Adam became a living soul, Jesus Christ a life-giving Spirit" (I Cor. 15:45).

Now by that he does not mean to deny that Jesus Christ had a soul similar to ours, but he means that He had in addition His Spirit, which is not only living but has in Itself the power to make alive.[67] Then he adds that "the first Adam was of the earth," since he "came from dust," and that "Jesus Christ is heavenly, having come from heaven."

There is no doubt but that this passage must be interpreted as was the other, that is, as having to do with the quality of Jesus Christ, and not with His substance. I mean with respect to His supernatural and divine power, which He has [received] from heaven as the Son of God and not from the earth as a mortal human. And in fact, as we have said, Saint Paul's foundation for confirming us in the hope of the resurrection would be nullified if Jesus Christ had a corporal substance other than ours.

They further allege that He was conceived by the Holy Spirit.[68] But this act[69] of the Holy Spirit did not shut out the substance of His mother. It is true that there occurred no union of man and woman which engendered Him according to the natural order of others. But that creates no obstacle, for by the miraculous operation of the Holy Spirit, He was formed from the substance of His mother, so that He is truly of the seed of Abraham and fruit of David's loins, as the same Spirit had earlier proclaimed of Him.

I am familiar enough with their reply: that this procedure would be impossible,[70] inasmuch as all human seed is cursed and corrupt, thus making the Lord Jesus descended from corruption.[71] But I reply that this miraculous conception overcomes this difficulty. For the Holy Spirit intervened in order to sanctify Him from the beginning and, in sanctifying Him, to preserve Him so that He might not be stained by any human pollution of any kind.

67. "to vivify."

68. See n. 58 above.

69. *vertu = force, acte de puissance, miracle.*

70. *inconvenient = impossible.*

71. Menno writes, "And so not the earthly, guilty, transgressing, accursed, and mortal flesh of Adam has satisfied God's righteousness . . . , but only the heavenly, innocent, obedient, blessed, and quickened flesh of Christ" (*Incarnation,* in *Complete Writings,* pp. 438f.).

For this reason, Saint Paul writes that He "took on the likeness of sinful flesh, in order to condemn sin in it" (Rom. 8:3). For in taking our flesh, He did not assume sin, inasmuch as the power of the Holy Spirit separated Him from the condition of others.

They also entertain a foolish and fantastic notion, for they think that humbling Him to that extent, i.e., giving Him a nature similar to ours, would bring dishonor to Jesus Christ. For this reason they imagine that it is more appropriate to His dignity to attribute a heavenly body to Him.[72]

I reply that it is a great folly to think that the glory of Jesus Christ could be diminished in any manner, or that His dignity could be wronged in any sense, by saying that He was humbled, or even destroyed, for our redemption and salvation. Moreover it is said of Him in the twenty-second Psalm that He is a "worm and no longer man, scorned by the people, and rejected by the common man" (Ps. 22:6).

Equally what Isaiah (53:3) says goes even further: that "He was despised," as a worthless person, "esteemed as leprous," "numbered among the transgressors." And what more could one say than what Saint Paul says? That He was "cursed" and "became a curse for us" (Gal. 3:13)?

If that impairs His honor, then we ought to be ashamed to admit that He was crucified for us. For the crucifixion involved a far more ignominious death than the gallows involves today.

Therefore let us not occupy[73] ourselves with these foolish notions of wanting to honor Jesus Christ according to our will,[74] or of fearing that we dishonor Him when we recognize that, from the standpoint of His human nature, He was abased for us. For from all eternity, He has been God of the same glory as His Father. Also, He has always remained such, without any loss [of glory].

That He put on our flesh and was humbled in it is a memorable testimony of His infinite goodness and of the incomprehensible love that He brought us. Consequently, instead of increasing[75] His shame one bit, it constitutes our principle reason for magnifying and praising Him.

72. See n. 71 above.

73. *amusons* = *occupons.*

74. *poste* = *gré.*

75. *derogue* = *enleve.*

In summary, then, if we want truly to acknowledge the Lord Jesus as our Savior, let us confess—following Saint John's exhortation—that "He came in the flesh" (I John 4:2) for the purpose of uniting us to God His Father, by means of the obedience which He rendered Him in our humanity, as in our behalf.[76] Whoever cannot make such a confession is Antichrist and ought to be held in abhorrence by us.

76. *personnes.*

6

On the State of Souls After Death[1]

It is time to come to the second issue which I promised to treat, which is, that the Anabaptists in general[2] all hold that souls, being departed from the body, cease to live until the day of the resurrection. There is, however, some difference between them. For some[3] do not think that the soul is a substance, or an entity[4] having essence, but solely the power that a man possesses while alive that helps him breathe, move about, and perform the other actions of life. The others,[5] acknowledging that the soul is an entity of essence,[6] nevertheless imagine that the souls of the

1. *CO* 7 (col. 111) provides no title for this section. Cf. Calvin's *Psychopannychia*, in *Tracts and Treatises*, vol. 3, pp. 413–490.

2. Christian Neff denies that the Anabaptists ever held this view: "Calvin, in his *Psychopannychia* (1544), counts the Anabaptists as one of the groups believing in the sleep of the soul, which is, however, obviously an error. . . . The fact is, there is no convincing evidence that such a belief was held by the Anabaptists or Mennonites anywhere" ("Sleep of the Soul," *Mennonite Encyclopedia*, vol. 4, p. 543). Williams, however, finds it "curious that the Mennonites deny that the position was ever held" (*Radical Reformation*, p. 597, n. 41).

3. See *Psychopannychia*, in *Tracts and Treatises*, vol. 3, pp. 419f., where Calvin identifies this group (thnetopsychists) in a manner similar to the identification here.

4. *creature.* See the *Institutes* 1.15.2 where Calvin elabortes on the idea of the soul as an essence.

5. See *Psychopannychia*, in *Tracts and Treatises*, vol. 3, pp. 419f., where Calvin again makes a similar identification of a second group (psychosomnolents), although in that version he lists the psychosomnolents before the thnetopsychists. See Williams's discussion in *Radical Reformation*, pp. 582ff. See also Conrad Grebel's reference to Gerard Westerburg's *The Slumber of Souls*, in Grebel's letter to Joachim von Watt, October 14, 1524—*Anabaptist Beginnings*, p. 41.

6. *une creature essentielle.*

deceased[7] sleep without any feeling or consciousness,[8] until the day of judgment.

For this reason,[9] if we want indeed to refute the Anabaptists entirely,[10] we must first of all demonstrate that souls have a proper essence, and, secondly, that after death, souls sense and recognize their condition and state. But before we enter into that more fully, let us note that the word "soul" is used in the Scriptures in different ways.

First of all it is used to mean "life," as when it is written in Job (13:14): "I carry my soul in my hands." Or in Saint Matthew (6:25): "Is not the soul more than food?" And in countless other passages. Sometimes it is used for "the will," or "desire," as when it is written in Samuel that "the soul of Jonathan was knit to the soul of David" (I Sam. 18:1). Or when it is said in Acts (4:32) that "those who believed were of one heart and soul."

Sometimes it is used for "the whole man." For example, when "seventy-five souls" descended with Jacob into Egypt (Acts 7:14). Or when the prophet proclaims that "the soul that sins shall die" (Ezek. 18:26). Sometimes it means "respiration," or "breathing," as when Saul says in Samuel, "I am seized with anguish, though my soul still lingers" (II Sam. 1:9). Or when Elisha[11] said, "Let the soul of the child return to him again" (I Kings 17:22).

Finally, when "soul" is joined with the word "spirit," it means "affection," as when Isaiah says (26:9), "My soul longs for thee at night, and I yearn for thee in my spirit." Or as when Saint Paul prays for God to keep the Thessalonians blameless "in body and in spirit and in soul" (I Thess. 5:23).

Equally, the word "spirit" is used in different ways, of which we need not go into now. Only let us realize that it is often used for "the soul,"[12] as we shall see in the use of passages soon to be cited.

7. *des trespassez = des hommes morts.*

8. *intelligence.*

9. *pourtant.*

10. *du tout.*

11. Calvin meant Elijah, not Elisha. Note in *CO* 7, col. 111, n. 2: "The author has confused here the two relations between the prophets Elijah and Elisha in I Kings 17 and II Kings 4."

12. See Calvin's usage of "soul" and "spirit" in the *Institutes* 1.15.2. Quistorp strongly questions Calvin's inclination to use "spirit" and "soul" interchangeably (*Calvin's Doctrine*, p. 65).

With that noted, let us see if the human soul does not have a proper essence given to it by God. And let us begin with the creation of man,[13] which should highly serve our purpose.

Now concerning the beasts and the other animals, God simply commands for them to be made. But when it comes to the creation of man, He enters into consultation, saying, "Let us make man after our image and likeness" (Gen. 1:26).[14] Now where shall we find this "image of God," except as a spiritual essence in man, in whom it has been imprinted? For the "image of God" certainly does not reside[15] in the body of man.

It is true that Moses adds next[16] (Gen. 2:7) that "man was made a living soul"—something he also says of the beasts. But in order to denote a special excellence, he says that God "breathed the power of life into his body," which He had formed from the earth.

Therefore, although the human soul may have qualities in common with those of the beasts, nonetheless, because it carries the "image" and "likeness" of God, it is indeed of a different condition.[17] Also, because its origin is different, the soul's pre-eminence is different, which is what Solomon means when he says that at death "the body returns to the earth, from whence it came, and the soul returns to God, who gave it" (Eccles. 12:7).

For this reason it is said in the Book of Wisdom (2:23) that "man is immortal, seeing that he has been created in the image of God."[18] [Of course] this is not an authentic book of the Holy Scriptures, but it is not improper for us to use it as a testimony,

13. See the *Institutes* 1.15.1–2.

14. Ibid.

15. Literally, "For with respect to the body of man this is not at all the place where the image of God resides." For Calvin the soul is the real man and bears God's likeness. See the *Institutes* 1.15.3. See Quistorp, *Calvin's Doctrine*, pp. 64f.

16. *consequemment* = *ensuite.*

17. Calvin distinguishes man from the animals in good Humanist fashion (see Quistorp, *Calvin's Doctrine*, p. 65).

18. Quistorp accuses Calvin of developing "a doctrine of the soul which is more philosophical than theological and which does not accord with Biblical anthropology" (Quistorp, *Calvin's Doctrine*, p. 75). Although Quistorp notes that the Bible nowhere states that the soul is "immortal" (ibid.), Calvin's argument in the *Institutes* (3.25.6) would surely rebuff this charge: he holds that since man's spirit has been formed after the image of God, more than a "transient life" has to be inferred. Calvin, who mentions Plato favorably (1.15.6), does seem to be influenced by him, defining the soul as "an incorporal substance."

as one of the ancient fathers.[19] However, we may only do so for this reason, that is, that if we understand the soul to contain what Saint Paul says about it, i.e., that we should be like God in righteousness and true holiness, then the "image of God," such as has been placed in man, can only be in an immortal spirit. That is the point[20] with regard to creation.[21]

Now there are many passages in the Scriptures that are by far clearer, as when Saint Peter says that "the outcome of our faith is the salvation of our souls" (I Peter 1:9). Or, when he says that the faithful "have purified their souls" (v. 22). Or, that "the desires of the flesh war against the soul" (2:11). Or, when he calls Jesus Christ "the guardian of souls" (2:25). For these statements would not hold good unless there were souls that had been saved and which had been assailed by wicked concupiscences and which had been cleansed of their stains and were being governed by Jesus Christ their guardian.

In addition, it is written in the history of Job (4:19) that "men dwell in houses of clay," a form of speech that Saint Peter equally uses when he says that he wants to warn the faithful "as long as he indwells his earthly tabernacle" (II Peter 1:13). If the principal part of man[22] did not indwell the body, as in a tabernacle, then Peter's words are groundless.

Furthermore, the apostle in the Letter to the Hebrews (12:9) makes the same point even more clearly when he says that the men who fathered us in this world are the fathers of our flesh, but God alone is the father of our spirits. I beg of you, if the soul were not an essence how could one utter these words? Then immediately afterwards, speaking of the citizens of paradise, he calls them "angels" and "the spirits of the just" (12:23). Could we want anything clearer than that?

Moreover, I do not see how we can interpret Saint Paul's exhortation to us, i.e., that we should purge our "flesh" and "spirit"[23] of every stain, unless we interpret the word "spirit" to

19. *docteurs.*

20. *voila.*

21. Calvin is a proponent of creationism, not traducianism. He believes that each soul is a creation out of nothing, a "beginning of essence out of nothing" (see the *Institutes* 1.15.5). Augustine also holds this view (see *City of God,* in *Nicene and Post-Nicene Fathers,* first series, vol. 2, p. 217).

22. Calvin means the soul. See the *Institutes* 1.15.2.

23. See I Thessalonians 5:23.

mean "a soul of essence."[24] For as the body is an object that can become polluted, so also is the soul a creature that, on its part, can become polluted and sanctified. The reason is similar, for as Saint Paul says in another passage, "The Spirit of God bears witness to our spirits that we are children of God" (Rom. 8:16).

But if we held to the principle that ought to be common among all Christians, it would not be necessary to enter into controversy over this matter, that is, whether the soul is an essence, seeing that this was the error of the Sadducees, which was expressly reproved in Scripture. For it is written in Acts 23:6 that Saint Paul, hoping to exculpate himself, affirmed[25] that he was being persecuted because he did not hold to the Sadducean sect. And Saint Luke, wanting to explain what that meant, says that "the Sadducees do not believe in the resurrection, nor that there are angels, nor spirits, nor souls" (Acts 23:8).

What more could we want? Saint Paul confesses that he is a Pharisee in these matters.[26] Thus it is clear that the Pharisees confess, as Saint Luke says, that souls are true entities of essence.[27]

Therefore, let the Anabaptists hold to the quarrel of the Sadducees, their predecessors, and maintain it against Saint Paul. And if they should ever win their case against him, then we shall see what we must say to them. In the meanwhile, we shall hold, in accordance with the whole teaching of God, that man is composed of and consists of two parts: body and soul.[28]

It is time to come to the second point, that is, the state of souls after their separation from the body. The Anabaptists think that they sleep as if dead. We say that they are alive[29] and have feeling. That such is the case, we claim the testimony of Jesus Christ, when He exhorts His disciples "not to fear those who kill the body but cannot kill the soul, but to fear Him who, having killed the body, can cast the soul into the fire of Gehenna" (Matt. 10:28).

24. *une ame essentielle.*

25. *protesta.*

26. *en ses articles.*

27. *creatures essentielles.* See the *Institutes* 1.15.2.

28. See the *Institutes* 1.15.2 where Calvin bifurcates the body and the soul. For him the soul takes precedence over the body, as it is the seat of conscience, intelligence, understanding, and will (1.15.6). Quistorp finds this view contrary to the union of body and soul emphasized in Scripture (*Calvin's Doctrine*, pp. 58ff.).

29. Literally, "have life."

If the soul were nothing, or instead were killed when it was separated from the body, then it would not be true that tyrants and persecutors have no power over it. Thus God has dealt with us graciously in not subjecting our souls to these[30] hangmen who would like to behave in a worse and more cruel manner than all the tyrants of the world, that is, by killing souls as well as [their] bodies.

But let us hear their noble sophistry.[31] "It is very true," they say, "that the soul dies momentarily,[32] but it does not perish at all, inasmuch as it must rise again."[33]

I ask them: and what of the body? For if the soul solely because of its hope in the resurrection does not die,[34] a similar hope[35] exists for the body, that it will not perish either.

Now our Lord Jesus carefully distinguishes between the two, saying that the body is killed, but not the soul. It was in this manner that Jesus Christ spoke to the Jews, saying (John 2:19), "Destroy this temple and in three days I will raise it up." Saint John adds that He was speaking "of the temple of His body"; thus He was setting the soul apart, indicating that it could not be destroyed. And in fact, at His own death He commended His soul to God His Father (Luke 23:46). And Saint Stephen, following His example, said, "Lord Jesus, receive my spirit" (Acts 7:59).

That, accordingly, is what we should think. It is God who is the protector of our souls, who preserves them from the tyranny of men, in order that when we die we might each commend our soul to Him.

Similarly, when Saint Peter says that our Lord Jesus "went in His Spirit to the spirits in prison" (I Peter 3:19), he clearly affirms[36]

30. *ses.* Literally, "his." Note in *CO* 7, col. 114: *"these* [in the] 1611 edition." That would make the Anabaptists the hangmen.

31. *belle cavillation.*

32. *pour l'heure.*

33. See *Psychopannychia,* in *Tracts and Treatises,* vol. 3, p. 415, where Calvin explains that although he has not seen the tracts propounding the view in question, he did receive notes on them from a friend.

34. Note the emphasis on the "hope in the resurrection" versus the preceding section's emphasis on the "immortality of the soul." Quistorp finds this contradictory (*Calvin's Doctrine,* pp. 81f.). One could argue, however, that Calvin at least balances the Platonic concept of the immortality of the soul with the New Testament emphasis on the resurrection of the body.

35. *raison.*

36. *testifié.*

by these words that souls are alive and conscious[37] after death. For otherwise they would not have been capable of receiving Christ's preaching, which, he says, Christ did in their midst.

I admit that this passage is held to be obscure and that it has been interpreted in different ways, but I am not claiming anything for my thesis that is not certain. For the apostle, having declared how Christ was humbled and having shown that it is necessary for all believers to conform themselves to Him, adds, as a consolation, that Jesus Christ was not vanquished by death, but instead overcame it.[38]

Therefore, in order to assure us that the power of the resurrection belongs to us, he says that not only have the living sensed this, but also the dead, and not only believers, but also unbelievers and rebels.[39] It is true that Peter does not distinguish between the two groups, but only mentions the second; nevertheless, this does not prevent us from concluding that Christ spoke to everyone in general. That he places the souls—the good and the wicked—"in prison" signifies the earnest desire which the faithful had for the coming of Jesus Christ, which held them as in anguish.

The meaning, accordingly, is this: that the power of the redemption that Christ accomplished appeared to the souls of the dead, to those of believers as well as unbelievers. But when Peter mentions this in particular, he omits the first.

Nonetheless, in order that we might not dispute the meaning, as it is unnecessary with respect to the present matter, I simply ask these good people whether the spirits of which the apostle speaks are not living souls? Besides, he adds another passage which is even clearer, that is, that "the gospel was preached to the dead in order that they might be condemned in the flesh, with respect to men, but might live to God, with respect to the spirit" (I Peter 4:6).

[Thus] we see how He subjects only the body to death, while preserving the soul alive.[40]

The same was pointed out earlier by Solomon when, reflect-

37. *sentent et congnoissent.* See the *Institutes* 3.25.6 where Calvin elaborates on the soul's nature after it is separated from the body.

38. This paragraph appears to be a commentary on I Peter 3:13–22.

39. See I Peter 1:19–20.

40. See the *Institutes* 3.25.6.

ing[41] on man's death, he separates the soul from the body at some distance, to the extent, he says, that "the dust will return to the earth from which it was taken, and the spirit to God who gave it" (Eccles. 12:7).[42] If some carp that the word "spirit" only means "life," even a little child can see that this corrupts the text.

It is true that if we only had the witness of Moses' statement, where he says (Exod. 3:6) that "God is the God of Abraham, Isaac, and Jacob"—a statement he makes about three hundred years after their death—that would suffice for those who don't want to be contentious. Still, whatever obstinacy that might exist to contradict this is deprived of all power by our Lord Jesus' interpretation of these words. For He points out that His Father is not the God of the dead, but of the living (Matt. 22:32).

I know they reply that "the dead" are called "the living" because of the hope of the resurrection. But that is nothing. For since the patriarchs were dead at the time Moses was speaking, it follows that they were living in a better life.

For this reason Saint Luke adds that "all live to Him" (Luke 20:38), denoting that our Lord preserves the lives of His own[43] by His grace and power. Which corresponds to what the apostle says: "If we live, let us live to the Lord; if we die, let us die to the Lord; so whether we live or whether we die, we are the Lord's, for Jesus Christ died and is raised, in order to rule over the living and the dead" (Rom. 14:8f.).

Now it is certain that Jesus Christ cannot rule over us if we are not alive. For this reason, if His empire extends to the dead, it follows that believers after their death subsist in some form of essence.

In fact if this were not so, the vision that Saint John receives in Revelation (6:9ff.) would have nothing of which to be composed. For he sees the souls of the martyrs under the heavenly altar, "crying out with a loud voice, 'Lord, how long dost Thou delay before avenging our blood?'" And then "God commanded them to be given white robes and to have patience for awhile until the number of their fellow servants should be complete."

There can be no doubt but that these "white robes" signify the beginning of glory that God grants the martyrs while they

41. Literally, "in discovering."

42. See the *Institutes* 1.15.2 where Calvin makes similar use of this text.

43. Literally, "his own in life."

await the day of judgment, for this is nothing new in the Scriptures.[44] As when Daniel says that he "saw the Lord dressed in a white robe" (Dan. 7:9). And even Jesus Christ was so [dressed] in His transfiguration on the mountain of Tabor (Matt. 17:2). Also, the angel who appeared to the women near the tomb was dressed in a white robe (Matt. 28:3). So also the angels who appeared to the disciples after the ascension of our Lord Jesus (Acts 1:10). And the same is said of the angel who appeared to the centurion Cornelius (Acts 10:30). Finally, in the parable of the prodigal son, it is written that when he had returned, his father ordered that one bring him his best robe, as a sign of joy and celebration (Luke 15:22).

Thus we see how all this repudiates the error of the Anabaptists, who, in the place of white robes, give souls pillows to sleep on.

Besides, when it is said that souls cry in asking vengeance of God, it is thereby shown that they can't be sleeping. For this cry cannot be interpreted as the cry of Abel's blood, since what the holy souls want is expressed in their cry.

This is sufficiently confirmed for us in the story[45] of Lazarus, where it is written that his soul was carried by God's angels to Abraham's bosom, and the rich man's soul went to hell (Luke 16:22). They think they have the perfect answer when they reply that this is a parable, that is to say, an example, and not a story of fact.[46]

But I ask of them, where have they seen in Scripture, in a parable or simply similitude, a man's own name mentioned as it is here? That is how the church fathers have understood it, as reason dictates. But even if I were to argue that it is a parable, it should still be interpreted as being true.

Our Lord says that Lazarus's soul was carried by angels to Abraham's bosom and that it found joy and consolation there. On the other hand, He says that the unbelieving rich man's soul suffers in great torment in hell. He says that there is a great gulf between the two. If souls have no sensations after death, of

44. Quistorp charges that Calvin spiritualizes the eschatological elements of the New Testament because of his horror of the radical excesses of his time (*Calvin's Doctrine*, pp. 109, 113, 123).

45. *histoire.*

46. *histoire.*

either good or evil, what becomes of this story[47] of our Lord's, except a fable and as a tale[48] from the book of Mélusine?[49]

Therefore this evasive reply of the Anabaptists is a blasphemy that dishonors our Lord Jesus, as if He had recounted for us a frivolous fiction without any meaning to it. Besides, it is a form of daydreaming that is repugnant to human intelligence, one that even little children can see through.

It is the same promise that was made to the poor thief, when he asked for mercy on the cross. For our Lord Jesus said to him, "Today you shall be with Me in paradise" (Luke 23:43). In this word "paradise" we don't merely have a figure of speech referring to a specific place, but rather the joy and happiness that those experience who live with Him. Even more, Jesus Christ did not defer this poor sinner until the day of the resurrection, but He appointed that very same day as the one for him to live eternally in His fellowship.[50]

The Anabaptists distort[51] this passage by citing what is written in another place, that "a thousand years are a day in the Lord's sight."[52] We are willing to grant that, but it must be noted that when God speaks to men He accommodates[53] Himself to their

47. *narration.*

48. *conte.*

49. *Mellusine.* Calvin's unusual reference indicates his familiarity with a body of French literature the Reformer rarely draws on. *The Oxford Companion to French Literature,* comp. and ed. Paul Harvey and Janet E. Heseltine (New York: Oxford, 1959), illuminates Calvin's reference: "Mélusine, a fairy of French folklore, the water-sprite of the fountain of Lusignan in Poitou, and the legendary ancestress and tutelary spirit of the house of that name. She consented to marry Raimond of Poitou on condition that he should never see her on a Saturday, on which day she resumed her mermaid-like shape. Her husband broke the compact, whereupon she fled. The legend was adapted in a prose romance by Jean d'arras (c. 1387) . . ." (p. 470).

50. See n. 34 above.

51. *caviller.*

52. See Psalm 90:4, II Peter 3:8. See n. 44 above. Cf. the *Institutes* 3.25.5 where Calvin elaborates on the one-thousand-year reign. Quistorp notes that Calvin saw chiliasm as "an impoverishment of the Christian hope" (*Calvin's Doctrine,* pp. 109, 113, 123, 158f., 160). John C. Wenger ("Chiliasm," *Mennonite Encyclopedia,* vol. 1, pp. 557–560) denies any trace of chiliasm "in the first generation of the main line of Anabaptists, whether Swiss, Dutch, or German, represented by such men as Conrad Grebel, Michael Sattler, . . . Pilgram Marbeck, . . . Menno Simons, . . . Jakob Hutter and Peter Riedemann." One must go to Hofmann and Hans Hut for such views. Wenger also denies that *The Schleitheim Confession* contains any trace of chiliasm.

53. For Calvin's "doctrine of accommodation," see H. Jackson Forstmann,

intelligence. So much so that we cannot find in Scripture where God has ever said, "I shall do such and such today—meaning in a thousand years from now!"

For example, if, when Jonah warned the Ninevites that "in four days" their city would be destroyed, they had interpreted this to mean "in four thousand years," that would have been a great folly on their part. Also when our Lord Jesus promised that He would be raised[54] "on the third day" (Matt. 16:21), we recognize that He was speaking in a manner common to men.

But I wander from my subject, inasmuch as anyone can see how the Anabaptists delude themselves by using such a subterfuge.

They advance still a further sophistry: "today" represents the time of the New Testament.[55] And to prove this they misuse the passage found in the Letter to the Hebrews (13:8), that "Jesus Christ is the same yesterday and today and for ever." But they do not realize that if one interprets the word "today" accordingly, the word "yesterday" would refer to the Old Testament time, and consequently it would follow that our Lord Jesus *had a beginning,*[56] which would be an absurdity. For we know that He is our *eternal* God, and even according to His humanity, He is called "the sacrificial lamb" from the beginning of the world (Rev. 13:8).

Furthermore, even according to their own view, we would have to conclude that the thief, whose sins Jesus Christ forgave, had to enter paradise before the resurrection. For the apostle mentions three time periods,[57] of which one, as I think, means the day of the Old Testament, and the other means the time

---

Word and Spirit: Calvin's Doctrine of Biblical Authority (Palo Alto, Cal.: Stanford, 1962), pp. 13f., 16, 55, 60, 97, 114f. Quistorp notes Calvin's use of accommodation to lessen the opportunity for an eschatological passage to be interpreted radically (*Calvin's Doctrine,* p. 124).

54. *ressusciteroit.* Literally, "would be resuscitated."

55. Possibly a reference to the Anabaptist conviction that the Reformation era represented a new age of "restitution" in which apostolic Christianity would truly be "restored." Some enthusiasts and revolutionaries espoused a radical interpretation of this idea. See pp. 296–297, n. 15, and p. 312, nn. 60, 61. See also Williams, *Radical Reformation,* pp. 375f.

56. Literally, "should have begun to be." Italics for contrast.

57. *temps.* Calvin appears to be following the Tychonian-Augustinian periodization of history; the last period consists of the time from the epiphany to the parousia. See Quistorp, *Calvin's Doctrine,* p. 160 (n. 4 in particular).

since the renewal of the world. Thus the word "today" means "our present time,"[58] which lies between the death of Jesus Christ and His final coming.

And that we might still better understand their tomfoolery, if Jesus Christ had promised the thief paradise on the day of judgment, it would have been fitting that He should have said, "in the age to come," and not "today." For that is the customary way that the Scripture speaks.

Who cannot see that they are defeated by such sound[59] reasoning?

Nevertheless, their impudence is such that they still advance another reply, i.e., that paradise was promised to the thief in the same way that God warned that Adam and Eve would die on the day they should taste of the forbidden fruit. Now it is certain that they did not die on that day but considerably later.

I reply that at the same instant Adam transgressed God's commandment he died with respect to his soul, while at the same time he was alienated from God, who was his true life, and came under the subjection of corporal death. Thus, in spite of their error and in spite of them, we have won this point: that on that day the thief was delivered from the misery into which Adam had fallen by his sins.

In summary, we conclude that just as death began to reign in Adam on the day of his transgression, so the thief, on the day the promise was made to him, began to be reinstated into the blessedness of paradise.

We see how Saint Paul lived in this hope, when he says that he "desires to be released in order to live with Christ" (Phil. 1:23). First of all he uses an apt expression[60] in saying that the faithful man is delivered by death from the bonds of his body, as he explains more clearly in another passage (Rom. 7:23; 8:22). Then he adds that his hope is to be with our Lord Jesus when his soul departs the body. And in fact, if this were not so, what he says in another passage would not hold true, that "neither life nor death can separate us from the love in which God holds us" (Rom. 8:38f.). For if in death we should perish, or our soul should lose its life, then in what would God's love for us consist?

58. *le temps ou nous sommes.* See Quistorp, ibid.

59. *claire.*

60. *belle proprieté.*

But this is by far more clearly[61] deduced from another passage where he writes (II Cor. 5:1ff.), "We know that if our earthly house of the tabernacle of our body is destroyed, that we have a house in the heavens from God, which is not made by hands. For this reason, while we live in this tabernacle, we groan with anxiety, not because we want to be unclothed but reclothed, in order that our mortality might be swallowed up by life. None-theless, we are always of good courage, knowing that while we are in our bodies we are separated from God. Besides, we walk by faith and not by sight. But we have this confidence and desire to be separated from the body and to come[62] into the presence of God."

[Now] because the "day of judgment" is mentioned here,[63] the Anabaptists attempt to entangle everything around it, in order to restrict all the apostles' words to this "day." But they can only do so much, since the truth is quite capable of maintaining itself against their slanders. For the apostle expressly says that the believer leaves the body and goes with God, from whom he has been separated[64] in this world. Furthermore, he adds, that "whether absent or present, we make it our aim to please God, while waiting of necessity to come before His judgment seat."

A man indeed would have to be obstinate and hardened against all reason not to want to accede to these words. And such is the case with the Anabaptists, who, instead of what Saint Paul says—that through death we draw near to God—make believe that we are drawn away from God and are farther from Him than we are in our present life.

That this is so, it is written that "whoever believes in the Son of God does not come into condemnation, but has already passed from death to life" (John 5:24). If eternal life has already begun in us, what an absurdity to say that death has interrupted it!

If we have already entered the kingdom of God, what purpose is served by making us leave it at death, or at least by making us withdraw from it, as crayfish?[65] "The kingdom of God is in you,"

61. *apertement = clairement.*
62. *iouyre = venir à.*
63. See II Corinthians 5:10.
64. *absent.*
65. Crayfish walk sideways or backwards.

says our Lord Jesus (Luke 17:21). What can this mean but that we already have the root of life which can never be destroyed.

The same is said in another passage: "This is the will of My Father, that whoever believes in the Son shall not perish but has everlasting life, and I shall raise him up on the last day" (John 6:40). Or again, "Whoever eats My flesh and drinks My blood has eternal life, and I shall raise him up on the last day" (John 6:54).

Let us note that He promises two things: eternal life and the resurrection. The Anabaptists accept one of these two and omit the other—as if one could separate them![66]

Christ speaks still more clearly elsewhere, saying, "I am the resurrection and the life, he who believes in Me, though he die, he shall live, and whoever lives and believes in Me shall never die" (John 11:25). Again, "Whoever keeps My word, he will never see death" (John 8:51).

I beg of you, can one speak more clearly than that? And ought a Christian want a firmer testimony for sustaining confidently his conscience?

A few might object that this only applies to the faithful. I admit that, and for my part I am content to instruct the children of God concerning their condition after death. Then afterwards, I will say something about the reprobate.[67]

But for the present, we see what Jesus Christ promises us if we are His. It is that in the midst of death our spiritual life will not be interrupted. And, what is more, as Saint Paul shows, it is then that our life enters into its greatest vitality.[68] "As our outer nature," he says, "is wasting away and our inner nature is being renewed day by day" (II Cor. 4:16). By these words he shows that although the present life wanes and becomes decrepit, the life of the soul grows and is strengthened more and more.[69] Thus it is contrary to this passage to conclude that the soul is extinguished when corporal life comes to its end.

Let me pursue this argument still further. We ought to grow[70] and profit daily in our Lord, always advancing closer to Him, as

66. See n. 34 above.

67. Calvin follows the same order in the *Institutes* 3.25.6–12.

68. *elle commence d'estre en sa plus grande vigueur.*

69. Quistorp refers to this view as "progressive glorification" (*Calvin's Doctrine*, p. 81).

70. *croistre = croître.*

if we were taking one step today and another one tomorrow, or as if we were climbing by degrees.

Now it is said of the present time, that "we walk in the light of His countenance" (Ps. 89:15). Again, "that His Spirit bears witness to us that we are His children" (Rom. 8:16). If it is the case that in death we lose this light and confidence that the Holy Spirit gives us, then it will be impossible for us to move forward. Similarly, Saint Paul says, that though we live in this world, nevertheless, "our dwelling place is in heaven" (Phil. 3:20).

Let us consider whether death must bar us from the kingdom of God, when formerly our dwelling place was there by hope. Certainly this mortal body is like a prison in order to humble our soul so low as to make it captive to earthly things. Therefore it is fitting that when it is freed and has left such a servitude it ought to be more disposed to contemplate God more privately. And when it is relieved of such a burden, it ought to be the more able to ascend to God. Thus it is the height of stupidity to tuck souls indolently in bed, as the Anabaptists do, making them sleep until the day of the resurrection.

But their error is still better overthrown by what the Scriptures teach about our regeneration. For when it pleased God to call us to participate in His grace,[71] it is written that He made us new creatures (II Cor. 5:17). How? By the power of His Word and of His Spirit, by Whom He mortifies our corrupt nature, causing us to be reborn that we might live in His kingdom.

Let us hear, now, how the two [i.e., Word and Spirit] operate in us. Saint Paul, in wanting to console us, says that "although the body is dead because of sin," nevertheless the Spirit of our Lord Jesus, living in us, "is alive because of righteousness" (Rom. 8:10).

I would argue that the present life is never perfect, so long as we are in this world, but inasmuch as the "Spirit of God" is a spark[72] of life which is given to us in order increasingly to vivify us until we arrive at perfection, it follows that our life can never be extinguished.[73]

As for the "Word," Saint Peter explains it more clearly, saying that "it is an imperishable seed," indeed an immortal seed, that God has set within us in order to exempt us from our natural

71. *nous appeller en la participation de sa grace.*

72. *estincelle = étincelle.*

73. *esteincte = éteinte.* Note the play on words between *étincelle* and *éteinte.*

condition (I Peter 1:23), which is, in the words of Isaiah, "that all flesh is like grass and all man's glory like the flower of hay" (Isa. 40:6), for when the Spirit of God blows upon man, he immediately withers and completely dries up.

Now as soon as the prophet has thus described us, he immediately adds that, to the contrary, "the Word of God abides for ever." Saint Peter cites this passage (I Peter 1:24f.) and explains that this eternal aspect of God's Word is manifest in us, inasmuch as by it we are "reborn" and possess it in our souls as an "imperishable seed," which neither dies nor ever perishes. How is this to be interpreted except as something obvious and completely resolved, that, being regenerated by God's grace, we are brought into His kingdom in order to live clinging to Him without end?

But nothing more fittingly and positively resolves this matter for us than our recalling the union and unity we have with our Lord Jesus. First of all we know that at baptism we are grafted into His body in order truly to become His members and to feel in ourselves as strong an effect of His power as a tree's branches feel from its roots. For we are united with Him to the extent that we become one in the same substance.[74] And no other reason need be cited save the one that He has declared by His own mouth: "Because I live," He says, "you shall live" (John 14:19).

Now we know that Jesus Christ's life was not temporary[75] nor at intervals. If then we live because He lives, it follows that it is without end. For it was necessary that He should die with us. For as He said earlier, "Whoever eats My flesh and drinks My blood abides in Me and I in him" (John 6:56). If Jesus Christ abides in us, then it follows that at the same time life abides in us too, following what He also formerly said, "As the Father has life in Himself, so He has granted the Son to have life in Himself" (John 5:26).

It is quite easy to see that the Anabaptists have never fathomed how we are united with our Lord Jesus. For this single principle is enough to reverse their false and pernicious opinion with regard to the fantastic sleep which they attribute to souls. For to the contrary we see the conclusion that Saint Paul deduces when

74. Note the emphasis Calvin puts on union with Christ to confirm the immortality and sentient nature of the soul after death (Quistorp, *Calvin's Doctrine*, pp. 81f.).

75. *temporelle = temporaire.*

he says that we are already citizens of heaven, "being made to sit in heavenly places with our Lord Jesus" (Eph. 2:6, 19; Phil. 3:20).

Therefore let us hold to what Saint Paul says, that "we are dead" with respect to the world, and that "our life is hid with Christ in God" (Col. 3:3). By this he means what he says elsewhere: "I no longer live, but Christ lives in me" (Gal. 2:20). Let us hold, I say, to this position, that possessing an inseparable union with our Lord Jesus, we are participants of that permanent life in Him.[76]

And let us remember that being raised, He dies no more and that death no longer has dominion over Him (Rom. 6:9), not only with respect to Himself but with respect to His members as well. Of course there is this difference: that in Him death is fully vanquished, completely overcome, while only partly so in us. Still, even in us, it has been overcome to the extent that it cannot reign over us.[77] Thus in awaiting the fulfillment of our redemption let us not doubt that the beginning that has been made in our souls will abide for ever.[78]

Thus far we have proven by sufficient testimony that souls, being separated from their bodies, nevertheless live in God. And we have reproved the error of the Anabaptists, who make believe that souls sleep, as if dead and without any consciousness. Now in order to satisfy everyone's request—insofar as we can—it remains to explain briefly what we ought to believe about the present state and condition of souls.

Now to begin with, I solemnly affirm[79] that I shall discuss it more soberly than many will want.[80] For I know how deeply curious some are, who would like every detail unraveled for them, down to the rooms and closets where souls reside while awaiting the day of judgment. Those who want to be fed on such

76. See n. 74 above.

77. Literally, "exercise its reign."

78. Quistorp sums up Calvin's view in the following manner: "Calvin teaches that man's soul, which is immortal in essence, does not perish nor sleep in death but insofar as it is born again in Christ already enjoys peace in the expectation of the resurrection of the body, which will bring it consummate blessedness" (*Calvin's Doctrine*, p. 81).

79. *proteste = affirme solennellement.*

80. See the *Institutes* 3.25.6 where Calvin expresses a similar caution. Quistorp notes Calvin's tendency to subordinte the eschatological to the ethical (*Calvin's Doctrine*, p. 125).

fables will deceive themselves if they look for them in me. For I love instead to hold fast to the simplicity of the Scriptures in order to teach what is expedient to know rather than to digress about in order to be perceived as subtle.

Now our Lord, foreseeing that it was not necessary for us to be more amply informed on this matter, was content to teach us simply that when our souls have departed from our bodies they nonetheless live in Him, awaiting the fulfillment of their beatitude and glory on the day of judgment, as we shall see. Therefore let us be content with that, and whatever statements can be made, and let us not go beyond these limits concerning the matter.

In order to proceed more clearly, let us begin by making a distinction between the souls of the faithful and those of the reprobate. When the apostle writes in the Letter to the Hebrews that "there remains only a terrible prospect of judgment" (Heb. 10:27) for those who, after knowing His truth, reject Jesus Christ and deliberately turn from Him, it is certain that he is not only speaking about this present life but much more about the time to come. For the wicked in this world do not always comprehend the judgment of God and are not startled or frightened by it, but when it comes time to die, they cannot avoid the fact that they are surrounded by this frightful and shocking impasse,[81] realizing the vengeance that has been prepared[82] for them.

Saint Peter and Saint Jude further testify to this when they say that God did not spare His own angels, who forsook their origin, but put them in the "nether gloom," locking them up, saving them for "the great day" (II Peter 2:4; Jude 6). In explaining for us the fate[83] of the devils, they also make clear the fate of the wicked. For it is one and the same. Thus we see that the unfaithful person's soul, being departed from the body, is like a malefactor who has already received his sentence of condemnation and now awaits only the hour when he shall be led to the gallows for execution.

It is true that even during this present life the wicked are often tormented by twinges of conscience and that the judgment of God persecutes them. But since they are intoxicated with vain

81. *destroit = situation difficile.*

82. *appareillée = preparée.*

83. *condition.*

thoughts, thinking they can flee and escape, they are not yet entirely God's prisoners but are vagabonds, fleeing the presence of the judge. But after death, it is not so. For God holds them as enchained, in such a way that they indeed see the punishment prepared[84] for them, from which there is no escape. Thus they are in extreme agony, awaiting the execution of their sentence.

The power to determine their fate[85] is not ours, nor a matter of our concern. Furthermore, we must not imagine that souls are similar to bodies, thus occupying a certain space. Let us be content to know that they are in hell, as was said of the wicked rich man (Luke 16:23), that is, in torment in Gehenna, seeing that they are experiencing the rejection of God, while yet awaiting a still greater revelation of His wrath.[86]

From this it is easy to deduce the state of faithful souls. So long as we are in this world, it is true that our consciences know joy and rest in God, but inasmuch as we are continually agitated by diverse temptations, such rest is disturbed by many cares. Moreover, since our salvation is based on hope, it is hid from us, to such extent that we do not walk "by sight," as Saint Paul says (II Cor. 5:7). But after death comes, since all warfare is ended and our enemies can no longer assault us, we hold it with the greatest of certainty.

Furthermore, we shall no longer hope then, as we do now, that is to say, above and against hope, but we [must] await this happy state which we [now only] sense and see in part. For this reason the soul of Lazarus received joy and consolation, though, certainly in the midst of the miseries of this world, he was throughout his life being comforted by God. But the "joy" our Lord means is the "joy" that the faithful soul has after death, when it sees itself delivered from all weakness, warfare, wicked lusts,[87] and the dangers of daily temptations, having a clearer and firmer comprehension of its blessed state[88] and immortal glory.

Hence, when we want to summarize in a word the condition

84. *apprestée = preparée.*
85. *le lieu ou ilz sont.* Literally, "the place where they are."
86. See the *Institutes* 3.25.9, 12.
87. *defiance = provocation, défi.*
88. *beatitude.*

of faithful souls after death, we can say that they are at rest,[89] not because they are in a perfect state of blessedness or glory, but because they are content with the joy and consolation that God grants them while awaiting the day of their final redemption.

If anyone would like this expressed in a similitude, the time in which we live in this mortal body is like a time of war. When we are stripped of our flesh, the battle ceases and ends and we gain the victory. But the day of triumph comes when Jesus Christ shall appear in His majesty in order that we might reign eternally with Him. But insofar as such similitudes only illumine and are not authentic,[90] let us take one from the Scriptures that will not only serve to instruct but also prove our point.

We know how Saint Paul allegorically treats the exodus of the Israelites from Egypt and their passage through the Red Sea (I Cor. 10:2). In the same way, then, let us understand that in baptism our Pharaoh is thrown into the sea, that is to say, that our old man is mortified, and we are buried with Christ and are thereby freed from the bondage of sin. But afterwards we enter into the wilderness, where we sojourn[91] during this mortal life. For we are poor and unworthy, save that our Lord daily bestows His benefits on us, in the same way that it was necessary for manna from heaven to rain on the people of Israel. Then when death comes, we enter into the promised land, a journey of no small difficulty. For it is then that we have to withstand the greatest assaults and the gravest perils.

Now after the people of Israel had entered the promised land, a long time elapsed before Jerusalem was built and the kingdom of the house of David was placed under judgment.[92] In the same way, faithful souls immediately after death experience some enjoyment of the heritage that has been promised to them, but inasmuch as the glory of Jesus Christ their king has not yet

89. Cf. Quistorp's analysis of Calvin's "rest of the soul" (*Calvin's Doctrine*, pp. 83–86).

90. Calvin always uses illustrations with reserve. See Erwin Mülhaupt, *Die Predigt Calvins, Ihre Geschichte, Ihre Form und Ihre Religiosen Grundegedanken*, Arbeiten zur Kirchengeschichte (Berlin: Walter de Gruyter, 1931), vol. 18, p. 39.

91. *conversons = séjourons.*

92. *fut mis sus.*

appeared and the heavenly city of God has not yet been established in its fullness,[93] they must wait until that day arrives.[94]

All these things in Scripture are comprehensible to those who have no desire to rebel against God. And not only does this doctrine receive sound approbation in Scripture, but the church fathers[95] also support it, among whom Tertullian says, "Both the reward of the good and the punishment of the wicked are in suspension until the resurrection."[96] Nevertheless, this does not prevent him from affirming here and there that the souls of the faithful do live in God. Consequently, in another place he says, "Why do we not interpret the bosom of Abraham as a temporary receptacle of souls, which would mean that there is a double reward, one immediately after death, and the other at the day of the last judgment?" And Irenaeus says, "Seeing that the Lord Jesus entered the shadow of death, where the souls of the departed were, and was afterwards raised corporally and ascended into heaven, certainly the souls of His disciples, for whom He did that, shall go to an invisible realm, which has been determined for them by God, and abide there, awaiting with patience the day of resurrection. Afterwards they shall be reunited with their bodies in order to come before the presence of the Lord. 'For the disciple is not above his master.'"[97]

Saint Chrysostom understands what a benefit and privilege it is for us that Abraham and Saint Paul are seated and waiting for the perfection of the church in order to receive their reward. For the Father declared to them that He would not give them their reward until we had joined them, as a father of a family sometimes says to his children, who have returned from work, that they must wait to eat until their other brothers arrive. "You are angry [He says] that you haven't already received your wages. What then of Abel, who won his reward far ahead of you and

93. *estat.*

94. Note that the glory of Christians will not be revealed apart from Christ's glory. Cf. Quistorp, *Calvin's Doctrine,* p. 19. See n. 34 above.

95. *anciens docteurs.*

96. See Tertullian, *The Resurrection of the Flesh,* in *Ante-Nicene Fathers,* ed. Alexander Roberts and James Donaldson (1885–1896; reprint ed., Grand Rapids: Eerdmans, 1950–1951), vol. 3, pp. 557–558. Tertullian states, "I will go further, and say that the soul does not even fall into sleep along with the body, nor does it with its companion even lie down in repose" (p. 558). See also p. 580.

97. See Irenaeus, *Against Heresies,* in *Ante-Nicene Fathers,* vol. 1, p. 411.

who has not yet received his crown? Or what of Noah and the other patriarchs? For they have waited for us until now and will go on waiting for others who will come after [us]. They have preceded us in the battle, but they will not precede us in the crown. For a day has been set for crowning all the children of God together."[98]

Saint Augustine writes that the souls of the saints are [kept] in secret receptacles until they receive the crown of glory on the day of judgment, but on the contrary the souls of the wicked await their punishment.[99] And in a letter he wrote to Saint Jerome, he says, "The soul, after the corporal death of the body, will attain rest, then later will take up again its body in order to attain glory."[100]

Saint Bernard [writes], "The peacefulness[101] which the souls of the saints presently enjoy is grand, but it is not yet perfect, for it will be perfect [only] when they sit on the thrones as judges. When they are stripped of their bodies, they are immediately brought into rest, but not into the glory of the kingdom." And in his following sermon he pursues this theme, saying that there are three states of the soul. The first is in the body, as in a tabernacle, the second [occurs] after death, as in the front gate of the temple, the third is in heaven with its glorious body. If anyone cares to pursue this, let him read Bernard's second and third sermons on the Feast of All Saints.[102]

Briefly, this is the standard tradition[103] that has always been held in the Christian church without any contradiction, that though we live in God by faith during this mortal life, immediately after death we shall receive joy and consolation, recognizing more clearly, and almost seeing with the eye, that heavenly

98. See Chrysostom, homily 28, *Homilies on the Epistle to the Hebrews,* in *Nicene and Post-Nicene Fathers,* first series, vol. 14, p. 492.

99. See Augustine, *The City of God,* in *Nicene and Post-Nicene Fathers,* first series, vol. 2, p. 248.

100. See Augustine, letter 166, in *Nicene and Post-Nicene Fathers,* first series, vol. 1, p. 525.

101. *doulceur = douceur.*

102. Cf. *Psychopannychia,* in *Quellenschriften,* p. 84, n. 2.

103. *la doctrine perpetuelle.* This tradition was challenged by Pope John XXII (in office 1316–1334). John's view that the souls of the departed must await the resurrection before they may behold the beatific vision was condemned by the Paris theologians in 1333.

blessedness[104] that has been promised to us, which we now contemplate as "in a mirror" and at best "dimly" (I Cor. 13:12).

The Anabaptists' delusion concerning the sleep of souls was never advocated by anyone, save by a heretical sect called the Arabs[105] and by Pope John of Rome some [two] hundred and thirty years ago.[106] But because it is something so offensive to both human intelligence and the Christian faith to hold that souls are put to sleep[107] at the very time they are closest to God in order to be more perfectly conscious of His goodness, all Christendom[108] has viewed[109] such a fantasy with horror.

Therefore let all who want to be obedient to God and to His Word continue in what I have pointed out from the Scriptures. Let them meditate on this beautiful promise, that "the righteous shall flourish like the palm and grow like a cedar in Lebanon," that those who are "planted in the house of the Lord shall flourish and shall bring forth their fruit; they shall be fat and robust in their old age" (Ps. 92:13f.).

Therefore since we see that our old age is renewed in us by the grace of God by a miraculous power, let us not be afraid when we see all nature fail.[110] Rather let us sing with David, "My soul, bless the Lord, who fills thy mouth with goodness and renews thee like the eagle" (Ps. 103:1, 5). In fact, we have the prayer that our Lord Jesus made to His Father for the same purpose, saying, "Father, I desire that they, whom thou hast given Me, might also be with Me to behold My glory"[111] (John 17:24).

Now since we have sufficiently proven the true doctrine concerning the immortality of souls, it is also necessary from the

104. *beatitude.*

105. *Arabiques.* See Eusebius, *Church History, in Nicene and Post-Nicene Fathers,* second series, vol. 1, p. 279.

106. See n. 103 above. Calvin literally writes "later," not "ago."

107. *assopir = assoupir.*

108. The Council of Florence (1439) concurred with the view that the soul, though separated from the body, was capable of consciousness before the resurrection of its body. The Fifth Lateran Council (in the eighth session, held in 1513), upholding the Florentine decision, condemned the view that the soul was mortal. See Williams's discussion of psychopannychism and Italian philosophical speculation on the immortality of the soul (*Radical Reformation,* pp. 20–25). See "John XXII," *New Catholic Encyclopedia,* vol. 7, pp. 1014f.

109. *eu.*

110. *deffaillir = tomber.*

111. *clarté.*

other side to examine the passages that the Anabaptists cite[112] and on which their error is founded.

First of all they claim that the term which the Scriptures use to define the human soul fittingly applies to animals' souls as well, as when it is said that "God created the great whales and all living souls" (Gen. 1:21). Again, that the animals entered the ark "two by two of all flesh, in which there was the spirit of life" (Gen. 7:15). And to confirm their thesis they utilize what Saint Paul says: that man is now corruptible, mortal, and bestial, but when he is raised he will be incorruptible, immortal, and spiritual, as it is written, that "the first man became a living soul" (I Cor. 15:45).

I acknowledge that the term "living soul" is often attributed to animals, because they also live in their realm. But there is a great difference between them and men.[113] For the human soul is called "living," because by it man reasons, judges, and discerns. The soul of animals has no other faculty than to give their bodies movement. Therefore it should not surprise us if the soul of a man who has reason, understanding, and will,[114] and the other unique powers of the body, should subsist being separated from the body, while the souls of animals should perish, insofar as they only possess corporal sensation.

For this reason Saint Paul cites the testimony of the pagan poet Aratus, "that we are the offspring of God" (Acts 17:29), in order to demonstrate the excellence of our soul. The fact that Saint Paul makes a distinction between a "living soul" and a "life-giving spirit"[115] is not done to denote that our present soul will perish, but simply to show that after the resurrection it will enjoy much more power.[116]

It is enough to know that we will be like God's angels, living without drinking or eating, no longer being subject to any change[117] or weakness (Matt. 22:30).

Secondly, they cite one of Ezekiel's visions where the prophet, describing the resurrection, says that God calls the spirit "from the four winds" to "breathe life into the dead" (Ezek. 37:9). But

112. *amenent = citent.*
113. See the *Institutes* 1.15.3.
114. Ibid., 1.15.6.
115. *l'esprit vivifiant.* See I Corinthians 15:45.
116. *vertu = force.*
117. *mutation = changement.*

the solution is easy, for Ezekiel in the customary manner of the prophets uses an exterior figure to symbolize the soul of man, as in his first vision, when speaking of the Spirit of God, he likewise calls it "wind." On this basis, whoever would argue that the Spirit of God is not an essence is without foundation. Thus it is a great folly on the part of these madmen not to observe a form of speaking that is so commonly used in all of Scripture.

Their third argument is, Granted the soul was created immortal, nevertheless it lost its immortality through sin. For Saint Paul says that "the wages of sin is death" (Rom. 6:23). But first of all I ask, "Hasn't the devil received this reward?" Yet he is not so dead as not to be constantly awake, searching about for whom he may devour. Second, I ask, "Is this death the end or not?" For if it is not the end, then—like it or not—they must admit to me that souls in death continue to feel the eternal fire and the gnawing pain of the worm. Thus it appears that the soul does not so die as to become insensitive to its punishment.[118]

As for the body, it is said that it will return to the earth from whence it came, in order to return to dust[119] (Gen. 3:19). But the death of the soul means to be alienated[120] from God and to be overwhelmed by the sense of His wrath, as the apostle explains in saying, "Awake, O sleeper, rise from the dead, and Christ shall give thee light" (Eph. 5:14). Certainly he is not referring to unconscious[121] bodies, but to those which being buried in sin carry death and hell with them.

Besides, it has already been shown that what we lost in Adam has been restored to us in Jesus Christ. For what was prophesied by the prophet, i.e., that He should overcome death for ever and would swallow it up (Hos. 13:14; I Cor. 15:54), that, the apostle proclaims, has been fulfilled. "He has destroyed death," says Saint Paul, "and has illumined life through the gospel" (II Tim. 1:10). Again, "If death reigned through one man's sin, then those who have received the abundance of grace shall reign in life through Jesus Christ" (Rom. 5:17).

That statement alone ought to suffice to shut their mouth. For since Christ has abolished the death that came [about]

118. *mal.*
119. *pourriture.*
120. Cf. Quistorp, *Calvin's Doctrine,* p. 75.
121. *insensible.*

through Adam, the entire problem is resolved in that comparison Saint Paul makes between them. That is, the power of Jesus Christ to *restore* is greater than Adam's to *destroy.* This is explained by him quite well. And immediately afterwards he adds that "there is no longer any condemnation for those who are in Jesus Christ, who no longer walk according to the flesh" (Rom. 8:1).

In fact, if death still had dominion over faithful souls, then the grace of God would have no reign or life, as he says, but rather the law of God would exercise its power over them, which is completely contrary to the teaching of the Scriptures.

Furthermore, they are mistaken, for often the word "to sleep" means "to die," as when it is written of Saint Stephen that "he fell asleep in the Lord" (Acts 7:60). Or again, "Our friend Lazarus sleeps" (John 11:11). Or still, "Do not be anxious concerning those who sleep" (I Thess. 4:13). In fact this form of speaking is more frequently used in the Bible's narratives[122] than any other.

My reply is that this "sleep" does not belong to the soul but ought to be attributed entirely to the body. For there are two expressions that are used in the same way: "to sleep with his fathers" and "to be with his fathers." Thus when it is said that a man "was laid with his fathers," it means he "was buried." But I do not want anyone to believe this unless I can prove it by the sure testimony of Scripture.

When Job said, "Behold, I [shall] sleep in the dust" (Job 7:21), he did not mean that his soul was about to go to sleep. Also, when he says in another passage that "all men shall lie down together in the dust, and the worms shall cover them" (Job 21:26), that only pertains to the body. The same holds true for what David says (Ps. 88:6), when he writes that [we are] "like the dead who sleep in their graves." And Isaiah, referring to Nebuchadnezzar, says, "All the other kings sleep in their glory and have been laid in their own tombs, but you, you have been cast out of your grave" (Isa. 14:18f.).

Thus we see, in summation, that the word "sleep" is applied through similitude to bodies which have become inanimate once the soul has left them.[123] It is a form of speech that the pagans always used. And from it is derived the word "cemetery" which

122. *histoires.*

123. See Quistorp, *Calvin's Doctrine,* p. 137.

we use. It means "the place where one sleeps,"[124] not because the pagans[125] understood souls to be sleeping there, but because bodies were laid out to rest in their sepulchers, as if in their beds. In the same way we ought to interpret that passage in Job—with which the Anabaptists arm themselves—where he says, "Once man lies down, he does not awake from his sleep, nor does he rise, until the heavens are changed" (Job 14:12).

They similarly make a shield out of one of Solomon's statements that actually contradicts their view more than any other passage in Scripture. In fact, I would not try to use it myself, except for the fact that they so impudently misuse it, as if it were made [only] for them. The words are, "I said in my heart concerning the sons of men that God wanted to show them that they are like beasts. For the death of a man and the death of a beast are such that their fate is the same. They come from the earth and return to it. Who knows whether the spirit of man ascends upward and the spirit of beasts descends below" (Eccles. 3:18ff.)?[126]

I reply, as I have already said, that Solomon could not have spoken more expressly in our behalf. For in desiring to reprove[127] the vanity of human intelligence, he says that man cannot comprehend by his natural reason or observation wherein he differs from the beasts. For primarily he enjoys his excellence over them after death. For the immortality of souls is something that transcends his capacity. Hence, since man is so confounded[128] by vanity as not to know whether his spirit ascends upward and lives for ever, or like that of beasts passes into corruption and perishes, we are forced to conclude that true wisdom lies in understanding the immortality of souls.

There is a passage similar to this one which he later adds, that "man does not know whether it is of God's love or hate, but this is hid and in suspense, because the same fate[129] comes indifferently to the good and to the evil" (Eccles. 9:1).[130] Thus, since everything is so uncertain, I ask whether a faithful man ought

124. *dormitoire = lieu ou l'on dort.*
125. *anciens.*
126. Cf. the *Institutes* 3.25.5.
127. *redarguer = blâmer.*
128. *convaincu = confondu.*
129. *toutes choses.*
130. See the *Institutes* 3.25.5.

not wonder, when adversity and tribulation overtake him, if God hates him? Of course not! For he has been promised that this is for his salvation, so that he can console himself and rejoice, being assured that tribulation is a sign of God's paternal love rather than a sign of His hate.

But Solomon speaks from a [human] point of view, wondering if we can know this based on human reason. And since all human life is marked by vanity, our only recourse is God and His Word. For he next explains what happens to those who are given over to such a fantasy, that "their hearts are full of impiety and contempt[131] for God," while they take hope in the proverb: "A living dog is better off than a dead lion" (Eccles. 9:4).

Now Solomon himself declares at the end of his book what we ought to understand with regard to this point. It is that "the body returns to the earth from which it came and the spirit ascends to God who gave it" (Eccles. 12:7).

The Anabaptist position is based primarily on the scriptural point that on the last day we are each rewarded according to our works. Hence they argue that since God postpones our beatitude and eternal life until the last day and likewise does not threaten the wicked [now] but preserves His vengeance for them until the last day, we must conclude that until then the good do not receive their reward nor are the wicked punished. Otherwise it would be meaningless to say that the people whose names are written in the book will be saved on that day or that it will be said to God's elect, "Come, inherit the kingdom" (Dan. 12:1; Matt. 25:34). Thus they conclude that since we do not obtain our salvation until the day of the final resurrection, that in the meantime our souls sleep and are without any joy of their beatitude.

I reply that their conclusion is illfounded. For although souls might not be in glory, it does not follow that they are not alive in God while awaiting His revelation.

But for a more ample response to this problem, let readers remember what I have reiterated[132] above, that our beatitude is still in the future,[133] until that day. There is no one who does not concur that the perfection of our beatitude consists in our being perfectly united with God. It is the goal toward which all the

131. *contemnement = méprise.*

132. *confessé.*

133. *est tousiours en chemin.*

promises of God point us. For what was formerly said to Abraham is equally addressed to us: that God is our highest[134] reward (Gen. 15:1). Hence the end of our beatitude, of our glory and salvation, is to belong wholly to God, to possess Him, and for Him to be wholly in us.

Now this will certainly not occur before the day of the resurrection. It is not without cause, therefore, that it is called "the day of salvation" (II Cor. 6:2). Thus it is said that at that time we shall inherit the kingdom of God, not that we shall not inherit part of it before then. For we already possess it partly by hope. But at that time we shall obtain[135] the full and perfect revelation.

But in order to be brief, what we have said above should suffice to answer their argument: that we are in a constant state of expectation and hope until Jesus Christ appears in [behalf of] our full redemption to receive us into the immortality and glory of His kingdom. In the meantime, however, as the apostle Paul says, we continue to have "our life hid in Him before God" (Col. 3:3).

It would appear that we have sufficiently answered them with respect to the day of the resurrection, were it not that they pursue [the matter] still further, producing Saint Paul's statement where he says that "if we are not raised, then we are the most miserable people of the world" (I Cor. 15:19). But this won't be the case, they say, if we are happy before the resurrection.

I reply that Paul has in mind the goal of the believers' hope, that is, that on the day of the resurrection they will obtain what God has promised them.[136] Thus, in the passage in question, if there were no resurrection, they would be denied all that they had hoped. We hold, thus, that faithful souls are happy enough while awaiting this day, but because of this waiting period,[137] which can be frustrating and vain, it follows that they become unhappy.

Since the entire beatitude of God's children proceeds from and depends on this, that on the day of the resurrection they will be like God and will enjoy their heritage, then it is not surprising if Saint Paul says that they will be the most miserable people in

134. *tresample.*

135. *aurons.*

136. See n. 34 above.

137. *leur attente.*

the entire world if there is no resurrection. In fact, he gives equal weight to these two ideas: that if there is no resurrection, then we only have hope in this world.

I am confident that each one of us can see at a glance that Paul's statement is without any contradictions. For he is saying that if we are deceived in our hope about the resurrection, then we are to be pitied. And we are saying that faithful souls are indeed happy because of that very hope, without which we affirm there could be no joy or beatitude. And there is nothing contradictory about that.

In addition they cite[138] what is written in the Letter to the Hebrews about the ancient fathers, that they "died in faith, not having received the promises, but having greeted them from afar and acknowledging themselves to be strangers on the earth" (Heb. 11:13). "Now people who speak thus make it clear that they are seeking their natural heritage and country, for if they had been thinking of the country from which they had come out, they might have been able to return to it. But they are hungering[139] for a better country, that is to say, for heaven" [Heb. 11:14ff.].

This passage is deceitfully corrupted by them and by their misleading glosses. For they hold it refers to the present time, whereas the apostle speaks of the time when the patriarchs lived[140] in this world. However, with respect to our argument, I am perfectly content to accept their gloss. For they argue that if Abraham and the other fathers are expecting[141] a heavenly heritage, then they don't have it yet. I reply to the contrary that if they are expecting anything, it means they are alive and are conscious of good and evil. What then becomes of "sleep"? We see how self-contradictory they are—like little children.

As for the rest, I fully concur with what the apostle later writes, that none of the ancient fathers yet enjoys what he awaited in this world, "since God ordained that they should not receive their perfection apart from us" (Heb. 11:39f.). And that is what we maintain: that the highest consolation of faithful souls consists in this glorious immortality into which we shall all together be gathered, when Christ appears at the judgment.

138. *obiectent* = *proposent.*

139. *appetent* = *désirent.*

140. *conversovent* = *habitèrent.*

141. *appetent.*

The passages to which I shall hereafter[142] refer will show how these madmen amass all the tricks of sophistry[143] they can—however shamelessly—in order to have some means of justifying their error. They say that if souls, being separated from their bodies, live with God, then Saint Peter inflicted a grave injury on Tabitha by raising her, since he withdrew her from fellowship with God and life's highest happiness in order to return her to this sea of misery (Acts 9:40).

I reply that this argument can be used against them as much as against us. For if her soul was asleep, unconscious of any evil, then one could say that she lost nothing by having to leave that rest in order to return to the struggles of this present life. I could say to them that they should be the first to resolve[144] this problem for me. But I know that one can't expect any sound answer from them.

As for our part, we can easily respond. For what Saint Paul says of himself is true of all believers: "whether it is more profitable for us to die, as it is far better for us to be with Christ" (Phil. 1:23). And at the same time he says that God, by healing Epaphroditus of his illness and retrieving him from death, had pity on him, although he was numbered among the faithful (Phil. 2:27).

The Anabaptists argue that it is an act of cruelty for souls to live after death. We answer that it is an act of mercy for it to please God to magnify Himself in us in this corporal life, making us instruments of His glory. Besides, it is not written that Tabitha was raised upon her own request, but at the request of those who cried over her loss at her death. Therefore let us hold that our Lord continually[145] bestows a singular grace on us by granting that we should live and die in Him.

Let us turn [now] to the passages they cite from David—although I am ashamed to mention them insofar as they misuse them so childishly. But it is necessary to mention them, insofar as they feather their nests with such passages when dealing with simple people.

They cite this text: "I said, 'You are gods, and sons of the Most

142. *doresenavant = dorénavant.*

143. *cavillations.*

144. *soudre = résoudre.*

145. *tousiours.*

High, nevertheless you shall die like men'" (Ps. 82:6). They explain that believers are called "gods" in this passage though they die like the reprobate and remain in that condition until the day of judgment.

But according to Jesus Christ's explanation (John 10:35), the passage refers to princes and ministers of justice who hold the title of "gods" because they serve as God's lieutenants in their work. And even if our Lord Jesus had said nothing about it, the usage of Scripture would demonstrate it to us. Even the text itself is so clear that it carries its explanation[146] with it. For the passage reproves those who exercise tyranny and iniquity and says to them that they shall die and leave behind the dignity of their office in order to render an account to God, as the least of all must.

They also cite this passage: "Put not your trust in men; the spirit of man departs and returns to earth, and on that day all their plans perish" (Ps. 146:3f.). They interpret the word "spirit" as "breath"—as if there were no other soul in man. Then they argue that if his "plans perish," it follows that the soul sleeps or is nothing.

I reply that the "spirit of man" means something other than "breath," as I have sufficiently proven. But inasmuch as this word is used here in that way [i.e., as "breath"], as it is in several passages, this doesn't mean that man comprises[147] nothing but "breath." As for what it said about his "plans perishing," nothing more is meant by this than that at death human enterprises are dissolved and go up in smoke, as is said elsewhere (Ps. 112:10): "that the desire of sinners will perish," in order to denote that it becomes of no effect.

Thus David does not say that men cease to think after death. But he means that all their deliberations come to nothing.

They cite another passage that is almost similar: "He remembered that they are flesh, a spirit that passes and returns no more" (Ps. 78:39).

Now I acknowledge that the word "spirit" means "wind" or "breath," but I deny[148] that this serves in any way to confirm their error. For by this manner of speaking the prophet wanted

146. *glose.*
147. *n'ait.*
148. *nie = renie.*

to emphasize the fragile nature of our condition and the brevity of human life.

It is written in the Book[149] of Job that "man is like a flower that sprouts from the earth and immediately withers and like the shadow that flees" (Job 14:2). Isaiah commands all preachers to cry that "all flesh is grass" (Isa. 40:6). If the Anabaptists can deduce from this that souls wither, then they see more clearly than Saint Peter, who proves that the souls of the faithful are immortal (I Peter 1:23), insofar as the prophet immediately adds that "the Word of God abides for ever."

There is a similar argument in what is said in another Psalm: "As a father pities his children, so also the Lord has had mercy on His servants, for He knows of what we are made. He remembers that we are dust, that our days are like grass, like the flower that quickly fades; for the spirit passes in us and is gone and no longer knows its place" (Ps. 103:13–16).

In all these sentences, let us note that man is admonished concerning his fragile nature, especially when God removes His hand and His strength from him, so that he might realize that he is nothing and even less than nothing unless God sustains him and preserves him by His grace. In fact, when we say that souls are immortal, we do not mean thereby, in any way, to slight[150] God, whom Saint Paul says "is alone immortal" (I Tim. 6:16). Rather we consider it a blasphemy to attribute immortality to the soul, as if it subsisted by its own power. Nevertheless it is appropriate for us to consider what particular quality[151] and nature God has given to souls: which is to subsist by His hand in order to enjoy immortal blessedness[152] or malediction.

But they think they have a mighty sword in what is written in another Psalm: "Dost Thou work a miracle for the dead by raising them that they might praise Thee? Who can recount Thy steadfast love in the grave or Thy justice in Abaddon?"[153] (Ps. 88:11f.). Again: "The dead will not praise Thee, O Lord, nor those who go down to the grave. But we the living will bless God" (Ps. 115:17f.). Or again: "What profit is there in my blood when I go

149. *histoire.*
150. *deroguer = faire tort à.*
151. *proprieté.*
152. *beatitude.*
153. *la terre d'oubliance.* Literally, "the land of no remembrance."

down to corruption? Does the dust praise Thee or declare Thy truth?" (Ps. 30:9). And still again from Hezekiah's song: "The grave cannot praise Thee and death cannot give Thee glory. Those who go down to the pit no longer await Thy truth. The living, the living, is he who confesses in Thee. The father recounts to his children Thy truth" (Isa. 38:18f.).

To resolve this matter we must note two things. The first is that by "death" we must not simply understand a natural death through which we all must pass, but a death that is purposefully punitive and a sign of God's wrath,[154] one that means a rejection of men, their complete perdition or loss. The second is that when it is said, "The dead will not praise Thee," the passage refers to that praise of God that is recounted among men who are conscious of His grace.

With respect to the first, it is true that the word "hell" often means "the grave," as we have translated it. But those who are trained[155] in the Scriptures know that the terms "dead" and "grave" mean what I have said they mean and especially so in the Psalms. Therefore those whom God has rejected and pursued with His wrath, not only with regard to the body but especially the soul, are called "dead," and the agony they experience is called "the grave."

For example, it is written, "Let death come upon them, and let them go down to the grave alive" (Ps. 55:15). Again: "Lord God, if Thou shouldst cease to save me I would be like those who go down to the grave" (Ps. 28:1). Again: "O Lord, Thou hast rescued my soul from the grave and hast delivered me from those who go down to the grave" (Ps. 30:3). Still again: "If God had not helped me, my soul would have dwelled in the grave" (Ps. 94:17). Again: "Our bones have been strewn about the grave" (Ps. 141:7). Again: "He has set[156] me in a dark place, like [the place of] the dead" (Ps. 143:3).

Now to the contrary it is said that those whom God blesses with His mercy live. "The Lord," says David in another place, "has commanded blessing and eternal life for His people" (Ps. 133:3). Again: "He delivered their souls from death and nourished them in famine" (Ps. 33:19).

154. Calvin emphasizes that the death of the soul is different from the death of the body. See Quistorp, *Calvin's Doctrine*, p. 75.

155. *exercez* = *éprouvés*. Literally, "tested."

156. *colloqué* = *placé*.

But there is one passage among the rest that expresses so well both meanings that it can suffice for both: "Can man pay the ransom for his soul, to live without end? Will he not see death, seeing that the wise [also] die? The foolish and the wise, I say, die together. They are laid out in the grave like sheep, and death devours them. But the righteous shall rule over them in the morning; their power shall perish in the grave, and their glory shall waste away, and the Lord will redeem[157] my soul from the power of the grave" (Ps. 49:7ff.).

The sum of this Psalm is that those who confide in their riches or power shall all die, whether poor or rich, whether foolish or wise, but whoever hopes in God will be delivered from the grave.

These things observed, we now have a solution for all the passages that the Anabaptists cite.

It has been seen that when the saints are startled by the apprehension of death they pray to God for Him to deliver them. Why do they have such a dread of death? Let us consider all of the examples of the faithful.

We do not read that they greatly complained or lamented when it came time to die, but they submitted patiently to God's good will, even David and Hezekiah, I say. Why then in these foregoing texts did they raise such lamentation[158] if not that in death they became aware of God's wrath and severity, which frightened them, and not without cause?

Now certainly a man who is aware of the rigor of God and is persecuted by His vengeance cannot praise Him, since we cannot render Him praise unless we sense His goodness. Secondly, when it is said in these passages that "the dead will not praise God," this does not mean that they will not praise Him in their heart, but that they will not recount to others His praises. This is what the other words in the text also mean. For "to narrate," or "to announce," or "to recount" to one's children means to celebrate orally the benefits of God so that the world might comprehend them.

The Anabaptists also produce two other verses from the Psalms. The one is, "I will praise the Lord throughout my life. I will sing praises to my God as long as I live" (Ps. 104:33). The

157. *retirera.*
158. *querimonies = lamentations.*

second: "Look away from me, that I may find courage, until I am gone and exist no more" (Ps. 39:13).

In place of their first passage, I can cite five that prove to them the contrary of what they allege. "Lord God, I will acknowledge Thee for ever" (Ps. 30:12). Again: "I will bless the Lord at all times, His praise shall continually be in my mouth" (Ps. 34:1). Again: "Each day[159] I will praise Thee for ever because of what Thou hast done" (Ps. 52:9). Again: "I will praise Thy name for ever and ever" (Ps. 145:1). Lastly: "I will forever sing praises to Thy name, forever and ever" (Ps. 61:8). David does not say that he will praise the Lord only during his present life, but he promises to do it for ever.

What does he mean, then, in the first text, someone might ask, where he promises to praise the Lord "as long as he lives" (Ps. 104:33)? I reply that those words do not exclude the praises that the saints render after death, because their manner of praising God is different from ours.

As for their second reference (Ps. 39:13), these are the words of a man [severely] pressed by the anguish of conscience, who begs of God that if he must be destroyed he may be left alone for a little while. It is similar to the example in Job where he says to God, "Leave me alone, that I may bewail my sorrow for awhile, before I go to the region of darkness, where there is only eternal confusion and horror" (Job 10:20f.). This in no way proves that souls came to an end.

There are several other passages in the book[160] of Job which they manipulate in their favor, on which I shall briefly touch as they come to my mind.[161] The first is, "Why did I not die at birth, or why did I not perish when I came forth from my mother's womb? For then I should have lain down in silence and rested in my sleep, or I should have been as an aborted child and like those who being conceived do not reach the perfection of life. I should have been in the place where the great and the small are at rest" (Job 3:11ff.).

But if, on the contrary, I should refer them to the fourteenth chapter of Isaiah, where he describes the dead coming before the king of Babylon to mock him (Isa. 14:9ff.), what would be

159. *derechef = de nouveau.*

160. *l'histoire.*

161. *memoire.*

their reply to me then? But I pass over that, content with the following simple exposition of Job's statement: that he, being pressed to the limit, and almost succumbing under his burden, only meant his present misery. For this reason, he makes it greater than all the others, as if it were his only [burden]. Therefore, he does not regard death with horror but rather desires it, as if it were the end of all misfortune, not thinking about what might follow.

This is the way people who are preoccupied with great anxiety and sorrow feel. For if in the heat of summer we long for a cool frost, and again in the winter, having forgotten how vexatious heat is, we long for hot weather, then it is hardly miraculous if a vehement passion should push us to such a yearning. Let us realize, then, that there is very little that a man, persecuted by God's hand, can do, except be so carried away as to forget everything else because of his sorrow.

A similar reason appears in several other statements he makes, as in the following: "Remember, Lord, that my life is only breath and that my eye will never return again to see good" (Job 7:7). Again: "Nothing remains for me but the grave" (Job 17:1). "All that belongs to me will go down to the depths of the pit" (Job 17:16), and other similar [passages]. For we see here that Job, being preoccupied with that distress which he sensed came from God's wrathful pursuit of him, could only see confusion and understood death as the total annihilation of his life, not thinking about what might happen afterwards, as has been said.

To want, therefore, to conclude that man's soul perishes with his body is not only an unacceptable act of stupidity, but also an act of impudence. However, with regard to this matter and all the others, I think I have so obviously reproved all that the Anabaptists allege that I can now bring an end to this matter.

I solemnly affirmed[162] at the beginning, and not without cause, that my intention was not to contradict point by point all the opinions that the Anabaptists hold. For that would be like entering a forest from which no one should ever come out. Besides, it is not necessary and would even constitute an enterprise more curious than useful if we sought to amass all the absurdities that each foolish head among them has imagined. Thus I have been content to treat briefly, as faithfully as I could,

162. *protesté.*

the articles held in common by those who are the most intelligent and sober or indeed the least scatterbrained among the entire sect. But as for those who are called the "Libertines," who are completely insane and without sense, I am reserving them for another tract.

Now to conclude, I beg all Christian readers to examine the whole matter in Scripture, as it is the true touchstone for testing every doctrine. I am confident that whoever will let himself be led by God's truth and will willingly submit to reason will find ample satisfaction with my repudiation[163] of the articles here.

Furthermore, I have sought, insofar as possible, to accommodate myself to the rudeness of the simple,[164] for whom I primarily labor. Thus the Anabaptists cannot cavil, as is their custom, that I have sought to win over the simple through subtlety or conquer[165] them by means of human eloquence, since I have used as popular and simple a means as I knew how.

But it is good that I should warn all the true[166] faithful of their malice. For the Anabaptists cannot make their cause appear good except by muddling[167] everything to the extent that their entire teaching is a confused mess. For like a body without a head, or arms or feet, they often use forms of speech that are absurd and outlandish,[168] without purpose, and that jump about like a cock-and-bull story. Interweaving different points, they cite only fragments[169] of Scripture. And they are so pleased with this [approach] that they make themselves believe that there is far more majesty in speaking this grossly than there is in developing their case in an orderly manner.

Now in order to confound them no better way exists than to expound and contradict the issues clearly and to restate[170] in an orderly manner one point after the other. Indeed, examine[171] and consider closely the sentences of Scripture in order to

163. *deduict.* Literally, "disavowed."
164. *petis.*
165. *opprimer = vaincre.*
166. *bons.*
167. *brouillant = barbrouillant.*
168. The Latin reads, *"absurdis et peregrinis."* See *CO* 7, col. 140, n. 1.
169. *couppez ou rompus.* Literally, "cut or broken."
170. *demener = remuer, dire.*
171. *poiser = peser, examiner.*

discover their true and natural sense,[172] using simple and clear words[173] that are familiar to common language.

When we do that they cry that we want to deceive them and to circumvent them by human astuteness and sophistry—as if it were the custom or intention of sophists to illuminate mysterious things anyway!

As for my part, I confess that insofar as I can, I attempt to set forth in an orderly manner what I say in order to make it as clear and understandable as possible. If the Anabaptists cannot accept that, then I do not know what to say except that "whoever does evil hates the light" (John 3:20).

Now in order to give a favorable pretext[174] to their doctrine, they have published along with their resolution the history of the death of a certain Michael[175]—an accomplice and member of their sect. In fact, they are in the habit of making a powerful defense[176] out of the fact that some have been killed for holding views which they would not retract, although if they had they might have escaped death and ransomed their life. Indeed, it is an effective[177] means of authorizing a doctrine for a man to abandon his life courageously[178] and freely in order to confirm his belief. For when we are told what the prophets, apostles, and other martyrs endured in order to maintain the truth of God, we are so much the more strengthened to adhere to the faith we hold, which they sealed by their blood.

I acknowledge, therefore, that we must not vilify the death of God's servants, since their death is "precious in His sight" (Ps. 116:15), and since their courage and constancy is no small aid in supporting our weakness. But since we can be thoroughly deceived by this unless we have another criterion, we must return to the foundation without which we should be unable to make sound judgments or be certain about the matter.

172. One of Calvin's favorite exegetical principles is to interpret a text in its "true and natural sense." See T. H. L. Parker, *Calvin's New Testament Commentaries* (London: SCM, 1971), p. 64.

173. Note Calvin's emphasis on *brevitas* and *perspicuitas*.

174. *couleur davantage.*

175. Michael Sattler. See *The Trial and Martyrdom of Michael Sattler,* in Williams and Mergal, *Anabaptist Writers,* pp. 138–144; and Yoder, *Sattler,* pp. 67–80.

176. *grand bouclier.*

177. *belle apparence.*

178. *constamment = avec fermete.*

Certainly a man's death, whoever he might be, is never so precious that it can or ought to prejudice God's truth in any thing, or be so beneficial as to approve of erroneous and perverse doctrines. Therefore let us hold to this: that although a sound and solid doctrine, being founded on reason, is confirmed later by the death of its adherents and confessors by whom it is maintained, nevertheless, the death of the whole world cannot prove a lie.

Indeed what separates the martyrs of God from the devil's disciples is that the martyrs die for a righteous cause. Therefore in the same way that it is laudable and courageous to suffer death when necessity calls for it in order to bear witness to the truth, so also it is an insane obstinacy to suffer for a wicked cause. So much so that whoever suffers for it the most is all the more to be reprimanded. In fact, when we let ourselves be carried away by this pretext, we lose complete judgment and esteem.

If it is necessary to be certain about the truth of God which we preach, then we have more than sufficient evidence in the death of our Lord Jesus, of all the prophets, apostles, and martyrs from the time of the early church to our own. And whatever is repugnant to it—whether sealed by blood or wax—will always remain a lie.

Against the Fantastic and Furious Sect of the Libertines Who Are Called "Spirituals"

Editor's Introduction

The translation of Calvin's treatise *Against the Libertines*[1] is based on the text in the *Calvini Opera,* volume 7, columns 149–248. For the most part the translation is straightforward and unadorned; accuracy and clarity were the twin criteria. All biblical quotations are from the text itself.

Purpose of the Treatise

Calvin was motivated to write his treatise *Against the Libertines* for a number of reasons. In his preface to the treatise he cites two. First, he felt compelled to oppose the sect because of its surprising "growth" and sheer "perniciousness."[2] As he knew better, he felt divinely called to repulse it. And second, as in the case of his treatise *Against the Anabaptists,*[3] he had been solicited by Reformed leaders[4] to rebut the sect.

1. *Contre la secte phantastique et furieuse des Libertins que se nomment Spirituelz,* par I. Calvin, a Geneve, par Iehan Girard, 1545; *Calvini Opera,* vol. 7, cols. 149–248.

2. Ibid., col. 150.

3. *CO* 7, col. 49.

4. See Valérand Poullain's letter to Calvin, May 26, 1544—A.-L. Herminjard, *Correspondances des reformateurs dan les pays de langue française,* vol. 9, p. 247, no. 1358. With this letter Poullain sent Calvin several writings of the Quintinists which Reformed brethren had sent him from Valenciennes. Poullain was hopeful that Calvin would read these and give the people of Valenciennes "some consolation which would sustain them in their misery and fortify them against these menaces [*pestes illas*] and support them." Farel (to Calvin, October 2, 1544—Herminjard, *Correspondances,* vol. 9, p. 335, no. 1395) also implored Calvin to write against these "disciples of Simon Magus," exclaiming, "If only [they] might

However, in chapter 4 of the *Libertines*, he hints at a third, somewhat more personal and discreet reason. He refers to the activities of Quintin of Hainaut and two of his followers who had found refuge in Marguerite of Angoulême's court.[5] Lest persons (viz., Marguerite) become "hurt by them through lack of information," he reluctantly concluded that he must break silence and publish an attack against the Quintinists.[6]

Williams hypothesizes that a tragic event, involving one of Calvin's colleagues at Strassburg, also prompted his decision.[7] Peter Brully, who had succeeded Calvin as the pastor of the French church at Strassburg, had been captured at Tournai while on a journey to the French-speaking Netherlands; he was burned as a heretic by the Catholic authorities on February 19, 1545. At the trial Brully had to defend himself against charges that linked his Protestantism with the antinomianism of the Quintinists. Stung by the irony of these events, Calvin was jolted into action.

Finally, the treatise had its inception in Calvin's decision of 1544[8] to write a two-volume refutation: one of the Anabaptists and the other of the Libertines. Having already delayed this "second treatise"[9] too long, Calvin finally published it.

Who Were the Libertines?

With few exceptions modern scholarship has largely ignored Calvin's treatise *Against the Libertines*. Only a limited number of

---

be extirpated utterly through you." Poullain again upon receiving a letter from Calvin expressed his joy (October 13, 1544—Herminjard, *Correspondances*, vol. 9, pp. 341f., no. 1398) that Calvin had agreed to write against the Quintinists.

5. Marguerite of Angoulême (1492–1549) was the queen of Lower Navarre and Nérac, sister of Francis I, and author of *Mirror of a Sinful Soul*. She protected evangelical Catholics such as Jacques Lefèvre d'Étaples, William Briçonnet, and Gérard Roussel, and befriended the Reformation. Calvin had occasion to correspond with her several times and had received her gratitude because of his endeavors to cultivate friendly relations between Francis I and German Protestants. See Williston Walker, *John Calvin: The Organiser of Reformed Protestantism* (New York: Schocken, 1969), p. 242.

6. *CO* 7, cols. 162ff.

7. George H. Williams, *The Radical Reformation*, p. 600.

8. *CO* 7, col. 54.

9. Ibid.

works have served to illumine it; however, before examining any recent studies, Calvin should be allowed to speak for himself.

Calvin was aware that Libertinism represented an aberrant movement within Protestantism that was much larger in scope than the sect he wished to expose. He was cognizant of this movement's presence in Holland, Brabant (Belgium), and Lower Germany,[10] but it was the French-speaking group he knew best and whose influence he wanted to eliminate.

To his knowledge the French-speaking Libertines could be traced to a Fleming named Coppin, a native of Lille, who began propagating the sect's views around 1525 in the region of his birth. Coppin was succeeded by a Quintin of Hainaut, a man of some gifts, who soon became the acknowledged founder of the movement.

Calvin did not know exactly when or how the movement came to France, but by 1534 Quintin and two of his followers, a Bertrand of Moulins and a Claude Perceval, were established in or near Paris, where Calvin reports that he personally met Quintin.[11] The three were later joined by a former priest, Anthony Pocquet. Calvin also learned from Étienne de la Forge, the Waldensian with whom Calvin stayed in Paris while working on Seneca, that the Quintinists had left their own country owing to "some crime rather than because of their message."[12]

Calvin did not know how long the Quintinists were active in France, but their prolonged presence concerned him. While there they had also continued to work in their own country, probably around Valenciennes, where, from what Calvin could learn, they had enjoyed a shocking success.[13]

Meanwhile Bertrand of Moulins had died, but Calvin understood that the remaining three had found refuge at Marguerite of Angoulême's court. Here Quintin served as an usher, Perceval as a valet, and Pocquet as a chaplain—all of which annoyed the Genevan a great deal.

10. *CO* 7, col. 159.

11. Ibid., col. 160.

12. Ibid.

13. See Poullain's letter to Calvin (May 26, 1544—Herminjard, *Correspondances*, vol. 9, p. 247, no. 1358) and Pierre Viret's to Rodolphe Gualther (September 5, 1544—Herminjard, *Correspondances*, vol. 9, p. 329, no. 1392) in which Liège, Tournai, and Valenciennes are identified as the towns in which the Quintinists had posed a definite threat.

Calvin also relates that Pocquet, who had formerly lived in Geneva, came to him in 1542, seeking his endorsement. Calvin was stunned to learn through Pocquet that Bucer had granted the Quintinists recognition. Calvin refused and Pocquet was required to leave.

Calvin estimates that the sect numbered about four thousand, but he fears that as many as ten thousand souls may have been tainted by their errors. He then describes the Quintinists as teaching an esoteric and pantheistic form of determinism, characterized by a crass antinomian and libertine ethic and tinged with a radical eschatology.

It is clear that Calvin was deeply biased against the Quintinists, pillorying them throughout his treatise in the hopes of crushing their influence in Marguerite's court as well as curtailing their movement wherever French was spoken.

Modern Assessments

In the early 1920s Karl Müller[14] subjected Calvin's *Libertines* to thoughtful criticism. In his estimation Calvin had created a false impression of the so-called Libertines. In actuality they were neither moral libertines nor pantheists but represented a mysticism similar to the pietism found in *Theologia Germanica*.[15]

How was it possible for a man of Calvin's stature to make such a mistake if this were so? Rather than lay the blame at Calvin's feet, Müller speculated that Calvin's view was the result of someone else's misunderstanding. Müller found the clue in the journey of two Dutchmen to Strassburg[16] and Geneva in 1544. They left behind certain Quintinist writings along with their own interpretations and requests for help.[17] Calvin read the writings in the light of the Dutchmen's views and arrived at his false impression.

Wilhelm Niesel[18] has weighed Müller's theory with appreciation

14. Karl Müller, "Calvin und die Libertiner," *Zeitschrift für Kirchengeschichte* 40 (1922): 83–129.

15. Ibid., pp. 85, 106, 128.

16. See Poullain's letter to Calvin (May 26, 1544—Herminjard, *Correspondances*, vol. 9, p. 247, no. 1358) in which he refers to this visit and "our Valenciennes brothers."

17. Müller, "Calvin und die Libertiner," pp. 122–129.

18. Wilhelm Niesel, "Calvin und die Libertiner," *Zeitschrift für Kirchengeschichte* 48 (1929): 58–74.

but is convinced that the Tübingen theologian was wrong. He notes that before the Dutchmen had visited Calvin, the Reformer was already familiar with the Libertines.[19] Furthermore, the introduction to his *Brief Instruction* and his full account of the sect's origins in the *Libertines* piece demonstrate that Calvin was fully cognizant of the group's views.

In Niesel's judgment Calvin began opposing the Libertines as early as his 1539 edition of the *Institutes.* In particular Niesel cites the Libertine doctrines of providence and regeneration (chaps. 9 and 18 of the *Libertines*) which Calvin refuted in the Strassburg edition,[20] and again the doctrine of angels and the devil (chap. 11 of the *Libertines*) which Calvin attacked in his 1543 edition of the *Institutes.*[21]

Niesel has reconstructed Calvin's contacts with the Libertines much as the Reformer himself had traced them. Niesel concludes that since Calvin had personally met Quintin in Paris, under no circumstances could the visit of the two Dutchmen in 1544 have been the main influence in shaping Calvin's low opinion of the Quintinists.

But is Calvin's word alone enough? Were there others who had a similar opinion of the Quintinists? Niesel cites three sources. The first is a letter which Bucer wrote on July 5, 1538, to the Queen of Navarre, in which he describes dangerous people in France in terms highly similar to Calvin's description of the Quintinists, even so far as to emphasize their "moral libertinism."[22]

The second is Michael Carnovianus's letter to Johann Hess in Breslau (1534), in which he recounts a trip he had taken in 1533 into west Germany, France, and the Netherlands to see how the Anabaptists (*Schwärmer*) and Catholics treated evangelical doctrines.[23] Near Paris he met a group of Anabaptists whom he describes as *"perversiores et pertinaciores,"* hence distinguishing between Anabaptists in general and a more perverse sect in the same way that Calvin would later distinguish between Anabaptists and Libertines.[24]

19. Ibid., p. 59. Niesel cites Calvin's letter to Farel (Herminjard, *Correspondances,* vol. 9, pp. 187f., no. 1337).

20. Niesel, "Calvin und die Libertiner," p. 60. See especially nn. 2, 3, and 4.

21. Ibid.

22. Ibid., p. 69. Niesel cites Bucer's letter in Herminjard, *Correspondances,* vol. 5, pp. 38f., no. 721; *CO* 10, cols. 215f.

23. Niesel, "Calvin und die Libertiner," p. 69, n. 3.

24. Ibid., pp. 69f.

Thirdly, Niesel cites Luther's letter of April, 1525, to his followers in Antwerp. In this correspondence Luther strongly denounced the doctrines of Loy Pruystinck, whom he accused of identifying man's reason and understanding with the Holy Spirit.[25] Niesel notes that the historian J. Fredericks[26] was tempted to associate Pruystinck's followers with Carnovianus's perverse Anabaptists near Paris, but Niesel cautions against this step in that the Loist documents nowhere require a "moral libertinism." Hence Pruystinck's followers should not be called Libertines but Spiritualists. Niesel, however, is willing to venture that the two groups did represent a form of "pantheistic spiritualism."[27]

In conclusion Niesel is confident that Calvin's Quintinists also represented a form of Spiritualism akin to the Loists, but at that point one should make no further conclusions. As for Müller's view, Niesel praises him for having made scholarship aware that the Libertines practiced a quietistic mysticism. "But now," Niesel writes, "we must emphasize that Calvin has discovered justly [*mit Recht*] the pantheistic basis of this Mysticism. Whether he was justified to complain that the Quintinists required a moral licentiousness [*sittlicher Zügellosigkeit*], we prefer not to decide. . . . The whole truth on this problem will only come once the writings of the sect, which go back before the year 1538, shall be found again."[28]

Since Niesel's article, George H. Williams in his encyclopedic *The Radical Reformation* has highlighted the main details concerning Calvin and the Libertines in largely the same manner that Calvin narrates them in his treatise. Williams has relied on Niesel's study and himself distinguishes between the Loists and Calvin's Libertines.

Williams prefers to designate the Libertines as "Spiritualizers"[29]

25. Ibid., p. 70. See n. 4 especially. Luther's letter may be found in *Briefe* (Weimar: Hermann Buhlaus Nachfolger, 1908), vol. 18, pp. 541–550. Luther cites eight Loist articles which Pruystinck taught. See Williams, *Radical Reformation*, p. 352, where these articles are listed and briefly discussed.

26. J. Frederichs, *Die Secte der Loisten of Antwerpsche Libertijnen: 1525–1545* (Ghent and The Hague: Graven, 1891). Cited by Niesel, "Calvin und die Libertiner," p. 69, n. 3.

27. Niesel, "Calvin und die Libertiner," pp. 71f.

28. Ibid., p. 74.

29. F. H. Littell's popularization of Ernst Troeltsch's term *spiritual*. See *Radical Reformation*, p. 351, n. 28.

and as a subgroup of Spiritualists. He does not believe that the "exact relationship" between the Loists and the Libertines can be worked out, but his survey of the Loists suggests there are similarities between the groups. He describes the Netherlandish Spiritualizers (Libertines, Loists, Familists, Spirituals, and Sacramentists) as "a loosely interrelated antinomian movement of the sixteenth century, compounding variously the self-deification of Rhenish mysticism, the libertarianism of the medieval Brethren of the Free Spirit and other groups, the ecclesiastical indifferentism of Erasmus, and the Christian antinomianism of Luther, and in some places . . . the Averroism of Padua."[30]

Singling out Loy, Williams states that he adopted an "Averroist view of the universal Intellect (*spiritus*)," holding "that man's intellectual nature is a spiritual substance and that everyone who is reborn possesses the Holy Spirit."[31] By separating man's spirit from his body, Loy concludes, the renewed spiritual man incurs no guilt for the excesses of the flesh. Therefore the spirit is declared sinless, and man can thus be absorbed into deity.

Examining Loy's *Summa doctrinae*,[32] Williams notes the particular emphasis Pruystinck placed on I John 3:9 ("No one born of God commits sin") and I John 1:8 ("Whoever says he has no sin is a liar"). Loy applied the first saying to the spiritual man, the second to the carnal man.[33]

Loy's beliefs demonstrate a remarkable affinity with many Quintinist doctrines as Calvin describes them. For example, Quintin also preaches a universal *esprit;* when fallen man is reunited with it, he is enabled to transcend distinctions between good and evil. Writing of the Libertines, Calvin cites the very texts emphasized by Pruystinck: "These fantastic people . . . to support their error, arm themselves with this verse of Saint John: 'Let him who is born of God, sin no more'" (I John 3:9). Several paragraphs later he also cites I John 1:8, 10.[34] As Calvin explains, a proper exegesis of these texts invalidates the Libertine claim to sinlessness. There is probably no direct tie between Calvin's

30. Ibid., p. 351.

31. Ibid., p. 352.

32. Williams (*Radical Reformation*, p. 352, n. 30) cites the edition of Ignatius Döllinger, *Beiträge zur Sektengeschichte des Mittelalters* (Munich: Beck, 1890), vol. 2, pp. 664–668.

33. Williams, *Radical Reformation*, pp. 352f.

34. *CO* 7, cols. 205f.; *Against the Libertines*, chap. 18.

Quintinists and Loy's group, but Niesel's judgment that they shared a pantheistic spiritualism or mysticism appears to hold up.

Williams also observes common features, such as piety and libertarianism, among the Loists, the Beghards, and the Brethren of the Free Spirit. He explains how Loy dressed in torn robes patched with jewels to symbolize his poverty and prophetic office.[35] This behavior too is of interest, as Calvin twice compares his Libertines to a band of "wandering beggars"[36] whose speech beguiles the simple.

The Loists were severely persecuted, especially in Antwerp in 1544 and 1545; as a result many fled. Williams thinks that the execution of the remaining Loists in February 1545 may have been an additional factor that prompted Calvin to write against the Libertines.[37]

Finally, Williams discusses the relationship between the Libertines and the Nicodemites (would-be Protestants in Catholic lands who complied with Catholic ritual—like Nicodemus they practiced their religion secretly). Williams asserts that in Calvin's view many Libertines were Spiritualists in Catholic lands who, like the Nicodemites, hedged on controversial issues.[38] But Williams does not think that the Nicodemites and the Flemish-French Spiritualists hedged on the same particular doctrines.

Williams concludes that Libertinism may be defined as a form of "speculative Spiritualism which threatened the ecclesiological and ethical discipline and solidarity of international Calvinism, particularly in Romance countries."[39]

More recently, Carlos Eire[40] has called attention to studies[41]

35. See *Radical Reformation,* p. 353.

36. *CO* 7, col. 168. The *Corpus Reformatorum* editors identify this group as having come out of Bohemia, possibly the Libertine sect of Peter Kániš, whose followers espoused a form of prefall sinlessness. See Williams, *Radical Reformation,* p. 208.

37. Williams, *Radical Reformation,* p. 354.

38. Ibid., p. 602.

39. Ibid.

40. Carlos N. N. Eire, "Calvin and Nicodemism: A Reappraisal," *The Sixteenth Century Journal* 10, no. 1 (1979): 45–69.

41. Ibid., p. 50, n. 21. In addition to the Müller and Niesel studies, Eire cites Norman Cohn's view that the Libertines were descendants of the medieval heresy of the Free Spirit (in *The Pursuit of the Millennium,* rev. ed. [New York: Oxford, 1970], pp. 170–171); Gerhard Schneider, *Der Libertiner: Zur Geistes- und*

which also shed light on the Libertines. Eire focuses primarily on Calvin and Nicodemism and carries the discussion beyond Williams's "brief"[42] study.

Eire explains that though the labels "Libertine" and "Nicodemite" may not necessarily imply mutually exclusive groups, the epithets do apply to different "attitudes" which in turn indicate "separate issues."[43] Furthermore, since Calvin dealt with Libertinism and Nicodemism as separate problems, Eire sees no reason for "ignoring the distinction." The point seems well taken in that Calvin's treatise supports such distinctions. In chapter 19 the Reformer refers readers to his tract[s] directed against wavering Nicodemites.[44] Eire concludes that Calvin's attack on the Libertines was directed against their "amoral behavior," not the problem of "simulation and compromise."[45]

Lastly, Allen Verhey[46] has also examined Calvin's treatise. Verhey's own study of the text and relevant documents leads him to concur with Niesel and Williams. In his view the Libertines addressed in Calvin's work are clearly the Quintinists as the Reformer has depicted them. Verhey's main interest, however, is the treatise's focus on the problem of determinism, an issue which caught Calvin's attention and which required him, perhaps because of his own doctrine of providence, to draw out its full consequences.[47]

These studies illustrate the broad background which lies behind Libertinism. For all the scholarly endeavor, however, Niesel's question remains partially unanswered. Is the "moral

---

Sozialgeschichte des Burgertums im 16. und 17. Jahrhundert (Stuttgart: Metzler, 1970); R. W. Collins, *Calvin and the Libertines of Geneva*, ed. F. D. Blackley (Toronto and Vancouver: Clarke, Irwin, 1968); and J. C. Margolis, "Reflexions sur l'emploi du terme Libertin au XVIe siècle," in *Aspects du Libertinisme au XVIe siècle*, Actes du Colloque International de Sommiers (Paris: Vrin, 1974).

42. Eire, "Calvin and Nicodemism," p. 52.

43. Ibid., p. 51.

44. See *CO* 7, col. 209. The two tracts are *Petite traité montrant que c'est que doit faire un homme fidèle connaissant la verité de l'Evangile: quand il est entre les papistes* (1543) (*CO* 6, cols. 541–578); and *Excuse aux Nicodemites* (1544), (*CO* 6, cols. 589–614).

45. Eire, "Calvin and Nicodemism," p. 51.

46. Allen Verhey, "Calvin's Treatise 'Against the Libertines,'" *Calvin Theological Journal* 15, no. 2 (1980): 190–219.

47. Ibid., p. 197.

licentiousness" which Calvin ascribes to the Libertines an authentic element of Quintin's pantheistic spiritualism, or is it an interpretation on Calvin's part, an inference from Quintinist doctrines? Is it possible that the "amoral" characteristics are manifestations of a Libertinism that is other than Quintin's, or at least similar to and in addition to his, which Calvin loosely attributed to him?

There is some evidence for this. Throughout the treatise Calvin describes elements of a Libertinism which apply to the Quintinist group but which also seem to relate to a larger body of Libertines. There are four specific elements that point to a larger group.

One element refers to the hermeneutical principle that "the letter killeth, but the Spirit giveth life."[48] Quintinists could obviously use this principle to their advantage and did, but it was hardly their principle alone, as will be shown below. The second has to do with the New Testament injunction to become like children, or to behave in a childlike manner,[49] thus justifying behavior which most Christians would not sanction. This too was not characteristic of the Quintinists alone. The third element has to do with the concept of "spiritual marriage,"[50] also observed among other groups, and the fourth with a radical application of the Anabaptist principle of the "community of goods."[51] In each instance Calvin cites these principles to demonstrate how the Libertines justify their reprehensible doctrines and immoral conduct. Further elaboration here will be helpful.

The first element refers to a principle of exegesis (the letter vs. the Spirit) which was vigorously debated among Anabaptists and Spiritualists. Debates between Marbeck and Schwenckfeld had occurred in 1540, and discussions between other Anabaptists and Spiritualists had taken place in Strassburg as early as 1530.[52] The Anabaptists tended toward the letter, the Spiritualists toward the Spirit. Hence Quintin's group was not the only group citing the Spirit over the letter. This was a common characteristic

48. *Against the Libertines,* chap. 9; *CO* 7, col. 173.

49. *Against the Libertines,* chap. 18; *CO* 7, col. 201.

50. *Against the Libertines,* chap. 20; *CO* 7, cols. 212ff.

51. *Against the Libertines,* chap. 21; *CO* 7, cols. 214ff.

52. See William Klassen's excellent article, "Anabaptist Hermeneutics: The Letter and the Spirit," *Mennonite Quarterly Review* 40 (1966): 83–96.

among Spiritualists. The second and third concepts were specifically associated with the excesses of the Anabaptist movement at St. Gall in Switzerland.[53] The third, in the form of polygamy, was practiced by a variety of groups.[54] The fourth was observed in varying degrees of intensity by the Swiss Brethren, Revolutionary Anabaptists, and Hutterites.[55]

Johannes Kessler, a chronicler of St. Gall's struggles during the Anabaptist-Zwinglian conflicts of the mid-1520s, cites all four of these phenomena as characterizing the Libertine mood that broke out in his native canton.[56] Ulrich Zwingli in his *Refutation of the Tricks of the Baptists*[57] also cites many of these same excesses as characteristic of the St. Gall community.

Zwingli in particular describes the St. Gall practice of *"matrimoniis spiritualibus,"*[58] which has striking similarities to the *"mariage spirituel"*[59] that Calvin ascribes to his Libertines. Zwingli also decries the crass manner in which the Anabaptists of St. Gall abused the "community of goods,"[60] just as Calvin disapproves the same practice employed by his Libertines.[61] Zwingli likewise reports a Libertine doctrine of sinlessness[62] that has affinities with Calvin's portrayal of Quintin's view.[63]

Moreover, in the treatise Calvin describes a spiritualized eschatology,[64] which he later associates with a document by Anthony Pocquet,[65] but which seems to belong to that general concept of

53. See Williams, *Radical Reformation,* pp. 127–134. See also Heinold Fast, "Die Sonderstellung der Täufer in St. Gallen und Appenzell," *Zwingliana* 9, no. 2 (1960): 223–240. Fast states that the excesses at St. Gall were interwoven with the Peasants' Revolt (1524–25).

54. Münsterites, Davidians, and Batenburgers. See Williams and Mergal, *Anabaptist Writers,* p. 29.

55. See *Against the Libertines,* chap. 21, nn. 3, 4, 5.

56. See *Johannes Kesslers Sabbata St. Galler Reformationschronik: 1523–1539,* ed. Traugott Schiess, in *Schriften des Vereins für Reformationsgeschichte,* nos. 103/104 (Leipzig: Verein für Reformationsgeschichte, 1911), pp. 51ff.

57. For bibliographical information, see p. 26, n. 80.

58. Zwingli, *Refutation,* pp. 169f.; *Corpus Reformatorum* 93, cols. 85f.

59. See *Against the Libertines,* chap. 20; *CO* 7, cols. 212f.

60. Zwingli, *Refutation,* pp. 167f.; *Corpus Reformatorum* 93, cols. 81, 84f.

61. *Against the Libertines,* chap. 21; *CO* 7, cols. 214f.

62. Zwingli, *Refutation,* pp. 129, 172; *Corpus Reformatorum* 93, col. 93.

63. *Against the Libertines,* chap. 18; *CO* 7, cols. 205ff.

64. *Against the Libertines,* chap. 22; *CO* 7, cols. 222–225.

65. *Against the Libertines,* chap. 23; *CO* 7, cols. 225–242.

restitution which was characteristic of Revolutionary Anabaptists as well.[66]

What can one conclude? Is it possible that the Libertines in these sections are the *libertins* of St. Gall? Can we suppose that Calvin had read Zwingli's *Refutation* by 1545[67] and was hence influenced by the Zurich Reformer's analysis and descriptions? Neither possibility, of course, can be proven. Both Kessler's *Sabbata* and Zwingli's *Refutation* describe a "German-speaking" Libertinism, where Calvin has distinctly limited himself to the "French-speaking" movement.

Perhaps one comes closer to the truth by concluding that these elements were not unique to a single group or locality but were characteristic of Libertinism in general. Hence it is quite possible for Quintin's group to have manifested these marks as Calvin has described them. Calvin certainly insists that his analysis is based on firsthand knowledge and experience. Other possibilities, two in particular, are also worth postulating.

1. Calvin may have attributed to Quintin's pantheistic and speculative spiritualism, which possessed elements similar to Loist views, a broader and more radical Libertinism than Quintin himself would have espoused. This possibility would represent something of a modified Müller-Niesel theory. In its favor are three factors. (1) Calvin himself distinguishes between two groups who were attracted to Quintin: those who enjoyed delving into Quintin's "speculations," and those who were simply "profane people."[68] The latter simply wanted an excuse for their Libertine attitudes and practices. Hence there were two groups in addition to Quintin and his immediate circle. Once having made this distinction, however, Calvin afterward tends to refer only to the Libertines in general. (2) Calvin acknowledges that he does deduce consequences.[69] Thus it is possible that Calvin inferred

66. See the bibliographical information on p. 296, nn. 13, 15.

67. A. Ganoczy, *La bibliothèque de l'Académie de Calvin* (Geneva, 1969), p. 196, reports that a four-volume collection of *Zuinglii opera* (publ. Froschauer, 1545) is listed among the works contained in the Bibliothèque de l'Académie de Genève. Cited by Stauffer, "Zwingli et Calvin," p. 145, n. 42.

68. *Against the Libertines*, chap. 5; *CO* 7, cols. 164f.

69. See *Against the Libertines*, chaps. 14–16; *CO* 7, cols. 186–198. Throughout the treatise Calvin frequently explains that because of the Quintinists' practice of "double dealing" and "double tongue," one gets only faint intimations of what they actually mean. In fact they reserve their central teachings only for their more advanced followers.

"moral licentiousness" to be a consequence of Quintin's views. (3) In a manner similar to his treatise *Against the Anabaptists,* in which he incorporated Melchiorite and psychosomnolent views along with his understanding of the Anabaptism of the *Seven Articles,* so too in his treatise *Against the Libertines* Calvin may have incorporated wider Libertine attitudes and practices than Quintin would have owned. Against this view, however, Calvin explicitly and repeatedly depicts Quintin as a flippant person who was quite capable of the amoral attitudes the treatise associates with Libertinism.

2. Calvin may have thought of Libertinism as certain heretical tendencies developing from a common core of theological and ethical attitudes. Central to this core were three aspects: (1) a pantheistic determinism, its ethical consequences and amoral behavior exemplified by Quintin's own life and demeanor; (2) a licentiousness characteristic of Libertine attitudes in general (cf. Calvin's "profane people"); and (3) an emphasis on Pocquet's spiritualized eschatology which denied the resurrection, put the speculative above the ethical, and thereby failed to edify either the church or the Christian life. In favor of this second view are the four broader elements discussed above which permeate the treatise, and the first and third factors cited in support of the modified Müller-Niesel theory.

There appears to be no simple solution. One seems almost compelled to recognize four subgroups: (1) Quintin himself; (2) Pocquet with his unique contribution; (3) the "speculators" who were attracted to Quintin's pantheistic and deterministic spiritualism; and (4) the "profane people" who seem to have indulged in the moral licentiousness which Calvin attacked. The last group may well have been the Quintinists at Valenciennes whose activities alarmed Poullain and Farel.[70]

Whatever their identity, Calvin's treatise makes it very clear that Calvin considered himself quite familiar with the Libertines' behavior, origins, acknowledged leaders, and principal doctrines. As for their affinity with the *libertins* of St. Gall, one can only note this. It is not possible to verify any connection.

70. See "The Genevan Libertines and the Quintinists" (pp. 184–185). One should not totally rule out the possibility that the Genevan Libertines (the Favres at least) might also be included in these "profane people."

The Structure of the Treatise and Libertine Theology

The treatise follows a clear outline.

I. The relationship between Libertinism and the early heresies of the church (chaps. 1–3)
II. The origins of Libertinism (4–6)
III. The spiritualistic hermeneutics of Libertinism (7–10)
IV. The principal doctrines of the Libertines
  A. God and creation (11–12)
  B. Providence and its consequences (13–16)
  C. The person and work of Christ the Redeemer (17–18)
  D. The Christian life (19–21)
  E. Eschatology (22)
V. Examples of Libertine literature (23–24)

After explaining in a short preface his motives for writing *Against the Libertines,* Calvin charges that Libertinism is nothing more than a sixteenth-century revival of Gnosticism. Rather than offering anything vital or fresh to the Reformation, Libertinism merely restates some early Christian heresies, specifically those of Cerdon, Marcion, and the Manichees.[71] Calvin points out that this resurrection of Gnosticism is not due to any cleverness on Quintin's part, nor to any knowledge of the church fathers or of the early heresies that he might have, but rather to his ignorance of Christian doctrine and church history. In his untutored condition Quintin has fallen prey to many delusions.

Cerdon, one of the early heretics, propounded a system of two principles which he called good and evil. He maintained that everything in the world came from the principle of good and shared its substance. Consequently, Calvin infers that Cerdon denied the resurrection (since by nature everything returns to its origin) and believed that Christ suffered only as a phantom. Although Calvin does not elaborate, he cites Cerdon's overt pantheism and Gnostic Christology for the purpose of clarifying and refuting similar doctrines in Libertine theology. Marcion,

71. See *Against the Libertines, CO* 7, cols. 156–158.

having been taught by Cerdon, possessed essentially the same views.

It is the Manichees who shed the most light on the Libertine movement. The Manichees' hermeneutics allowed them to reject the Old Testament and retain from the New only those portions which served them. Their theology posited a dualism of light (good) and darkness (evil) which acted in combination on all men. The human soul was composed mainly of light; when purged of the influence of darkness, the soul was able to return to its divine origin. The Manichean ecclesiology recognized two orders: the elect, to whom alone the highest wisdom was revealed, and the auditors, initiates who were gradually learning the tenets of the faith. The auditors were informed that their failure to grasp the esoteric points of faith was not due to any deficiency in Manicheism but to a deficiency in themselves.

Calvin's theme in chapters 1–3 is that the Libertines "have only revived these old heresies," borrowing somewhat from each one, but exceeding them all in "folly and impudence." He points out that the Libertines have even constructed two essential principles on "the foundation of the Manichees": man's soul is synonymous with God's Spirit, and everything else is either "of the world, or of Satan, or is nothing."[72]

In chapters 4–6 Calvin traces the origin of the Libertine movement. As already noted, he does not presume to critically analyze the sects of Holland, Belgium, and Lower Germany. It is the French-speaking group, led by Quintin and Pocquet, whose influence he wishes to curtail.

The limitations of Quintin and Pocquet make the rapid growth of the group puzzling and difficult to account for. Calvin explains this phenomenon by describing two types of people that are drawn by such groups. One type is continually tempted by "foolish curiosity." Calvin notes that unfortunately these people grow discontent with "the simplicity of the Scriptures" and therefore indulge in "frivolous speculations."[73] Those of the second type, whom Calvin designates as "profane people," have grown tired of carrying Christ's yoke. They simply want an easier

72. Ibid., col. 158.
73. Ibid., cols. 164–165.

moral path to follow, a concession which Libertinism is quick to grant.

Chapters 7–10 contain Calvin's analysis of the Libertines' hermeneutics. Four of their procedures are explained and criticized.

1. Calvin charges that the Quintinists employ a style of language that conceals their true purposes. Like the "loud-mouthed boasters" of II Peter 2:18 and Jude 16, the Quintinists are described as speaking in a "high" or "haughty style," using "an unbelievable tongue," a "unique jargon," warbling "like birds," "garbling" their words, "babbling," and "bantering." "When you hear them speak," warns Calvin, "you will only be hearing high German."[74] One is tempted to surmise that the Quintinists practiced glossolalia, but what Calvin seems to be saying is that the Quintinists' lofty, obscure language hinders communication and prevents understanding.

2. Calvin explains that the practice of simulation is central to the Libertines' methodology. They attempt to give everything a double meaning. Two Scripture verses provide them justification for this practice: Psalm 2:4 ("He who sits in the heavens laughs at them") and Matthew 10:16 ("Let us become wise as serpents"). Jesus Himself, note the Quintinists, used parables which even His disciples failed to understand until He explained them.

Calvin argues, however, that simulation only sanctions their speaking with a "double tongue" and finding "double meanings" throughout Scripture. Moreover, this practice reveals their profound misunderstanding of Jesus' use of parables and makes Him guilty of simulation as well. Hence, instead of teaching what is "clear, pure, certain, and open,"[75] they deliberately obscure God's plain Word.

3. Calvin claims that the Libertines' key hermeneutical principle is, "The letter kills but the spirit gives life."[76] Instead of emphasizing a passage's "natural" and "simple sense," they prefer its "spiritual sense." Consequently, in the absence of any sound hermeneutical norm, they freely engage in lofty speculation, coming up with allegorical interpretations and finding new revelations in Scripture.

74. Ibid., col. 169.
75. Ibid., col. 172.
76. Ibid., col. 173.

Problems caused by their faulty hermeneutics are compounded by their failure to understand the Spirit's role as interpreter of Scripture. The Spirit was sent to illumine both what Christ taught and what the prophets proclaimed. The Holy Spirit works not by adding anything new to the Scripture but by enabling man to better understand the Word. Thus the "Spirit and the Scripture," states Calvin, "are one and the same."[77] Any principle of interpretation that ignore's the Word's natural and plain sense is to be rejected.

4. Calvin charges that the Quintinists' conception of the word *Spirit* is so loose (they regard God's Spirit as indwelling and constituting everything) that they empty it of meaning. Hence they can justify extremely reprehensible behavior as "spiritual."

In many respects the ten chapters we have just reviewed serve as an introduction to Calvin's refutation of the Libertines. Chapters 11–22 proceed to describe and criticize the major articles of Libertine doctrine.

In chapters 11–12 Calvin explains the Libertine belief in one single divine Spirit, or universal essence, which indwells every creature. This one living Spirit extends everywhere and constitutes everything.

Calvin condemns this pantheistic view as heretical and akin to "ancient pagan suppositions." It is totally contrary to the biblical revelation of man as a unique and distinct being, created in time, who exists as a creature separate from God's essence. At no point is man's soul or essence ever to be confused or blended with God's.

But if, as the Libertines suppose, the Spirit indwells everything, how do they account for the "devil," the "world," "sin," and the "old man"? These are understood to be misconceptions of fallen man's reasoning or *cuider.*

Cuider is a crucial term, if not a principal Libertine doctrine. An archaic word, it functions as both a verb and a noun. According to J.-D. Benoit[78] its modern equivalent as a verb is *croire* ("to believe") and as a noun *croyance* or *opinion* ("belief" or "opinion"). Cotgrave's famous 1611 *French-English Dictionary* lists many possibilities: as a verb, "to thinke, weene, deeme,

77. Ibid., col. 176.

78. See Jean-Daniel Benoit, "Glossaire, Tables et References," in *Institution de la Religion Chrétienne* (Paris: Vrin, 1963), vol. 5, p. 410.

imagine, suppose, presume, have an opinion of, make a ghesse at"; as a noun, "a thought, conceit, ghesse, . . . imagination, opinion, supposition, presumption."[79]

Calvin implies that the Libertines used the term *cuider* to designate something which is not "real" but only the product of human "imagination" or "fantasy." Things are *cuider* because people "conceptualize" them incorrectly; that is, these things are not what people "presume" or "suppose" them to be. For the Libertines the "devil," the "world," "sin," and the "old man" are *cuider.*

Of course Calvin rejects this view as utterly foreign to Scripture, where the "devil," the "world," "sin," and the "old man" are hardly human suppositions but represent real entities or conditions, distinct and separate from the reality of God.

In chapters 13–16 Calvin touches upon pantheistic determinism, the central nerve of Libertinism. He sees that pantheism (the proposition that God's Spirit indwells all and constitutes everything), if allowed to go unchallenged, threatens to undermine a responsible doctrine of providence. Thus Calvin sets about to discredit pantheistic determinism by showing that it is incompatible with biblical revelation and by tracing its philosophical and theological consequences to their logical extremes. It is not an overstatement to claim that these chapters constitute the heart of the treatise. For they not only expose the philosophical foundation of Libertinism, but they also contain Calvin's clearest articulation of the doctrine of providence.

As Allen Verhey points out in a recent study of these chapters,[80] it is rather commonplace to view Calvin as a determinist who ultimately denies human freedom. But chapters 13–16 permit one to challenge such a view.

At the same time this section poses an impregnable problem for the historian who wishes to know whether Calvin's descriptions of Libertine doctrine even approximate Quintin's true position. In his honest zeal to demonstrate the theological ramifications of Quintin's mystical pantheism, Calvin has perhaps confused his own projected consequences with Quintin's actual views. Nonetheless, Calvin insists that his presentation of Quintin's

79. See the listings under *cuider.* The work does not contain page numbers.
80. Verhey, "Calvin's Treatise 'Against the Libertines,'" pp. 190–219.

determinism is accurate. Calvin goes so far as to depict Quintin as a flippant, irresponsible, and theologically shallow opportunist whose demeanor and activities are in keeping with the consequences Calvin foresees.

Calvin argues that Quintin's pantheistic determinism undercuts the Christian doctrine of providence. Calvin perceives that if everything without qualification is attributed to God, then there are three unacceptable consequences: (1) the God of providence becomes synonymous with all that is tragic, evil, and demonic; (2) conscience becomes unnecessary; and (3) distinctions between good and evil lose all their significance. Calvin assumes tht the Quintinists do indeed accept these consequences. A brief examination of each will be helpful.

1. It is apparent to Calvin that if God is the unqualified cause of everything, He is responsible for all that is tragic and evil. This view is repugnant because it obviously attacks God's goodness. But the Scripture repudiates pantheistic determinism by revealing the way in which God actually does govern the world. In fact, it attests to His working "in a threefold manner."[81]

First, God works through the natural order. Writes Calvin, "There is a universal operation by which He guides all creatures according to the condition and propriety which He has given each at creation."[82] Nevertheless, Calvin warns, this "natural operation" does not replace or militate against free will, for "this universal operation of God's does not prevent each creature, heavenly or earthly, from having and retaining his own quality and nature and from following his own inclinations."[83]

Second, God causes His creatures "to serve His goodness, righteousness, and judgment."[84] That is to say, by "a special ordinance . . . He guides all things in accordance with what he deems to be expedient."[85] The activities of nature and men are instruments by which God exercises His moral will in both global and private affairs. Or, what pagans knew as Fortune Christians may ascribe to Providence.

What the Libertines fail to grasp, explains Calvin, is that (1) God does not work so effectively in these instruments as to

81. *Against the Libertines, CO* 7, col. 186.
82. Ibid.
83. Ibid., col. 187.
84. Ibid.
85. Ibid.

erode their ability to act in their own behalf. For God does not use men as if they were stones, but as "thinking creatures," who are endowed with reason and will and who act in their own right. And (2) God's use of evildoers in no way sanctions the motives or actions of such persons. The failure to draw this distinction is a glaring flaw in the Libertine position.

The third way in which God operates is through His Holy Spirit, by means of whom He regenerates a fallen humanity and draws it to Himself.

2. The second consequence of pantheistic determinism is that "one's conscience need no longer be concerned about anything."[86] Calvin rejects this notion on two counts: one, that God gave the Israelites the law for the purpose of guiding and quickening consciences; and two, that He Himself implanted conscience in every human life, thus making man a moral being. Hence any theology that minimizes conscience is to be wholly rejected.

3. If God is the unqualified cause of everything, then it becomes unnecessary to condemn anything, and Christians are excused from the task of making moral judgments. Indeed, according to Calvin the Libertines cite or allude to a number of New Testament passages (Matt. 7:1, 5; John 8:7; Rom. 14:10) to support their "principle that it is wrong to pass judgment."[87] On the contrary, Calvin replies, these passages do not obviate altogether the need to make judgments; they merely forbid hypocritical judgments. God still wills moral discernment and concern for one's neighbor.

In chapters 17 and 18 Calvin discusses the Libertine view of Christ's person and work, particularly His work of regeneration.

Calvin accuses the Quintinists of holding a Gnostic view in that they perceive Christ as a union of *cuider* and the Spirit which indwells everything. Calvin seems to suggest that they view Christ as a phantom, that is, as not actually suffering and dying, but only appearing to.

This Spirit-phantom fulfills the role of a "model." "It all comes down to this," writes Calvin, "that what Christ has done and suffered is only a farce or a morality play, acted out upon a stage,

86. Ibid., col. 192.
87. Ibid., col. 194.

which represents the mystery of our salvation for us."[88] In fact, in the Libertine view, explains Calvin, "we are all Christs, and what was done in him, he has performed in us." That is why Jesus said, "It is finished," or still better, "All is finished."

This view of Christ's work is, so to speak, a "second-Adam Christology," in which Christ's act is regarded as redemptive because it awakens in all human beings (who are no less divine than He) the awareness of their reconciliation as something which has already ontologically occurred. Christ simply displays for others what is ontologically true. This conception of redemption goes a long way toward explaining the Libertines' view of regeneration, for to them regeneration is simply a "return to that innocent state which Adam enjoyed before he sinned."

According to Calvin, the Libertines teach that before the fall Adam existed in a state of innocence. In this condition of innocence his actions and will were not regarded as good or evil, but were simply the result of God's spiritual indwelling. In this state Adam saw "neither black nor white." However, when Adam and Eve ate of the fruit of the tree of the knowledge of good and evil, their eyes were opened and they "saw sin." They began seeing white and black, that is, making distinctions between good and evil. As a result, they became slaves to sin. This condition of distinguishing between good and evil, as well as being a slave to these distinctions, is *cuider,* from which all believers are set free in Christ. Hence one may now do what Adam did before he sinned, which is to follow one's natural sense of direction.

Calvin charges that such a Christology or soteriology is Gnostic and fails to account for the radical nature of sin. There can be no perfection in this life, only forgiven sinners.

Calvin turns in chapters 19–21 to examine the vast personal, religious, social, and economic repercussions of Libertinism. In Calvin's mind its ethical consequences are as damaging to the Christian life as its deterministic and philosophical consequences are to the doctrine of providence. If God causes everything, and distinctions between good and evil are purely *cuider,* or "imagined," then anything is legitimate.

A consequence of this line of thought is that there is no need nor room for normative principles. This is most apparent in the Libertine views of Christian liberty, vocations, and the fellowship of believers. Calvin observes that in the absence of any norm the

88. Ibid., col. 199.

Libertines "extend Christian Liberty to include everything [as being] lawful for man, without any exceptions."[89] In addition, the absence of norms leads to three diabolical conclusions concerning vocations: (1) no vocation is evil; (2) no evils attach to any vocation; and (3) "every inclination in man, whether . . . natural or a bad habit, is a calling of God."[90] Furthermore, the lack of principles erodes every just order of society and undermines the institution of marriage in particular—a matter which Calvin illustrates at considerable length. Finally, Calvin accuses the Libertines of operating with such license as to make a mockery of the fellowship of believers, the New Testament practice of holding goods in common. Calvin explains that the Libertines emphasize this practice, as do the Anabaptists, in order to deceive the simple-minded and to avail themselves of the fruit of others' labor.

Calvin rejects these Libertine positions. He offers instead a Reformed view of Christian liberty, according to which Christians are still bound to the law, but not so rigorously; of vocations, according to which Christians are to avoid those callings repugnant to Scripture; and of goods, according to which Christians do have the right to possess and to use private property, but are to remember to share their goods with the world's indigent.

The last doctrine Calvin reviews and critiques is the Libertine view of the resurrection. According to their teaching, the resurrection has already occurred. Since the redeemed person knows himself or herself to be already in union with the one single spiritual essence which indwells all living beings, a future resurrection is not only a misunderstanding of Christ's resurrection but a totally unnecessary event.

It is apparent from Calvin's rebuttal that the Libertines cited several verses to support their argument: John 11:26 ("Whoever believes never dies, but has passed from death to life"), Ecclesiastes 12:7 ("The spirit of man will return to God who made it, while the body will return to the earth from whence it came"), Ephesians 2:19, and Colossians 3:1. Calvin dismisses the Libertine interpretation of these verses as a bald falsification of the biblical facts. He reiterates that God has created souls as life forms

89. Ibid., col. 206.
90. Ibid., col. 212.

distinct from Himself. Calvin then reaffirms a future end time filled with judgment and grace. Moral humanity moves in faith and hope toward this future.

In chapters 23–24 Calvin presents one of Pocquet's booklets word for word, warning readers to be alert to the errors this tract and other Libertine publications contain.

Pocquet's booklet is rambling, obscure in many places, and imbued with an eschatological emphasis that these are "the last days." Calvin notes that the piece does not clearly explain the arcane and, in his view, erroneous doctrines of the Libertines. Rather, it is meant to win over the unwary with its sweet promises. The tract breathes the esoteric air of mysticism, stating that "we are all members of Christ," and that Christ was "made every man." Although it teaches that "everything is [caused by] the will and providence of God," it does not flaunt an amoral attitude or endorse an antinomian ethic.

Pocquet refers to the Libertine conception of sin and Adam and Eve's enslavement because of *cuider.* He also makes an appeal to live in the Spirit, to be vivified by the second Adam, and hence to lay aside any fears of death or hell. Pocquet goes so far as to claim that the fear of death and hell is "an error," and states that "one can make fun of it as a vain thought." He finishes by emphasizing union with Christ and a life of love, peace, and purity.

Calvin concludes by warning Christians not to be "diverted from the pure simplicity of Jesus Christ." He reminds his readers that God has made them "rational creatures," endowed with "gifts of intelligence." They must not surrender these gifts or exchange them for ignorance that can make them subhuman or irrational. He also implores them to accept only "good and useful doctrines," teachings that are morally and biblically sound, as criteria for belief. If Christians will make such doctrines normative, then they will be able to avoid the excess of speculation and the defect of the profane.

God has made men creatures of reason and has implanted consciences within them. Any theology that compromises these gifts of God, as Libertinism does, must be rejected by biblical Christianity. Indeed, one of Calvin's favorite epithets for the Libertines is *"phantastiques."* It could be translated "fanatics," but Calvin's point is that the Libertines are more than "fanatical"; they are literally "fantastic," or "unbelievable." They have so transcended the bounds of reason and common sense that they have discredited their own position.

An Evaluation

Certainly Reformed theology today can glean much of value from this treatise. In a time of cults, moral permissiveness, and an overemphasis on tongues Calvin's admonitions are relevant in two ways: (1) to the task of the church as it seeks to formulate and be guided by sound theological principles; and (2) to the Christian life for the same reasons which Calvin propounded in his own day.

But to judge Calvin's fairness to the Libertines is very difficult. It is possible, if not likely, that Calvin attributed to the Quintinists a Libertine attitude which Quintin and his followers would have disowned. Even so, Calvin's work retains its full integrity. For Calvin understood, with incisive perspicacity, the "consequences" Quintin's views would have entailed. Hence, when pressed, Calvin accepted the challenge and refuted Libertinism with his typical astuteness.

The Genevan Libertines and the Quintinists

A problem associated with any final assessment of Calvin's polemic against Libertinism must be mentioned. It has to do with the precise relationship between Geneva's Libertines (the Favre family and the Perrinists who were opposed to Calvin's reformation of the city) and the Quintinist Libertines attacked by the Reformer in his treatise.

Calvin's struggle with the Genevan Libertines or Perrinists is dated traditionally between March 21, 1546, and June 3, 1555, after which the Perrinists were both defeated at the polls and condemned later by the Little Council.[91]

The central questions appear to be, What is the relationship, if any, between these two groups of Libertines? To what extent do the Genevan Libertines share views with the Quintinists? Were the Genevan Libertines inspired or influenced by the Quintinists? and if so, how? What role, if any, did Calvin's treatise *Against the Libertines* play in furthering the distance between himself and

91. See Walker, *Organiser*, pp. 295–353.

the Favre family or Perrinists? What influence, if any, did the treatise have in contributing to their defeat? Is Calvin's reference to the "profane people" who eagerly became Libertines in order to indulge themselves a veiled reference to the Favres of Geneva, with whom he might have sensed he was about to clash?

R. W. Collins's book, *Calvin and the Libertines of Geneva*, traces the Reformer's conflict with the Genevan Libertines.[92] Although Collins identifies some of the Genevans as "spiritual Libertines" (e.g., Pierre Ameaux's wife),[93] he neither raises nor discusses any of the questions posed above. Certainly the answers to these questions would help clarify the identification of the Libertines of Calvin's treatise as well as shed light on the Genevan Libertines.

It must be acknowledged, however, that the tendency in Reformation studies is to emphasize a sharp distinction between the Genevan Libertines and the Libertines of Calvin's treatise. Williston Walker, following F. W. Kampschulte's lead, classified the Genevan Libertines as a political faction which opposed Calvin for political reasons.[94] Both John T. McNeill[95] and George H. Williams[96] have adopted a similar position, which is also the view of this introduction. Still, the question of the precise relationship between the two groups and the influence Calvin's treatise might have played in the defeat of the Perrinists is worthy of study.

Mysticism

The treatise *Against the Libertines* should also prove to be a valuable resource for exploring anew both Calvin's rejection of mysticism and his concern for the believer's "spiritual union" with Christ. Though he was opposed to the spiritualistic pantheism of the Quintinists and, in François Wendel's words, "had already shown himself . . . hostile to any glorification or deification

92. Collins, *Calvin and the Libertines*, pp. 153–200.
93. Ibid., p. 154.
94. Walker, *Organiser*, p. 295.
95. John T. McNeill, *The History and Character of Calvinism* (New York: Oxford, 1970), p. 169.
96. Williams, *Radical Reformation*, pp. 604f.

of man,"[97] Calvin nonetheless wrote, in the *Institutes*[98] and elsewhere,[99] quite eloquently of the "mystical union" that believers have with Christ.

Perhaps a careful study of the *Libertines* piece may shed light on Calvin's rejection of any mystical identification of man with God or Christ while sharpening an understanding of his use of the terms *mystica unio* and *union sacrée.*

97. François Wendel, *Calvin: The Origins and Development of His Religious Thought,* trans. Philip Mairet (New York: Harper & Row, 1963), pp. 235f.

98. 3.11.10.

99. *Commentary on I Corinthians,* 6:15.

Preface

Saint Paul is within reason when he writes that "there must be factions[1] in order that true Christians may thereby be recognized" (I Cor. 11:19). For the appearance of trouble among Christians or of any false teachings provides an occasion for discovering how and with what affection those who are called Christians have received the Word of God.

For some, steadfastly persevering in the truth [of God's Word] as declared to us, demonstrate through experience that it has taken living root in their hearts, while others, allowing themselves easily to be seduced and tossed about here and there by every wind, show by their inconstancy that they have never received it except in a thoughtless manner.[2]

I will not at this time develop this matter at any length, but I will only take examples that are openly known to us.[3]

For twenty years now the devil, in order to extinguish or suffocate the holy teaching of the gospel, which he could see was coming again from above, or indeed in order to defame it and make it odious to the world, has given birth[4] to a number of diverse heresies and wicked opinions. Many people who had formerly been faithfully instructed in the pure teaching of the Scriptures were immediately swept away. Others, being disposed to resist all of these scandals with firm constancy, have been so much the more strengthened by God and His Word.

1. *sectes.*

2. *a la volee = sans réfléchir.*

3. *nous voyons a l'oeil. L'oeil* here should be translated "with evidence," "openly." With this sentence Calvin succinctly describes the methodology he uses to develop his polemic against the Libertines.

4. *a suscite = a fait naître.*

Our Lord, as I have said, permits and arranges[5] for this to happen, both for the approbation of His own as well as for exposing the hypocrisy or vanity of those who profess to be faithful, prior to any scandal[6] that should bring their unfaithfulness to light. It is true that we find some who are surprised by pure ignorance and simplicity. Still, there is no doubt that our Lord permits them to fall in order to humble them in the future and to help them profit better, in order to have a firmer and more solid foundation in His Word, correcting their past indifference and presumption.

Thus none can excuse himself when he is led astray[7] from the right path and clings to lies and falsehood. He cannot say that it is not his fault or that our Lord should not punish him for not loving and fearing Him as he ought, as will surely be said by and by.

Be that as it may, whenever any wicked and pernicious sect begins to multiply, and especially grow, the task of those whom our Lord has constituted for the edification of His church is to oppose[8] and to repulse that sect vigorously,[9] before it is strengthended and further taints[10] and corrupts.

In fact, inasmuch as the church is provided with pastors, it is not enough for them to serve[11] and administer the good pasture of Jesus Christ's flock, unless they also keep on the lookout for wolves and thieves, in order to cry out against them and to chase them away from the flock whenever they come too close.

However, strictly speaking, heretics are not only like thieves or wolves, but are much worse. For since they corrupt the holy Word of God, they are like poison, murdering poor souls under the pretext of grazing them and providing them with good pasturage.

Furthermore, inasmuch as Satan never ceases to plot by every means the dissipation of that holy unity which we have in our Lord Jesus by [means of] His Word, it is absolutely necessary, for

5. *dispose.*
6. *la matiere.*
7. *debauche.*
8. *d'aller au devant.*
9. *vivement.*
10. *gaster = gâter.*
11. *proposent.*

the preservation[12] of the church, that this very same Word should serve and be used as a sword and shield in order to resist such machinations.

Now insofar as it has pleased our Lord, by His infinite goodness, without consideration for what I was, to add me to the number of those He has commissioned, not only to publish His truth to the world, but also to maintain it against all adversaries, I must engage myself in this charge according to the ability He has given me. Moreover, several of the faithful,[13] being warned of and clearly seeing in part the horrible dissipation that these evildoers have created, have never ceased soliciting me until such time as I have promised them to take up the matter.

12. *conservation.*

13. See the letters of Valérand Poullain, Pierre Viret, and William Farel (Herminjard, *Correspondances,* vol. 9, pp. 246ff., no. 1358; pp. 327ff., no. 1392; pp. 334f., no. 1395; pp. 341ff., no. 1398). See also Williams's discussion of these letters and the Quintinist activities they report (*Radical Reformation,* pp. 599ff.).

1

On the Perniciousness of the Libertine Sect

Although all heretical sects are mortal pests in Christianity, nevertheless we do not read anywhere in all the early histories where there was ever a sect as pernicious as that which is today called the Libertines.

Not only is it malicious, but it is so monstrous[1] and churlish that there is not a man of sane judgment who can think of it without feeling horror. Still, one need hardly be astonished, as if it contained anything new. For the core[2] of the doctrine, its origin, dates from the time of the apostles, at least in part, as I shall soon show. The rest of it is similar to what the Valentinians,[3] Cerdonites,[4] and Manichees[5] held, who have troubled the church for over fourteen hundred years.

Truly the Libertines are ignorant and stupid people who have neither engaged in careful research nor learned their nonsense from it.[6] And in all likelihood, they do not even know that it has always existed.[7] At all events, what they know has not come through [their] reading. But the same master, who has of old raised up ancient heretics, as I have said, has rarely taught such a lesson as he has taught them.

For since we know through our Lord's warning that this father

1. *enorme = excessive, monstrueuse.*

2. *la somme.*

3. A Gnostic heresy founded by Valentinus, who first came to Rome c. A.D. 136. See p. 196, n. 10.

4. Cerdon was Marcion's teacher. See p. 195, n. 4.

5. Named for their founder, Mani, a Persian, c. 216–276. See p. 196, n. 12.

6. *n'ont pas tant visité les papiers qu'ilz ayent peu apprendre leurs follies de là.*

7. Literally, "always been mentioned."

of lies has existed from the beginning, there is no doubt that all the errors that have ever been and presently are have been forged in his workshop. Thus it is hardly a surprise if he has stirred up anew this wretched sect and has raised up ignorant persons to put it in force. For it has never been necessary for a man to be instructed in a school other than his to know how to blaspheme against God in destroying His truth through malicious tricks.[8] For the word "lies," of which he alone is the principal progenitor,[9] comprises all forms of combat against the truth.

But since it is one thing to talk and another to demonstrate one's point, it will be expedient to see, by means of solid and clear proofs, whether what I have said is true, that is, that the Libertines introduce nothing new with respect to the principal articles of all their teachings, but rather since the time of the apostles there have existed similar heretics, who soon afterwards were joined by others who have held diabolical delusions, with which the Libertines today seek to infect the world. Also by this means we shall see what constitutes their sect in order to be able to pass judgment on it.

8. *cauteles* = *ruses.*
9. *docteur.*

2

On the Similarity Between the Libertine Sect and the One Mentioned by Saint Peter and Saint Jude

We see in Saint Peter's Second Letter (chap. 2), and in that of Saint Jude, that in their time there existed a sect of evildoers who, under the name of Christianity, led simple folk into dissolute living, removing their discretion between good and evil and benumbing their consciences through flattery, in order that, without scruples, each might indulge his appetite, abusing Christian liberty in order to give free rein to every carnal license, and taking pleasure in introducing a confusion into the world that overturns all civil government,[1] order, and human decency.[2]

For Saint Peter uses these words: "Like brute beasts, who are born to be caught, they revile in matters of which they understand nothing, deriving their happiness from their decadent[3] pleasures" (II Peter 2:12f.). Then he compares them to "mists driven about by a storm," to "waterless springs." And because they have "boasted so loudly," as if to carry their hearers higher than heaven, they "entice them with carnal passions and cause them to fall into concupiscences, from which they had just been pulled out, by permitting[4] them liberty, while they themselves are slaves to every corruption" (II Peter 2:17ff.).

1. *police.*
2. *honnesteté.*
3. *caduques.*
4. Note in *CO* 7, col. 155, n. 3: "'promettant' [in the] 1611 [edition]," correcting the original reading, *permettant,* in order to make it conform to II Peter 2:19. The translation preserves the original reading.

And Saint Jude concurs, saying that "they revile whatever they do not understand and that they have no other understanding save their carnal attitude,[5] like brute beasts, corrupting themselves in all that they think" (Jude 10).

Whoever knows anything about the Libertines upon a careful study of these passages will be able to discern that in these passages the Holy Spirit wanted to provide us with a description of this sect in order to put us on guard. As for myself, I would never have fully and keenly understood all these things if I had not recognized them in this sect.

But because not everyone recognizes them, it would be wise[6] if they would become familiar with these qualities,[7] insofar as they can recognize the truth. For, first of all, with regard to this "loud boasting" which is mentioned here, we ought to note that from the first time one hears them, it seems quite clear that they have been ecstatically entranced above the highest clouds. For beyond the fact that they only speak as if entranced,[8] they use a language so foreign that those who hear it for the first time are astonished. And they frequently use this method for the express purpose of arousing their hearers' admiration in order to win[9] their hearts before anyone realizes how abominable their doctrine is.

But once they have frothed through their boastful prefaces,[10] they immediately sink into the abyss of leading the world into a surly life, void of discernment. For they make believe that man needlessly torments himself whenever he is scrupulous about anything; rather each person ought to be led by his spirit [or fancy].

Thus confounding all order, they mock both the fear of God and the faithful and have as little respect for His judgment as they have for any decent human consideration. And they promise liberty, that a man might freely give himself to all that his heart desires and covets, without experiencing difficulty, as if he were subject neither to law nor reason. For in their view, law and

5. *sentiment.*
6. *il sera bon.*
7. Literally, "to appropriate these qualities."
8. *que d'esprit.* Literally, "as by spirit."
9. *d'entrer dedans.* Literally, "to enter into," "to get within."
10. *proemes = préfaces.*

reason constitute a bondage which they do not want to hear mentioned.

If anyone thinks that I am attributing[11] false teachings to them, I shall demonstrate, within a finger's breadth,[12] that I am only reciting their own ideas, using those manners of speech that are customary and understandable, instead of those which they disguise in their jargon,[13] which will be deciphered in their place.

11. *impose = impute, attribue.*
12. *apres au doigt.*
13. *gergon = jargon.*

3

On the Similarity Between the Libertines and Several Early[1] Heretics

Wild heresies[2] appeared so soon after the time of the apostles that it is amazing how such idiotic nonsense[3] was ever able to enter into human understanding. Nevertheless the Christian church was for some time somewhat vexed by them. But since everyone recognized how absurd they were, they held them in horror. So much is this so that for the past twelve hundred years not a single person in the entire world has willed to adhere to a heresy—or at least has not dared to profess one—until today, when these wretches, who are called the Libertines, were incited by Satan to blaspheme, not simply in a way similar to the others, but by adding still further damnable errors.

To begin with there was a Cerdon[4] who emphasized two principles, one which he called good, the other evil. He maintained that everything in the world came from the [good] one and shared its substance. In saying this he denied the resurrection, because he thought that everything that had come from the one returned to its origin. Thus he held that Jesus Christ had appeared and suffered only as a phantom.[5]

1. *anciens.*

2. *heresies sauvaiges.*

3. *des resveries tant lourdes. Lourdes* should be translated as "idiotic," not literally as "heavy."

4. See Eusebius, *Church History,* in *Nicene and Post-Nicene Fathers,* second series, vol. 1, pp. 182f. Cerdon, Marcion's teacher, came to Rome c. 138. Cf. Irenaeus, *Against Heresies,* in *Ante-Nicene Fathers,* vol. 1, p. 352.

5. *phantasie.* Literally, "fantasia."

Next came Marcion,[6] who disguised somewhat Cerdon's ideas, as he wanted the glory of inventing new theories rather than being known for dressing up what his predecessor had said badly; he was similar to him.

Close to this same time appeared the Gnostics, who were thus called because they attributed to themselves a superior understanding.[7] However, the faithful called them Borborites[8] to denote that they respected them about as much as they did frogs on the bank of a marsh. The Borborites also held that the soul is of the substance of God, positing two principles, one good, the other evil, and maintaining that souls that are kept pure in the human body return to the nature of a good God, while those that are soiled by the impurities of the world return to an evil [nature]. Besides, they employed an obscure jargon for babbling[9] spiritual things, which no one could understand.

There was not a great difference between Valentinus[10] and Apelles,[11] except that each added something of his own to what others had said in order to make himself appear as the author of a new sect so that he might attract attention.

Now because from earliest times the Manichean[12] sect was already renowned among the others, enjoyed a multitude of followers, endured the longest, and picked up ideas[13] from everywhere, filling itself with copious false doctrines, it is essential for us to treat it as a unique mirror in order to show what we maintain.[14]

The Manichees, rejecting the Old Testament and scoffing at the law and the prophets, accused God, who is revealed there, of cruelty and an excessive harshness. From the New Testament they accepted here and there what was in agreement with their

6. Marcion was a Gnostic who came to Rome c. 140. See Eusebius, *Church History*, pp. 182ff. Cf. Irenaeus, *Against Heresies*, pp. 352f.

7. *une excellente congnoissance par dessus les autres.*

8. In the French there is a play on the words "Borborites" and *borbier*, the latter meaning "swamp" or "marsh." See Irenaeus, *Against Heresies*, p. 353.

9. *gasouiller = gazouiller.*

10. A Gnostic heretic at Rome during the bishoprics of Hyginus, Pius, and Anicetus, i.e., c. 136–165. See Eusebius, *Church History*, pp. 182f.

11. Apelles was a disciple of Marcion. See Eusebius, *Church History*, pp. 182f.

12. Named for the founder Mani, a Persian, who lived c. 216–276. See Eusebius, *Church History*, pp. 316f., n. 1.

13. *pieces.*

14. *pretendons = mettons en avant.*

ideas and cut out whatever displeased them or was contrary to their views. Next they created two different gods: one the origin of good, the other the origin of evil.

Similarly they posited[15] two souls in man, one which came from the good god and which they said had been tainted by inferior things, but which nevertheless they wanted to purify until by degrees it returned to its first origin. As for the other, they said it could not be corrected but would forever return to the realm of darkness,[16] of which it consisted.

Now their purifications amounted to wicked sorceries and damnable acts of shamefulness similar to the other heretics whom I have named above. As for the souls of those who were not of their sect, they said these would go into brute beasts.

Furthermore, their sect was divided into three orders or classes. They called their great teachers Macarians,[17] which means "blessed ones." And when they exercised the function of priests,[18] they called them Catharites.[19] In addition they had two kinds of novices.[20] The ones to whom they revealed the secrets of the school were called *elect.* The others, whom they enticed[21] over a long period of time in order to win them, they called *hearers.*[22]

Although this is still not the place to infer[23] point for point the teachings of the Libertines, nevertheless at the moment we need to note that they have only revived these old heresies which I have reviewed. They have taken something from each, creating a mass of confusion, only in the end to outdo all the others, transcending them in folly and impudence.

At first they boldly rejected the Scriptures, even giving nicknames to each apostle in order to scoff at their authority. Saint

15. *constituoyent.*
16. *au commencement des tenebres.* Literally, "to the beginning of darkness."
17. *Macariens.* Based on the Greek μακάριοι, "happy," "blessed."
18. *purger = purifier.*
19. Based on the Greek καθαροί, "pure."
20. *d'Escholiers = d'Ecoliers.*
21. *amielloit = allêchait.*
22. Augustine belonged to this rank. See Augustine, *On the Profit of Believing,* in *Nicene and Post-Nicene Fathers,* first series, vol. 3, p. 348.
23. *desduire = déduire.* Literally, "to deduct," "to describe," "to infer." *Infer* best describes Calvin's methodology.

Paul was "Broken Pot,"[24] Saint Peter "Denier of God,"[25] Saint John "the Doting Lad,"[26] Saint Matthew "Usurer." And they were unashamed to blaspheme thus openly. But seeing that people were shocked to hear them speak in this way, they decided to operate more covertly.

For example, in order not to seem to be rejecting Scripture, they have changed it into allegories, going out of their way to find obscure meanings,[27] turning a man into a horse and a cloud into a lantern's horns. Such guile they share with the Priscillianists,[28] who of old used such an approach and differed thereby from the Manichees.

We shall later examine[29] how they manage to twist and turn the Scriptures by such allegories. My present comments are made simply to point out the path they have followed and to identify their predecessors.

As for God and the substance of souls, though the Libertines in no way speak as the Manichees do, nevertheless what they babble between their teeth is tantamount to what they say, that is, that there is only one spirit who is God, and on the other side is the world; that all creatures are nothing unless the spirit of God, indwelling men,[30] sustains them until it is withdrawn from them; and that all else that men possess that is beyond this[31] is either of the world, or of Satan, or nothing.

If a man belongs to their sect, they make him God, saying that his soul is God's spirit. If not, they disregard him, as if he were nothing more than a horse, because only the world would be in him, which is nothing.

If we were to observe their life, we would find that they build all their illusions on the foundation of the Manichees with regard to these two principles—except they have discovered an easier means for making themselves gods than the Manichees had. For

24. *pot cassé.*

25. *renounceur = renieur.*

26. *iouvenceau et follet.*

27. *sens esgarez = sens écartés.*

28. Priscilla was a Montanist prophetess held in high honor by all Montanists, who were thus known in some quarters as Priscillianists. See Eusebius, *Church History*, p. 231, n. 18.

29. *traicterons.*

30. *estant aux hommes.*

31. *outre cela.* Literally, "beyond this"—*this* meaning the spiritual indwelling of God.

whereas the latter went to great lengths in their purifications and exorcisms, the Libertines purify themselves by doing nothing other than closing their eyes to the distinction between good and evil and by lulling their consciences to sleep in order to overcome any fear of hell. And lo, they are purer than angels!

Everything Christians hold concerning eternal life and the resurrection is but a fable to them. For they fantasize that man's soul, which is divine, will return to God Himself[32] at death, not for the purpose of living as a human soul, but in order that God might live as He always has[33] from the beginning, as we shall more amply see later.

As for the different degrees of discipleship, they follow a form similar to the Manichees. For they are very careful not to move too quickly when explaining to anyone what they have on their stomach, but they take a long, suspended time and subject to equivocation those whom they hope to bring into their sect, without revealing to them the watch-word[34] until they see that they have sufficiently bewitched them to the point that they will believe whatever they want them to. Only those who are under *oath*[35] discover their mysteries, with the exception that their major teachers reserve to themselves several points in order to justify their position and to preserve their dignity.

For the moment these comparisons will suffice. But the order we are following will require us to speak of them more fully later on.

32. *Dieu, s'en retourne à soymesme.* That is, God will return to Himself.

33. *il a faict.*

34. *le mot du guet.*

35. *Serment* is capitalized in French, suggesting a Libertine order, rank, or class.

4

On the Origin of the Libertine Sect and Its Principal Leaders[1]

It is true that if in general I should hope to include and review everyone who goes under the title of Libertine, as well as those whose ideas are similar to their misguided fantasies, of which I plan to treat in this book, I could not do it. For the sect has comprised different groups, some in Holland, some in Brabant [Belgium], and some in the other regions of Lower Germany.[2] But because I shall write solely about those of the French tongue, I shall desist from making a long account concerning what has appeared in these other countries, as if it were a superfluous thing. And I shall content myself to explain[3] briefly the means by which this poison got into our tongue and who the first abettors were who spread it about.

To begin with, about twenty years ago, or more, a certain Coppin,[4] a Fleming and native of Lille, began to stir up this filth[5] in the region of his birth. He was an ignorant man and had no other means to advance himself than his audacity—for as the proverb says, "A fool doubts nothing."

Afterwards he was helped by another named Quintin,[6] who

1. *Quel a esté le commencement de la secte des Libertines: et qui en sont les principaux capitaines.*

2. See Williams's discussion of the Netherlandish and Flemish Libertines (*Radical Reformation,* pp. 351–355). Williams point out that these groups had some affinities with the evangelical Spiritualists of Germany.

3. *advertir* = *avertir.* Can mean "to warn," as well as "to inform."

4. Coppin was active in Lille about 1529. See Williams, *Radical Reformation,* p. 354.

5. *ordure.*

6. Quintin of Hainaut was a tailor; he later served as an usher in the court of Marguerite of Angoulême (1492–1549). See Williams, *Radical Reformation,* pp. 354, 599. Calvin alludes to the Quintinists in the *Institutes* (3.3.14; 3.20.45).

created such a commotion that he obliterated the memory of the other, so much so that he is considered the [movement's] first and principal contriver. And he—as he is a fierce villain—is extremely pleased with this reputation and is careful not to mention his predecessor,[7] as if he had learned nothing from him. He is from the country of Hainaut or one of its quarters.

Now I do not know how it came about that he came to France, but I saw him there a little over ten years ago. He was accompanied by a Bertrand of Moulins,[8] who since[9] then has recently[10] become either God or nothing, according to their view, since he has departed this world.

Now not only would I not want to attribute[11] any crime to them, but I would want to prevent anyone else from doing the same. Nevertheless, I cannot close my eyes[12] concerning what I have heard from the late Étienne de la Forge,[13] whose memory ought to be hallowed among the faithful as a holy martyr of Jesus Christ. He said that they left their country owing to some crime rather than because of their message.

I also understand that a third person was part of their group, a man named Claude Perceval.[14]

They have worked so successfully that they have infected many people in France, so much so that there is hardly a place where they have lived that ought not be completely afraid of their corruption. Still at the same time they have continued to plot and to practice in their own country in order to seduce every poor simple idiot, or any whom they can find, who might be disposed to follow them. And they have been so successful that it is a horror to hear about the infection there.[15]

7. *maistre.*

8. Bertrand of Moulins was a French-speaking tailor; he later served as a valet in Marguerite's court.

9. *puis* - *depuis.*

10. *n'agueres* = *naguère.*

11. *imposer* = *attribuer, imputer.*

12. *dissimuler* = *fermer les yeux sur.*

13. Étienne de la Forge was a Piedmontes Waldensian who was martyred in 1535. Williams explains that Calvin lived with de la Forge in Paris while working on the commentary on Seneca (*Radical Reformation,* p. 599, n. 48).

14. Claude Perceval was also engaged, with Quintin and Bertrand of Moulins, in spreading Libertine doctrines among French-speaking people. He was active in Strassburg and stayed in Martin Bucer's home. See Williams, *Radical Reformation,* pp. 354, 599.

15. An apparent allusion to Valenciennes. See Poullain's letter to Calvin, May 26, 1544—Herminjard, *Correspondances,* vol. 9, p. 247, no. 1358.

It is true that they have had a helper whom I have not yet mentioned—a little priest named Monsieur Anthony Pocquet,[16] whom I also met three years ago.[17]

These then are their principal "scholars"[18] or patriarchs. Since then others have attempted to achieve a renown as great as theirs. But, as I have said, I shall refrain from speaking about the Flemish, Dutch, and Brabantine [Belgian] groups.

In the French tongue alone, one can find a number of their savants[19] who are good for about three days[20] [of argument and teaching], all of whom want to be the greatest. But this is of no surprise, for it is not necessary to be a scholar or intelligent to attain esteem among them. It only takes impudence to acquire it. In fact, all whom I have mentioned are as ignorant as they can be. And their arguments are without rhyme or reason, containing about as much sense as herring fishermen's disputations on astrology.

What has transformed Quintin and his tailor-companion[21] into scholars has been their desire to be fed in ease and the fact that work does not agree with them. That is why they have decided to gossip the way priests and monks do while singing, since they have taken this on quite willingly, the one being an usher and the other a valet [in Marguerite of Angoulême's court].

As for Monsieur Anthony, he thought how nice it would be to ponder his speculations after chanting the Mass. For people in his occupation[22] have little else to do. But once it has been shown below in what their wisdom consists, we will more clearly see how easy it is for one to do this in order to acquire instant and great renown.

16. Antoine Pocquet was born in Engheim c. 1500. He was a former Catholic priest and doctor in canon law. He served as a chaplain in Marguerite's court. See Williams, *Radical Reformation,* pp. 354, 599.

17. Anthony Pocquet visited Geneva in 1542 or 1543.

18. *docteurs.*

19. *docteurs.*

20. *qui se sont passez au bout de trois iours.*

21. *compaignon de coustumiers.* An allusion to Bertrand of Moulins and his role as valet in Marguerite's court.

22. *son estat.* An allusion to Pocquet's office as chaplain in Marguerite's court. See Calvin's disdain of such posts (*Institutes* 4.5.10). Calvin charges that canons, deans, chaplains, and provosts constitute a drain on the church, for they do not preach the gospel, nor do they oversee discipline or truly administer the sacraments.

There are two reasons that prompt me to name these wretches, who otherwise are unworthy of anyone giving them a single word of recognition, so much so that the paper would be soiled by their names. First of all, many who have no idea what the word "Libertine" means recognize the name of Quintin. Second, it is expedient that such dangerous beasts should be marked so that everyone might recognize them for fear of being hurt by them through lack of information.

Furthermore, I know quite well that I will not please everyone by publishing their names in this way.[23] But what should I do when I see four scamps who are already the cause of the ruin of four thousand men and of whom at least three are still seeking constantly to overthrow God's truth, who scatter the poor church, who deceive all whom they trap in their nets, who sow damnable blasphemies, and, what is still worse, put everyone into a horrendous confusion? Am I to keep silent or conceal it?

What cruelty on my part it would be if, in order to spare them or to please everybody, I should allow them to destroy and ravage everyone without warning that we should be on guard against them? If I were to know of brigands who had seized a road, ought I not reveal them for fear that poor travelers might fall into their hands? Should I hide poisoners who have conspired to murder an entire people?

Now there is no brigandage as evil, nor poison as pernicious to the world, as this accursed doctrine which tends to scatter and destroy not only Christianity but also all human propriety[24]—not even among the Turks and pagans has such ever been!

But if I were to remain silent,[25] then I would deserve being thought of as a murderer, since I should be consenting to evil. [Hence] should I not sound a word, seeing that they abuse the name of Jesus Christ in order to introduce under His shadow an abomination greater than any the world has known, and by means of which He is subjected to such disgrace that He is considered worse than a devil from hell? In remaining silent, I

23. Calvin knew that he would offend the sensibilities of Marguerite. See his letter to her, dated April 28, 1545, in *Letters of John Calvin,* ed. Jules Bonnet, vol. 1, pp. 453–458.

24. *honnesteté = convenance.* See Edmond E. A. Huguet, *Dictionnaire de la langue française du seizième siècle,* 7 vols. (Champion: Didier, 1925–1967), vol. 4, p. 497.

25. *en ce faisant.* Literally, "in doing this."

should be less faithful[26] than a dog that doesn't care if its master is attacked, or at least does not bark.[27]

Therefore I am compelled to cry out with a loud voice that if ever there were any heretics who overflowed with—I won't say simply perverse and false opinions but—excessively horrible blasphemies, these three have surpassed them. And never were there monsters whom one ought to hold in such abomination as Quintin and his gang.

Since I can only edify the church of God by fighting against those who machinate to destroy it, I would be cheating myself[28] if, to the best of my ability, I were to discredit the pope and his accomplices, but should pardon those who are by far the more serious enemies of God and the greatest spoilers of His truth. For even the pope retains some form of religion. He does not remove hope in eternal life. He teaches the fear of God. He observes some distinction between good and evil. He recognizes our Lord Jesus as true God and true man. He attributes authority to the Word of God. But the goal of Quintin and his gang[29] is to turn heaven and earth upside down, to annihilate all religion, to efface all knowledge of human understanding, to deaden consciences, and to leave no distinction between men and beasts.

I have waited long to address this because I had truly hoped that these absurd delusions might have peacefully disappeared without the world's having to be dazed[30] by them. But since our Lord has permitted these vermin to multiply so extensively that there is almost a public epidemic,[31] one can no longer keep silent.

Consequently,[32] no one must take pleasure in the fact that I am exposing such evildoers, unless they can demonstrate that they are prepared to prevent them from hiding their iniquity. If there were a way of not publishing their turpitude in order to oppose them, I would take it voluntarily.[33] But since it is neces-

26. *plus lasche = plus lâche.*

27. *n'abaye = n'aboye.*

28. *il me feroit beau voir.*

29. *ceux cy.*

30. *esventé = etourdi.*

31. *contagion.*

32. *pourtant = par conséquent.*

33. Note how much Calvin wishes he could avoid publishing a tract against the Libertines. See p. 203, n. 23.

oppose them, I would take it voluntarily.[33] But since it is necessary for me to single them out[34] in order to prevent them from doing evil, none should be offended.

In fact, that I have delayed so long in doing this shows of necessity that I am constrained. If at the beginning I had been so excited as to write against them—although that would have been my right—nevertheless some rudeness[35] might have miscolored my argument precipitously.[36] But now, since such a long time has elapsed, I have no other choice. For if anyone is offended by this, how will he be able to free himself of the suspicion of being one of their accomplices?

Rather, whoever has a drop of true zeal must try to expose them, whether they are great or small. And everyone, including children, ought to spit in their face,[37] as a sign of abomination whenever they see them pass on the street, in order to shame those who, in supporting them, have caused the perdition of ten thousand souls—beyond the scandal and loss they have caused the gospel and the greater harm they could still do if God by His infinite goodness were not intervening.[38] And since they can cause so much harm,[39] am I to protect the honor of those who have put the sacred name of God and His Word to the greatest shame that has ever been imagined since the beginning of the world?

In addition to all this, there is a still more urgent reason that presses me to act. For insofar as I have been able to perceive, these scum have the audacity to pass themselves off as servants of God in order to deceive the simple. As in the case of Monsieur Anthony Pocquet who, about twelve years ago, having lived in this city for awhile and spread his wicked teaching, so practiced from the start and sought by subtle means to gain my endorsement[40] in order to advance himself among those who defer in some authority to me, as if I approved of his diabolical errors.

Now he did not act his part so well that I was at least not able

34. *ie les monstre au doigt.* Literally, "to point at them [with scorn]."
35. *chagrin = rudesse, méchanceté.*
36. *hastivité = rapidité.*
37. See *CO* 7, col. 163, n. 3: *conspuere in faciem.*
38. *n'y prouvoit.*
39. *blasme = blâme.*
40. *d'avoir tesmoignage de moy.*

to recognize him for a dreamer and madman, as I remonstrated at our *congregation,*[41] though I did not know of his wickedness then, but have since been informed that he came from the country of Artois and Hainaut where he sowed his poison.

When he came he was unable to get anything out of me. He alleged to me that our brother Martin Bucer[42]—whose name should be honored throughout Christendom—certainly accorded him what I was refusing.[43] Of course, while concealing his venom he was attributing[44] false teachings to this good servant of God in order to serve his own advantage later and for the purpose of gaining an entrance among those who have some fear of God.

I beg of you, ought I keep silent when I see with my own eyes how these brazen villains parade their adulteries[45] before us, without our realizing it, for the purpose of corrupting poor souls? Think of the benefit they derive from our silence, insofar as they are so shameless as to want to wrest our approval by their wicked teachings!

Consequently it is quite in order to remove their mask behind which they hide in order the more easily to conduct their accursed enterprise, which overturns both God's honor and the salvation of souls.

41. Note in *CO* 7, col. 163, n. 5: "This designates the weekly meetings of the pastors and laity in which they discussed scriptural passages and ecclesiastical questions." These Friday meetings were exegetical exercises open to the public. It is unfortunate that the ministers did not begin to keep a register of their meetings until 1546 (*Register of the Company of Pastors of Geneva in the Time of Calvin,* ed. and trans. Philip Edgcumbe Hughes [Grand Rapids: Eerdmans, 1966]).

42. The Strassburg Reformer (1491–1551) who befriended Calvin in 1539 and whose ideas and writings influenced him.

43. Karl Müller discusses the Libertines' association with Martin Bucer in "Calvin und die Libertiner," in *Zeitschrift für Kirchengeschichte,* pp. 90–98.

44. *abuse.*

45. *macquereaux = paillards.* Literally, "adulterers," or even "fornicators."

5

On How It Is Possible for This Bestial Sect to Have Such a Large Following and on the Character of Such People

Now someone will say to me, "Since this doctrine is so absurd and repugnant, not only to the entire holy Scripture, but also to all humanity, and since its leaders[1] are coarse[2] and ignorant people, how have they managed to acquire so many followers, even from among persons who earlier tasted the simple doctrine of the gospel?"

First of all, [it has happened] because[3] our Lord permits sects to emerge in order to test everyone's faithfulness and to distinguish the good from the evil. Also, it is essential that such come about so that those who appear to accept[4] the gospel and appear to wear the Christian's robe may be shown to be what they are, in order that the Christian church might be purged of such filth and that they might become an example to others, to the end that we might learn never to play with God.

Now beyond this common factor,[5] and almost the mother of all heresies—being arrogance or presumption—if we look closely at the matter, we will find that there are two reasons[6] why so many people have fallen into this error. One is that many have given themselves to a foolish curiosity, applying their minds to vain and superfluous questions, instead of searching for those

1. *docteurs.*
2. *rudes = incultes.*
3. *comme.*
4. *tenir.*
5. *la racine commune.* Literally, "the common root."
6. *vices.*

things that edify. Not being content with the simplicity of the Scriptures, they have fluttered about in the air by [indulging in] frivolous speculations in order to satisfy their foolish lusts, or in order to demonstrate their subtlety and high intelligence.

The other reason is that some, having had a partial beginning in the pure teaching of the gospel, have misused it, not only treating it as a profane science, but in order to give themselves up[7] to a carnal license and lead a dissolute life. Indeed, knowing that the gospel does not permit that, but rather serves as a bridle for restraint, they wanted to find an easier way out,[8] in which it would be permissible for them to indulge in every turpitude.

In fact, almost all the disciples of this sect are comprised by these two types, i.e., those who are *fantastics,*[9] who only want to fidget around with extravagant questions and who derive all their pleasure by engaging in useless things, and those who are *profane people,* who have grown tired of carrying Jesus Christ's yoke, and instead have sought to put their consciences to sleep in order to serve Satan without any remorse or scruples.

Still someone might ask, "How does it come about that those whose studies and inquiries involve them in areas which are not theirs to know let themselves be stupefied by such puerile follies, which would not even deceive the most ignorant and coarse people of the world? Indeed, it seems a strange warning that those whose searchings divert them from God,[10] in order to follow their own will, can accept such absurd delusions."

To that I reply that it is a just vengeance of God's to place them in such a reprobate condition, in which they differ in no way from beasts, except by retaining their human form. In fact, what a dishonor this first group does God! For they search across country for new questions, as if the heavenly wisdom He reveals to us in the gospel were too simple and too base for them.

Indeed, seeing that God is not good enough to be their master, is it not a just vengeance that He should deliver them over to Satan and send them to his school? When their understanding cannot be content with the limits of truth, is it not fitting that it

7. Literally, "to slacken upon the reins."
8. *quelque retraicte.*
9. *phantastiques.* Italics for emphasis.
10. *cherchent de s'eslongner de Dieu.* Literally, "search far away from God."

should enter into a labyrinth of complete deception, void of any path or address?

As for those who have misused the teaching of the gospel in order to debauch themselves, or who have been unable to bear it because of its austerity, is it not fitting that even their natural sense should be taken away along with their distinction between good and evil?

Let us realize, therefore, that it is in this manner that our Lord avenges the outrage that has been committed against His Word, or the contemptuous way in which it has been treated, or the manner in which it has been polluted by dissolute living.

Now when men have accordingly barred[11] themselves from the Word of God, which is the only light[12] for guiding us in the right path, it is appropriate that the judgment given by Saint Paul should be executed on them, i.e., that God give Satan the efficacy to do with them whatever he chooses [I Tim. 1:20].

In summary, those are the principal reasons that Quintin and his accomplices have such a long string of followers at their rear. Besides, the cunning with which they operate helps them too. For from the very first they speak such a strange language that simple folk are enraptured by them, as they are confident that they can raise them into heaven to be with the angels. And holding their hearers suspended in this condition for a long time, until they have bewitched them, they make them believe that the moon is made of green cheese.

Without a doubt they have enveloped many in this way. For they inordinately promenade[13] about those who are easily led around, enthralling them with their obscure jargon of which one cannot understand a thing, almost dazzling their eyes, to the extent that they can no longer see either white or black. Nevertheless, being so grossly ignorant and advancing such idiotic and absurd dreams, they would never succeed in winning people as much as they do except for the fact that our Lord has willed to punish those who allow themselves to become entrapped, as He cast them into a reprobate state[14] since they have not willed to cling to Him or to His teaching.

11. *exclus.*
12. *clarté.*
13. *pourmenent = promenent.*
14. *sens reprouvé.*

Finally, there is a special reason which pertains to princes, or lords who govern in their name, and to all persons who administer justice. It is that whenever they attempt to prevent the holy teaching of God from entering their countries, persecute those who proclaim it or who provide the means of coming to its knowledge, strive to abolish and extinguish it, and suppress it by every means that they can, our Lord punishes them by causing their countries to be infected by these vermin.

And isn't that a fitting judgment? For since they reject the benediction [of God], His malediction comes upon them instead. They don't think about that. They are content to think that they will attain the goal of their enterprises through fire and sword. But they are self-deceived. For sometimes when they machinate and plot,[15] the Word of God proves the stronger and overcomes and destroys all the impediments that they have put forward in an effort to block God's approach.[16] And the church in the midst of persecutions grows.

In the meantime, God causes the wicked sects in their countries to multiply even more in order to deprave[17] and corrupt all their subjects, until they arrive at a [state of] confusion that no living man can remedy. For as a consequence of the counsel they pursue, there follows the indifferent punishment of all who oppose the superstitions of the antichrist, so that they gain nothing. For the only way to exterminate wicked sects and heresies is to yield[18] to God's pure truth, which is the unique light that dispels darkness, as experience truly demonstrates.

15. *facent.*

16. *pour luy coupper le chemin.* Literally, "to cut the road in front of God." The metaphor of an army blocking a road is reminiscent of Calvin's personal experience. In 1536 the war between Francis I and Charles V had closed the road to Strassburg. Calvin, planning to go to Strassburg, had to alter his plans and detour; he thus came to Geneva.

17. *gaster = gâter.*

18. *qu'en donnant lieu.* Literally, "by giving place."

6

On Remedies for Not Falling into the Errors of the Libertines, or on Remedies for Withdrawing If Anyone Has Already Succumbed

Since our Lord has promised to manifest Himself to those who seek Him in fear and humility, if we want to come to Him, then let us take this route. Let us strive to come to the knowledge of our Lord Jesus, not by presuming to mount so high by our own understanding, but by praying Him to render us capable of growing[1] in His teaching. For we cannot do this if we have not renounced the presumption of wanting to be wise beyond measure.

Let us desire nothing save to know one sole God through[2] our Lord Jesus, and to aspire to no other goal—as in truth God does not teach us any other knowledge by His Word.

Let us not have so quarrelsome a spirit, or such sensitive ears, that we cannot consent to this simple and pure truth in which the infinite treasures of God are enclosed.

Let us not profane the Word of God by changing it into a vain and unfruitful knowledge, or by using it in any other way than to edify.

Let us not receive it in vain by scorning either the threats of God's judgment that it contains or His grace which is presented to us in it.

In brief, let us realize the end for which the gospel has been given to us, and let us receive it as God intends us to do. Let us

1. *profiter.*
2. *en.*

consider what our disposition ought to be, and pray God to create such within us.

Therefore, let us not be afraid that heretics might have the power to pierce our eyes and make us turn from God. And, above all, let us not fear that God will forsake us so much as to [allow us to] slip into the abyss of this bestial Libertine sect.

This admonition is addressed to everyone. Our Lord, by His infinite mercy, has already begun to visit our hearts[3] through His Word. [But] some have decided to take the gospel as a pastime. Seeing what has happened to them, let us be warned[4] by their example.

We have a similar mirror in counting-house clerks, in idle office and shop workers, as well as among merchants and artisans. Therefore, in order that we might not become like reeds buffeted by every wind, let us take root in our Lord Jesus. And lest we become like little children, being vulnerable to every deception, let us grow and be confirmed in Him.

I say, "in our Lord Jesus," such as He was proclaimed long ago by the prophets and is clearly conveyed to us in the gospel.

Now if there are some who have already been seduced by means of their thoughtlessness, let them take no pleasure in their wrong. May they not become hardened against God. May they not close their ears to the holy admonitions that they will hear[5] in this tract. May they not become intoxicated with their own knowledge and thus be incapable of making judgments. May they not totally degrade their consciences, which are already benumbed. But may they be awakened by Him who is the sun of righteousness, who has come into the world to enlighten us.

May everyone together patiently note the warnings that I shall offer, to the end that they might serve them as guideposts in order that they might not be overtaken by impudence. For I truly hope, if it pleases God, to paint these monsters so vividly that everyone will be able to perceive them from afar in order to be on guard against them.

3. *courtz*

4. *mirons nous = réglons nous.*

5. Note in *CO* 7, col. 168, n. 1: "All the French editions have *voir* [see]. Read: *oir* [hear]."

7

On the Quintinists' Language and Style of Speech

To begin with, in the same way that the "wandering beggars,"[1] as they are called, possess a unique jargon which is only understood by their brotherhood, so much so that they can deceive a man while speaking face to face with him without him realizing it, so also the Quintinists possess an unbelievable tongue[2] in which they banter, to the extent that one understands it about as little as a bird's song. Not that they do not use common words as others do! But they so disguise their meaning that one can neither determine what their subject matter is or whether they are affirming or denying something.

Now it is true that they do this out of malice in order to entrap the simple by treachery and stealth. For they never reveal the abominable mysteries which are hidden under their words except to those who are already under oath. In the meanwhile they take a novice and leave him to gape[3] and wonder, his mouth agog, without understanding anything. Thus by using guile they hide behind such obscurities the way brigands lurk in caves.

Truly these are the "loud-mouthed boasters" whom Saint Peter and Saint Jude compare to scum and froth (II Peter 2:18; Jude 16). For there is little else to them. But thinking that they have bewildered the good sense of others by their high style,

1. *gueux de l'hostière = mendiants constituant une sorte de confrérie.* See Jean-Daniel Benoit, "Glossaire, Tables et References," in *Institution de la Religion Chrétienne,* vol. 5, pp. 431–432. See also *CO* 7, col. 168, n. 2, which explains that the term *gueux de l'hostière* refers to a group from Bohemia. This group appears to have been an order of mendicant friars who had a peculiar way of preaching.

2. *une langue sauvaige.* Literally, "a wild tongue," or "savage tongue."

3. *bailler = bâiller.*

they are carried away themselves, so that even they understand nothing of what they babble.

I remember once in a large group[4] how Quintin, seeing that I was successfully rebutting his idle talk and wanting to obscure lucidity, told me that I found his ideas unacceptable[5] owing to a lack of understanding.[6] To which I replied that I understood better than he, since he knew nothing that he was saying and I at least recognized that he wanted to seduce[7] the world by means of absurd and dangerous follies. In fact, one will thus find that they have delved[8] so deeply into their silly speculations and so enveloped themselves that they do not know where they are, for they are still up in the clouds.[9]

Therefore let this be a means of recognizing them. For when you hear them speak in this way, you will only be hearing high German.[10] For God created the tongue for the purpose of expressing thought in order that we might be able to communicate with each other.[11] Consequently, it is a perversion of God's order to pommel the air with a confused sound that cannot be understood, or to try by subtle means to go around one's elbow to get to one's thumb in order to awaken one's hearers and then leave them in such a state.

Besides, the Scriptures ought to be our guide with respect to how God's mysteries are handled. Therefore let us adopt the language that it uses without being lightheaded. For the Lord knows quite well that if He were to speak to us in a manner befitting His majesty, our intelligence would be incapable of reaching that high. Thus He accommodates Himself to our smallness. And as a wet nurse coos[12] to her baby, so He uses

4. *en grande compagnie.* A possible allusion to the company of pastors at Geneva and their Friday *congrégations.*

5. *mauvais.*

6. *par faute de l'entendre.*

7. *embabouilner = séduire.*

8. *se fourrent = pénétrent.*

9. *ne touchent ne ciel ne terre.*

10. *le haut Allemant.* Literally, "high German."

11. Calvin explains his philosophy of language in his exposition on the ninth commandment in the *Institutes* 2.8.47–48. Cf. *John Calvin's Sermons on the Ten Commandments,* ed. and trans. Benjamin W. Farley (Grand Rapids: Baker, 1980), pp. 216–217.

12. *begaye.* Literally, "stammers."

toward us an unrefined[13] way of speaking in order to be understood.

Whoever, therefore, reverses this order only succeeds in burying God's truth, which can only be known in the manner that He wills to reveal it to us. That is why we must labor to unravel their obscurities in order to drag them if necessary by force into the light,[14] so that their abominations, which they make a point of hiding, might be known to all the world.

Similarly, every Christian must be warned that when he hears them garbling as they do he must cut them off immediately at the spigot and say to them, "Either speak the language that the Lord has taught us and which He uses in His Scriptures, or go speak to the rocks and trees!"

13. *grossiere.*
14. *clarté.*

8

On the Libertines' Great Malice and Impudence in Glorying in the Fact That They Have a Double Heart and a Double Tongue

But they overflow still more. For they have no difficulty in saying one thing first and then another thing later and in changing their position to the delight of their hearers. What is more, they are very proud of this and hold to it fiercely. For one of the principal articles of their theology is the necessity of having the art to ape themselves in order to deceive the world.

I don't know if I ought to call that impudence or malice. For since simplicity is the highest virtue we can recommend, it is a sign of a completely perverse nature when a man is so given to bending himself about that, like a serpent, he slips out of the hands of those who are trying to hold him.

On the other hand, they must be incredibly impudent to feel no shame when they are accused of lacking constancy[1] in their words. It is the same source for their double dealing[2] which they permit themselves when they give the appearance of doing whatever it takes to please men. For example, they engage in idolatry without any scruples. They pretend to accept all the superstitions of the papists, since according to their view all external matters are within the liberty of Christians.

As for this topic, I will discuss it in a later chapter, only I would like to say one word about it here. For readers should be warned

1. *tenure.*

2. *simulation = dissimulation.* Note the trace of Nicodemism in this and the two subsequent paragraphs.

that, whether in their jests or words, the Libertines delight in scoffing[3] at the world and in constantly changing their position,[4] so much so that one is unable to tell exactly what they maintain.

In fact, if Quintin were held a prisoner today, whether by Christians or the papists, and one should want to get him to confess,[5] he would only make a gesture of mockery. For he would surely escape, since he would grant either group whatever it wanted to hear. And in doing so he would not contradict their teachings. For the first article of their faith, as I have already said, is the necessity of the art of being able to disguise themselves and to speak with a double tongue—a practice that even pagans condemned. For even they recognized and declared that nothing is more contrary to nature[6] than for a person to change his identity by guile. So much is this so that according to their view it would be better to resemble a lion than a fox.

But they are not content with this, for they dare claim that they have derived this principle from God, arming themselves with what is written in Psalm 2:4: "He who sits in the heavens laughs at them," citing this text as a proof that God is a simulator. That is how they use Scripture.

The prophet uses this expression to signify that God delays His judgment on the iniquitous and the persecutors of His church, leaving them unpunished for awhile, not because He is sleeping or is powerless to act, but because He is amused by their audacity while He awaits the coming time of their ruin. And this is done for our consolation in order that we might not lose courage when we see the wicked in authority and God's aid does not seem apparent. But these villains interpret it to make God into a scoffer[7] who mimics[8] Himself for the purpose of deceiving the world.

They attribute[9] the same to Jesus Christ. To support this they cite the response He made to His apostles, that it was to them that He had clearly revealed the secrets of the kingdom of God, but since it was not fitting for the people to hear the simple and

3. *beffler = bafouer.*
4. *retourner leur robbe à tout propos.*
5. *qu'on se vousist tenir à ses confessions.*
6. *à une bonne nature.*
7. *gaudisseur = railleur, bon vivant.*
8. *contreface = imite.*
9. *imposer = imputer, attribuer.*

clear truth, He spoke in parables (Matt. 13:11; Mark 4:25; Luke 8:18; 19:26). Thus they suggest that[10] when our Lord Jesus used parables He was calling white black, or meant one thing for another, in order to kill time with His hearers or make them imagine what was farthest from His mind.

We know there is a question concerning what Christ intended His similitudes or parables to mean. But we know the purpose they served. In the first place, they gave color and majesty to His ideas by arousing the minds[11] of His hearers and making them more attentive. Second, they gave the same hearers a point to consider and left it up to them to determine their meaning.

Doubtless they require exposition, since their contents are obliquely presented in figures. But what prevented the people from understanding them was their failure to make allowances for the figures and their preference to remain in their ignorance rather than to inquire and be taught.

As far back as the Old Testament, God solemnly affirmed through Isaiah His prophet that He never spoke by stealth nor in darkness, nor did He ever command the people of Israel to seek Him in vain (Isa. 45:19). Thus are we going to dishonor our Lord Jesus by saying that He came into the world to obscure, or rather to extinguish, the clarity that was already from of old? or to blur what was clear? or to confuse what was beyond doubt?

How does that harmonize with the fact that He is the "sun of righteousness" (Mal. 4:2)? and the "light of the world" (John 8:12)? and that His office is to enlighten darkness? Does it not constitute an outrageous blasphemy?

Besides, what Saint Paul says of the gospel is the opposite[12] of what they pretend. For he testifies that the gospel is a clear and shining doctrine that manifests God's face for us in Jesus Christ without [containing] any veil to obscure our view[13] (II Cor. 3:14). Then he adds that if there is anyone who still cannot see anything in this great light,[14] then he must be blinded by the devil.

I leave it to readers to consider how great the difference is between Saint Paul and these mischief makers.

10. *comme si.*
11. *espritz.*
12. *il s'en faut beaucoup.* Literally, "very far from it."
13. *ce regard.*
14. *clarté.*

We should take pride in possessing a doctrine that is clear, pure, certain, and open to[15] everyone, and should say that those who use obscurity utilize a shameful veil in order to cover up their turpitude. They go to great lengths not only to distort their teaching in such a way that one can no longer discern its beginning or end, but they twist it about and subject it to sleight of hand.

As for Jesus Christ being an example with which they arm themselves, He would have to renounce Himself to adhere to them. For His nature is not contrary to His gospel. And as I have already pointed out, He did not speak in parables in order to maintain two meanings,[16] or babble unintelligently, but rather the better to impress His teaching upon the hearts of the faithful and give it a greater luster. And although unbelievers might not have understood any of it, nor profited from it in any way, that does not make His parables confused enigmas: rather one must consider the source of their failure [to understand].

Now He explains this, as He so often reiterates, "Let him who has ears to hear, hear" (Matt. 13:9). By this He means that there are many who are deaf,[17] with whom one must have the gift of gab before they begin to listen.

Finally, He concludes that, with regard to this matter, Isaiah's saying is verified: "For they are blind in their understanding and hardened in their hearts, to the end that they might perish in their unbelief" (Matt. 13:14; Isa. 6:9ff.).

Consequently, if the Libertines want to be esteemed as true imitators of our Lord, let them do as Saint Paul [did]. Let them remove and cast away all veils, which are signs of shame, and let them teach us a pure and clean gospel, one which is not difficult to understand, except for those who are alienated in their minds because of their own unbelief (II Cor. 4:3). Otherwise I accuse them of blaspheming Jesus Christ in their wanting to ape Him.

In addition they cite this passage: "Let us become as wise as serpents" (Matt. 10:16). But since in this same passage Christ requires us to be "innocent as doves," let us hold the two together, then it will be easy for us to see that He does not want us to have a malicious cunning for beating about the bush in order to

15. *facile à = enclin à.*
16. *deux visages.*
17. *sours = sourds.*

deceive the world; rather He simply admonishes us to do nothing out of inconsideration.

If anyone desires a more ample exposition of this wisdom with respect to what it means, then let him seek it from Saint Paul where he says that since we live[18] in the midst of this world, which is completely perverse, let us be on guard lest we are deceived, and let us walk wisely, knowing what the will of God is (Eph. 5:6). But these scum, under the pretext of this sound teaching,[19] boldly lie whenever it is to their advantage. And not only do they excuse themselves of all their simulations and lies, but they also glory in them, even to the point of putting an innocent man in danger of death, to see if he can escape it.

18. *conversons* = *habitons.*
19. *belle doctrine.*

9

On the Authority the Libertines Give Holy Scripture

We have already said that from the very beginning the Libertines scoffed whenever anyone quoted Scripture to them, not concealing the fact that they accepted it as fable. Nevertheless, they readily made use of it when they found a passage they could turn to their advantage.[1] But this did not mean that they believed in it. They did it only to trouble the simple and to unsettle them in order to win them more easily.

If anyone replied to them by citing Scripture, they would respond that we shouldn't be subject to the "letter that kills but to the Spirit who gives life."[2] In fact, the swine Quintin assigned[3] insulting nicknames[4] to each of the apostles in order to make them contemptible. For example, in his knavery he called Saint Paul "Broken Pot,"[5] Saint John "the Doting Lad,"[6] Saint Peter "Denier of God,"[7] and Saint Matthew "Usurer."[8]

That is how this disgusting wretch dared to blaspheme with his own foul mouth! And those who should have punished him so severely as to have made him an example to all fed him and kept him.[9] It is against my own will that I even mention it! But if I should spare them, certainly God would spare neither them nor me.

1. *leur sens.*
2. See p. 170, nn. 48, 52.
3. *imposé = imputé.*
4. *quelque brocard.*
5. *pot cassé.*
6. *iosne sottelet.* Can also mean "silly boy" or "stupid ass."
7. *renieur de Dieu.*
8. *usurier.*
9. *luy donnent estat.*

Now when they saw that all true believers[10] considered it a detestable sacrilege to trample the sacred Word of God under foot, in accordance with their article of faith that permits them to speak with a double tongue, they put on that tight-fitting garment[11] under which they currently hide. They did this to give the impression that they accepted holy Scripture, but in accepting it they turned it [to their advantage] after the example of their predecessors, the Priscillianists, of whom we have spoken, and changed it into allegories.

In fact, they have so deformed it that they give about as much honor to the Word as if they denied it altogether. For they consistently maintain this principle: that Scripture, taken in its natural sense,[12] is but a dead letter and only kills. Thus they abandon it in order to come to the life-giving Spirit.

Now in doing so, they pursue a double purpose. First of all [they mean] that one should not hold to the simple sense[13] of Scripture, but one should play around with it by means of allegorical interpretation. Second, [they mean] that one should not be content with what is written, or acquiesce in it at all, but one should speculate higher and look for new revelations.

Although this sect is certainly different from the papists', inasmuch as it is a hundred times worse and more pernicious, nevertheless both of them together hold this principle in common: to change Scripture into allegories and to long for[14] a better and more perfect wisdom than we find in it. And together both as a coverup appeal to Saint Paul's statement that "the letter kills" (II Cor. 3:6).

Now in tearing out this passage and applying it to themselves they corrupt it terribly. Thus it is necessary, first of all, to point out the apostle's intention, and then we can look again at the conclusion[15] they deduce from it.

10. *tous bons cueurs.* Literally, "all good hearts."

11. *fourreure.* Literally, "case," "sheath," "tight-fitting dress." Calvin seems to be suggesting "snakeskin" here.

12. *sens naturel.* Determining the natural sense of a text is one of Calvin's cherished principles of biblical interpretation. See T. H. L. Parker, *Calvin's New Testament Commentaries,* p. 64.

13. *simple sens.* Could also be translated "natural sense," "plain meaning," "natural meaning."

14. *d'affecter = aimer, désirer.*

15. *la consequence.*

The apostle in this passage makes a comparison of the law and the gospel—if one separates Jesus Christ from the law. He calls the law "the letter," because without the grace of God it is a cold doctrine, without efficacy, inasmuch as it does not penetrate the heart. In the same way in another passage he calls circumcision "literal," insofar as it is done to the body and is only an external ceremony (Rom. 2:29).

On the contrary, he calls the gospel a "spiritual" doctrine, since Jesus Christ is included in it and vivifies the Word, making it efficacious[16] in our hearts by His Spirit. Then he says that the law, remaining literal, "kills," inasmuch as we can only find condemnation in it. For he immediately adds that this is "a preaching of death" (II Cor. 3:7). While on the contrary, the gospel "gives life," since it makes available[17] the grace of Jesus Christ, by which it bears fruit in us to salvation.

That is Paul's simple sense[18] from which nothing else should be drawn out, unless we ought to learn not to divide the Word of God so as to cut it off from Jesus Christ who is its soul, as he adds later, and by whom alone it has the power to become beneficial to us.

But these great [Libertine] expositors! What? They want to use this passage to introduce us to a method of making Scripture serve one's own advantage,[19] or they want to make it read like a plot. For there is about as much substance[20] to allegories as there is to bottles of water that babies drink with a straw.

Certainly Saint Paul never had their interpretation in mind. Thus let them refrain[21] from citing this [text] as a witness to their method.

Their second understanding[22] is even more diabolical. For they seek to turn us away from Scripture in order to make us err[23] by following their imaginations, or rather in order to lead us beyond the limits of Scripture to the end that each might

16. *profiter.*

17. *apporte.*

18. *simple sens.* See p. 222, n. 13.

19. *nez de cire.* "Ce qu'on peut tourner et façonner a son gré" (Benoit, "Glossaire," p. 404).

20. *fermeté = soutien, force.*

21. *se deportent = renouncent.*

22. *entendit.*

23. *vaguer = errer.*

follow his own interests and the devil's illusions instead of following the truth of God. [Thus] in order that every Christian might be warned to resist such a pernicious temptation, we must note to what end our Lord has promised us His Spirit.

Now He did not promise the Spirit for the purpose of forsaking Scripture, so that we might be led by Him and stroll amid the clouds, but in order to gain its true meaning and thus be satisfied. In Jesus Christ's own words: "When the Spirit of Truth comes, He will enable you to understand the things which you have heard from Me" (John 14:26). [Hence] we see that He does not promise His apostles a spirit that will create new doctrines for them; rather the Spirit only confirms them in the gospel which was preached to them.

Furthermore, after His resurrection, when He opened the understanding of His two disciples (Luke 24:27, 32), it was not in order to inspire them with strange subjects[24] not found in Scripture but in order to help them understand Scripture itself.

In fact, to whom has been given the greatest abundance of the Spirit if not to the apostles? Nevertheless, the Spirit did not cause them to lay aside Scripture or create in them mistrust for it. But on the contrary we see that the Scripture became the focus of their entire study and obedience. And we hold to the same obedience.

As for Saint Paul in particular, never once did he want to lay aside Scripture, for he found its authority so good that he recommends it to us in order to persuade us to know and to hunger to know only what it contains. For he says, "It is useful for our instruction, exhortation, repentance, and for making us perfect in every good work" (II Tim. 3:16), saying that it is the foundation on which our consolation and patience should rest if we would be firm in hope.

As for the word "Spirit," it appears from what he calls his "ministerial preaching of the Spirit" (II Cor. 3:8) that Spirit and Scripture are one and the same.[25] For after admonishing the Thessalonians not to "quench the Spirit," he adds that they should "not despise the prophets" (I Thess. 5:19f.). By this he means that we choke out the light of God's Spirit if we cut

24. *choses.*
25. *il ne signifie point une chose diverse de l'Escriture.*

ourselves off from His Word. That is, provided[26] it is [properly] preached to us. For preaching and Scripture are the true instruments of God's Spirit.

Therefore, let us consider anyone a devil who wants to lead us astray from it, whether directly or indirectly, and let us flee from them as we would a poison. Let us hold, I say, to the pure and plain[27] Word of God, where He has clearly revealed His will to us. And let us pray that by His Holy Spirit He will want to implant it in our hearts, which is His true office. Let us say to Him with David: "Lord, open my eyes that I may behold the marvels of Thy law" (Ps. 119:18).

26. *ie dis selon que.*
27. *simple.*

10

On the Libertines' Frequent Abuse[1] of the Word *Spirit* Which Is Constantly in Their Mouth

Beyond what shall be said here, it should be noted that the Libertines do not know how to broach a subject without immediately using the word "Spirit," and with difficulty they cannot sustain two sentences without repeating it. And even in repeating it they change its meaning,[2] for in the same way that village priests frequently make a single *marmouset,*[3] which they have in their parishes, serve for five or six saints, so also these clowns apply the word "Spirit" to anything they choose in order to benefit themselves in every way. Indeed, they use it like a table gravy[4] over all their food.

They say that the Word of God is "Spirit." It is true that our Lord Jesus once used this word when He said that His words were "spirit and life" (John 6:63). But we clearly know[5] that what He meant was that His words were "spiritual" and "life giving." For the issue had to do with eating His body. But the Capernaumites thought He meant eating it in a physical way. Hence He explained to them that this was not the case.

Now there is no controversy over the point that all of God's teaching is "spiritual." Indeed, we teach as much. But these fantastics have something else in mind, whose meaning escapes us,

1. *abusent en plusieurs sortes.*
2. Or *ce n'est pas en une signification seule.*
3. A *marmouset* is a grotesque figure.
4. *une saulse commune.*
5. *sait sans difficulté aucune.*

unless they are trying to create a new Word, something like a phantom. For they call Jesus Christ "Spirit."

True, Saint Paul in one passage (II Cor. 3:17) attributed this term to Him, but not that simply. For he calls Him "the Spirit," that is to say, the soul of the law, because without Him the law is dead, as we have previously said. But these beasts confuse everything without reason, making no distinction between the Son of God and His Spirit.

I have not mentioned all the ways in which they use this word, for there would be no end to that, only I have cited these examples in passing in order to warn the faithful that whenever they hear the word "Spirit," they should consider the way in which it is being used, lest they embroil themselves in confusions for which there is neither rhyme nor reason.

Furthermore, it should be noted that in their confused application of the word "Spirit" to whatever comes into their head, not only do they confound their hearers' understanding by confusing matters that ought to be held distinct, but they also cajole them into believing that they are completely "spiritual" and "divine" and are almost as holy[6] as angels. And the better ones frequently become "enraptured" at first, until they perceive the true end of this spirituality.

I say the above because today it is a great scandal to all true believers[7] to see a large number of fickle persons subjecting the Word of God to such a sensuous understanding,[8] twisting Christian liberty into a dissolute license of the flesh, chatting casually about the gospel, living shamelessly, and blaspheming God in their deeds while praising Him with their lips (Titus 1:16).

Therefore when a zealous person falls into the hands of these suitors and hears them talking primarily about the "Spirit," and that the Word of God is nothing but "Spirit," and that Jesus Christ is equally "Spirit," and that we must be "Spirits" with Him, and that our life must be "spirit[ual itself]," his first impression is that the Libertines are deeply zealous persons who are concerned lest the Word of God become polluted and compromised[9] by the scandalous lives of false Christians. Being thus

6. *demy ravis.* Literally, "half-enraptured," "half-delighted."
7. *tous bons cueurs.*
8. *en leur sensualité.*
9. *mise en vitupere.*

deceived, he forms a good impression of them and is won over[10] by their friendliness and by the fact that they require nothing by way of faith.[11]

But soon afterwards, the Libertines begin to disgorge their venom and fall from their lofty manner of speaking, as Saint Jude says (v. 10), to a churlish doctrine. For, as we shall see, there is no whoremonger or highwayman or even infamous desperado who would ever be so unbridled as to approve of all the damnable crimes that these "great spirituals"[12] commit.

"What then?" someone may ask. "Must we regard the word 'Spirit' with suspicion?" I would not say so, and I would be reluctant to think it. Hence at the very beginning I said that we must be very prudent and careful not to reject the word or scorn it but should discern how people make use of it.

Therefore if we see a man simply going about, pointing out that the Word of God is "spiritual" and can mold our hearts in faith and holy living, if he speaks of calling upon the name of God, of repentance, of good works, and of all the Christian practices according to their pure Scriptural usage, if he treats these matters clearly[13] and frankly, if he reproves the vanity of those who only honor the Word of God with the tip of their tongue, and admonishes them to approach it differently, let us hear him with a good heart. Let us help him repair and correct all the corruptions that presently reign.

But whenever we hear anyone obscuring the Word,[14] we ought to cut him off immediately and ask him what he means. If he continues to beat around the bush and to twist his words about, the way a snake coils its tails, then let us drag him into the light, even against his own will, as if we were dragging a thief or a malefactor out of his hiding place.

That is how we should differentiate between light and darkness, lest in trying to ascend to heaven by their method we

10. *l'induira.*

11. *leur adiouster aucunement foy.*

12. *ces bons spirituelz.* This phrase, set in the context of the Libertines' abuse of the word "spirit," clarifies why Calvin dubs them Spirituals. See also the last sentence of this chapter.

13. *nayfvement = clairement.*

14. *parler par ambages.* Literally, "speaking in an obscure manner."

tumble into an abyss of dreadful abominations.[15] Thus we can now understand how and why they have acquired the title "Spirituals," of which they are so puffed up that the term "Christians" no longer means anything to them.

15. *toutes abominations.*

11

On the First Article of Libertine Doctrine: That There Is Only One Immortal Spirit. With a Statement Explaining How This Is Contrary to the Truth of Scripture

It is time to consider[1] the inference[s] that can be deduced from this wretched sect's general articles of faith. To begin with, they maintain that there is only one divine spirit[2] that exists and indwells every creature. In saying this they eradicate the essence and nature of both human souls and angels. Even if I were not to sound a word of reproof against this error, there is not a person of sound judgment who would not hold this absurdity with horror. But it is essential to point out the hidden abomination of this position, along with showing to the contrary what the Scripture says.

It is true that among the ancient philosophers[3] there were a few who were fantastic enough to think that there was only one spirit, extended everywhere, and that all living creatures having movement and feeling were part of it, from which they had come and to which they would return. But inasmuch as experience and reason oppose this, there never was a man of sober judgment—even among the pagan philosophers—who did not reprove such a folly.

1. *venir.*
2. *esprit, de Dieu.*
3. Calvin does not cite specific philosophers or philosophical schools.

We have already singled out above[4] several sects which from ancient time troubled the Christian church with musings which, if not exactly similar, were close to this view: that souls and heavenly spirits, being of God's very own substance, were taken like coals from a fire.[5]

Now the Libertines, in order to surpass in impudence every heretic who has every lived, have returned to this ancient pagan supposition that there is only one spirit everywhere. Now we shall not here examine the objections which ensue from this position—objections which I shall examine in their proper place. But for the present I shall only touch on the essence.

Hence, when they posit[6] a single spirit, they are supposing that angels are only inspirations or movements and not creatures possessing [their own] essence. Instead of our souls they say that it is God who lives in us, who gives strength to our bodies, who supports all those actions in us that pertain to life.[7]

Now, beyond those other pretexts, of which we shall soon speak, they maintain as a principle that both Scripture and nature teach us that the eternal Spirit of God is the source and origin of everything. This we readily concede. But it does not follow from this that He did not give each creature a unique being and substance.[8] It is quite another thing to say that every creature comes from God and that what God has created is God Himself.

Saint Paul says that "in Him we live and have our being,"[9] by virtue of which we are rightly called "His offspring" (Acts 17:28). But this does not mean that God is the spiritual nature that indwells man.

True, we subsist in Him, insofar as we do not have our foundation in ourselves [i.e., are not self-caused]. But there is a vast difference between being the "work" and the "worker" himself.

For the moment, I shall desist from speaking of angels. But to

4. See chapter 3.

5. Ibid.

6. *etablissent.*

7. See Artistotle's definition of the soul as a nutritive and sensitive agent (*De Anima* 2.4, 5).

8. *un estre et une substance propre aux creatures.* Literally, "a being and a unique substance to the creatures." See p. 122, n. 21.

9. Literally, "We are in Him and live in Him."

deny that man's soul is an authentic,[10] created substance is another matter. And that Christians should doubt[11] this is a matter of grave alarm.

Nevertheless, since this is the case, let us listen to their grand arguments:[12] *there is only one God who [truly]*[13] *exists.* I admit that. But we do not cease to[14] subsist in Him, as He created us at a specific time[15] for this purpose and upholds us by His power.

Saint Paul, they argue, calls God alone immortal (I Tim. 6:16). I certainly agree with Saint Paul. But he means that God alone has this privilege in Himself and by virtue of His own nature, so much so that He is the source of immortality. But what God has in Himself He has communicated to our souls by His grace when He formed them in His image.

That is their "valid argument" by means of which they so confuse everything that they change God into a creature and do away with the human soul.

Now when it comes to correcting[16] this diabolical view, there are so many sound arguments that we only have to arm ourselves with the testimony of Scripture. The human soul is subject to ignorance, but God is not. It is subject to the passions, but God is not.

And what shall we say of [the soul's] inconstancy and diversity? What of [its] fragile nature and weakness? And what finally shall we say of sin?

They gain nothing by quibbling that sin is an awareness[17] in man but not [an awareness in] the Spirit of God. For whether Quintin himself or a similar apostate of their sect comes forward, is he really able to know and do everything? Certainly Quintin's jargon would lead you to think so, but I reject the notion that God knows what is going on in heaven but is Himself unaware of anything in man. But they fantasize that God is changeable,

10. *vraye.*

11. *doubte = doute.*

12. *belles raisons.*

13. In *CO* 7 (col. 180, n. 1) it is indicated that the Latin text was made to read *qui vere sit* for the French *qui soit.* The addition of the adverb "truly" suggests that the Libertines meant that there is only one truly existing substance, God.

14. *laissons de = cessons de.*

15. *une fois.*

16. *redarguer = convaincre de faute.*

17. *le cuider = une opinion.*

since He is completely different in this world than He is in heaven.

Should I not gain a great deal of spare time if I would refrain from refuting such monstrosities? But in order not to consume too much time in vain, I am satisfied with pointing at them in disgust.[18]

Besides, the teaching of Scripture is simple and clear: that God has made our souls after His likeness and they so indwell our bodies that when they depart from them, each goes to the place which it has prepared for itself [by virtue of how it lived] in this world—some to consolation and rest, others to the anguish and torments of hell. And I have dealt with that so amply [in my tract] *Against the Anabaptists* that it would be superfluous to mention it any further.

18. *de les avoir monstrez au doigt.*

12

On What the Libertines Think About the Devil, the World, and Man, Until the Latter Becomes a Member of Their Sect.[1] And on the Contrary, What Ought to Be Held

Someone might well ask, "What then is their opinion of the devil?" My reply is that they use the title and speak of him, but in accordance with their meaning. For they interpret[2] the "devil," the "world," and "sin" as imagining something to be real that is nonexistent.[3] And they say that man is such until he is remolded in their sect.

For this reason they understand all of these things under a single word, i.e., *imagination.*[4] By this they mean that whenever we think[5] of the devil or of sin, these are only frivolous fantasies which we have conceived. And not only do they speak of devils as they do angels—taking them as inspirations without essence—but they think they are only vain thoughts which we ought to forget as dreams.

As for sin, they do not simply say that it is a privation of good,[6]

1. Literally, "when he is not of their sect."
2. *prennent.*
3. *pour une imagination qui n'est rien.*
4. *cuider.* Can also mean "belief," "supposition," "thought." *Cuider's* alternate meanings should be kept in mind. See the discussion of this word on pp. 177–178.
5. *on a quelque opinion.*
6. See Augustine's discussion of evil as a privation of good (*Enchiridion,* in *Nicene and Post-Nicene Fathers,* first series, vol. 3, pp. 240).

but in their estimation it is a notion that evaporates and is gone once we move on to something else.

In brief, they speak of these things in the same manner that Saint Paul speaks of idols. For when he says that "an idol is nothing" (I Cor. 8:4), he means that it exists only as a conception, without reason or foundation, in the minds of the ignorant. Therefore we can dismiss it.

In this way the Libertines, pretending to eliminate[7] the distinction between good and evil, teach that we no longer have to be held back by such an idea[8] since sin has been abolished, and that it is a folly to be tormented by it any longer, as if it constituted something real.[9]

In a parallel manner they compose man of his body and of his suppositions,[10] saying that natural man's soul is possessed with the devil and the world; consequently, it is only a smoke that passes and constitutes nothing lasting.

Let us now turn to the pure teaching of the Scripture. It teaches us that devils are evil spirits that constantly war against us in order to lead us into perdition. And as they are destined to eternal damnation, they continually machinate to drag us toward a similar ruin.

For example, they are instruments of the wrath of God, the executioners who punish unbelievers and rebels by blinding them and by exercising a tyranny over them that incites them to evil (Job 1:6, 12; 2:1, 7; Zech. 3:1; Matt. 4:1; Luke 8:29; 22:31; John 8:44; 13:2; Acts 7:51; 26:18; II Cor. 2:11; I Thess. 2:18; I John 3:8). Beyond these the Scripture is full of other passages, and references are so common that we hardly need to cite them. The matter is clear enough,[11] unless one chooses to renounce the Scripture.

But we need to note Satan's craftiness here. There is nothing he wants more than to surprise us unawares.[12] For what better means is there for making us believe that he does not exist than for us to doubt him?

7. *oster* = *oter.* Literally, "to get rid of."

8. *plus amuser a cuider.*

9. *c'estoit quelque chose.*

10. *cuider.*

11. *toute liquide. Liquide* means "clear," "evident," "easy to understand." Perhaps "transparent" would also suffice.

12. *au deprouveu* = *au dépourvue.*

Consequently we see how hateful this doctrine is, not simply because it is contrary to the truth, but because it is so pernicious as to escape our thoughts. Thus it tends to expose poor souls to the devil as a prey inasmuch as it makes them believe that there is no spiritual enemy who battles against us, precisely when we are as sheep in the midst of wolves or, as the Scripture calls them, "roaring lions" (I Peter 5:8).

The word "world" is used in a variety of ways in Scripture. When it is used in a "bad" sense it means the corrupt nature in human beings which is the result of sin, from which proceed all those vices that are committed by men: ambition, avarice, hate, slander,[13] gluttony, pride, lechery,[14] conceit,[15] and the fountain of all evil—unbelief.

To shroud[16] all the concupiscences of our vicious nature and all the earth's perversity under the word "imagination"[17] is like wanting to inhale the sea in a single snort. But in the same way that they attempt to efface the memory of devils to the end that one no longer wills to be on guard against them, they also want to put under foot what is said in Scripture concerning those arms and weapons by means of which this enemy assaults us, not in order to destroy them, but only to the end that one no longer thinks about them, until one is mortally wounded by them and has received an incurable disease.

They even go further concerning sin. I beg of you, what does it mean to call sin "an imagination"[18] except to disguise it lest we should perceive the evil it causes?

The Scripture is quick to warn us how dangerous a poison sin is, thus it exhorts us to be diligent and to resist it. It carefully delineates its nature, root, and fruits. And not without cause, for the need is paramount.[19]

Thus one can see by what "spirit" these wretches are led when they want not only to obscure this essential doctrine, but to annihilate it altogether.

As for man, the Scripture clearly teaches us that from the

13. *detraction* = *médisance.*
14. *paillardise.* Can mean any sexual promiscuity.
15. *presumption* = *presomption.*
16. *ensepvelir* = *ensevelir.*
17. *cuider.*
18. *cuider.*
19. *est plus que besoing.*

time he turned away from God his soul has been full of ignorance and vanity, full of perversity and rebellion against God, given over to evil, oppressed and vanquished by weakness. Nevertheless it continues to call him a creature of God, possessing in himself those natural conditions which God placed in him, unless all of it is corrupted and depraved by sin.

Consequently, according to Scripture, man's soul is a spiritual substance endowed with sense and reason, in order to understand and pass judgments, and endowed also with will, in order to choose and desire those things that his life wants.[20]

True, the Scripture immediately admonishes us that our intelligence is perverted because of sin—so much so that we are blind and that our will is corrupt, even to such an extent that only iniquity flows out of it. Nevertheless the soul continues to exist in its essence and to retain the inseparable qualities of its nature, according to the order that God has established.

Consequently, to reduce the soul to an imagination[21] is an impudent act of resisting the truth, beyond the fact that by doing so the Libertines cause man to misunderstand himself to the end that he no longer cares about his soul, which our Lord hoped we would prefer above all the world (Matt. 16:26).

20. *son mouvement la poulse.*
21. *imagination.*

13

On the Libertine View That a Single Immortal Spirit Comprises Everything. And What Pestilence Is Hidden Under This View[1]

After creating a single spirit among themselves,[2] by means of which they destroy the nature of both the angels of heaven and the devils of hell, as well as human souls, the Libertines maintain that this single spirit constitutes everything. By this they do not mean what the Scripture means when it says that at the same time all creatures subsist in Him, are equally guided by Him, are subject to His providence, and serve His will, each according to its order. But they mean that everything in the world must be seen directly as His doing.[3]

In making this claim they attribute nothing to the will of man, no more than if he were a stone. And they cast aside every distinction between good and evil, since nothing can be badly made in their view, seeing that God is its author.

Now in order for this to be more clearly understood, I shall cite several examples illustrative of their idea.

This notorious swine Quintin[4] once found himself in a street

1. See Allen Verhey and Robert G. Wilkie's translation of this and the next three chapters in *Calvin Theological Journal* 15, no. 2 (1980): 205–219. Verhey introduces these chapters with a helpful discussion of the Libertines and Calvin's view of determinism (ibid., pp. 190–205).

2. *à leur poste.*

3. *oeuvre.* Literally, "work."

4. *grosse touasse de Quintin.* This was rendered in Latin as *porcus ille,* "well-known swine" (*CO* 7, col. 183, n. 1).

where a man had just been killed. By chance a faithful believer was also there who said, "Alas! Who has committed this wicked deed?" Immediately he replied in a jesting way, "Since you want to know, it was I."[5] The other being completely surprised said, "How can you be so flippant?" To which he replied, "It isn't I, but God."[6] "Why," asked the other, "must you attribute to God evils that He has commanded should be punished?" At which this swine disgorged even more forcefully his venom, saying, "Yes, it's you, it's I, it's God! For whatever you or I do is God's doing! And whatever God does, we do; for God is in us!"[7]

If you concede this point, then we must either attribute sin to God or dissolve the world of sin, inasmuch as God does everything. Thus, any distinction between good and evil is eliminated. From which it follows that it is illicit of us to find anything wrong, seeing that everything is the work of God. Hence men can do whatever they wish without hesitation,[8] not only because they are beyond any danger of sinning, but because to restrain desire would be to limit[9] God.

For example, if someone has committed lechery we must not reprimand him. For that would be to blaspheme God. If a man covets his neighbor's wife, let him enjoy it if he can. For he is certainly doing nothing other than the will of God. Indeed, what he does is a divine act.

As for goods, whoever can bamboozle[10] them, whether by subtle or violent means, let him go at it boldly. For he does nothing of which God disapproves. Let whoever has seized whatever he can have no fear of retribution. For it is unfitting to correct God.

It is true that they then turn all these fantastic speculations to their profit and advantage. For, whatever might happen, if they do not want to be affected by it, they imagine that not even their

5. Calvin preserves Quintin's colloquial Picardy patois, perhaps to dramatize Quintin's haughty and surly attitude. The text reads, *Puy que tu le veu savoir: cha esté my* (*CO* 7, col. 184).

6. Again the patois: *Che ne suis-ie mye: chet Dieu.*

7. The patois: *Ouy, chet ty, chet my, chet Dieu. Car che que ty ou my foisons, chet Dieu qui le foit: et che que Dieu foit, nous le foisons, pourche qu'il est en nous.*

8. *à bride avallée = sans frein.*

9. *empescher.* Literally, "to obstruct," "to impede," "to oppose."

10. *attrapper.*

God does anything prejudicial against them. If anyone suffers from either harm to himself or from a loss of his goods, they scoff at it, saying that all of that is good. And if we should pity such a person, that would be to oppose God. But if anyone so much as hurts their little finger, they forget all of these lofty arguments and overflow with more anger than anyone else.

Let me recount a humorous incident that will serve to illustrate what possible profit their daydreams provide them. There was a certain cobbler in Paris who had been so cajoled by this sect that in his opinion nothing was any longer evil. Now it so happened one day, that, having decided to call upon Étienne de la Forge,[11] with whom he had some acquaintance, he found him sorely vexed because his servant had run off and had stolen his money. But the main cause of de la Forge's sadness lay in his fear that the servant might deceitfully use his credit.

The cobbler asked what he thought he would do. He answered him in three words, as he was a man of few words. My cobbler immediately sprang back, prepared to bound over the clouds, and argued with Étienne de la Forge that he was blaspheming God by calling his works evil and that, since God causes everything,[12] one ought not esteem anything as evil. Étienne de la Forge, knowing that he would gain nothing by reasoning with him or by entering into a dispute, immediately cut off his conversation with him.

Several days later God willed that this cobbler philosopher should be robbed by one of his own servants. Immediately he frantically ran about here and there, seeking some news of his whereabouts. Not finding him, he went to Étienne de la Forge's house in order to unburden his heart[13] and to pour out his complaints.

As he was beginning to hurl strong insults at the thief and was

11. The *Corpus Reformatorum* editors provide the following footnote: "Étienne de la Forge, of Tournai, was a rich merchant of Paris and a great friend and protector of Calvin. He 'held the advancement of the Kingdom of God with the greatest esteem' and printed at his own expense the books of the Bible and distributed them with his alms. He was a victim of the persecution that followed the placard incident and was burned alive at St. John's cemetery at the beginning of 1535 (*Histoire des Martyrs* 1619, p. 113; v. *Hist. eccles.* I. p. 21; Colladon, *Vie de Calvin*, ed. Franklin, p. 18)"—*CO* 7, col. 185, n. 1.

12. *faisoit tout.*

13. Literally, "courage."

already in the process of doing so, Étienne de la Forge interrupted him, saying, "What? Must you blaspheme so? Can we accuse God, since it is God who does everything? Instead we should praise Him."

The poor man,[14] being confounded by his own words which he had used [earlier], went away completely crestfallen,[15] his tail between his legs, and at the same time unreformed by it.

This example teaches us how our Lord confounds these madmen by experience itself, and yet it serves them to no avail as they only continue hardened in their folly, seeing that the devil possesses them and prevents them from seeing what is before their eyes.

Now it should be noted that three accursed consequences follow from this article. The first is that if this is the case there would be no difference whatsoever between God and the devil, as in fact the God whom they invent for us is an idol worse than the devil of hell. The second is that men would no longer have a conscience for abstaining from evil, but like beasts would follow their sensual appetites, without any discretion. The third is that we would be unable to make any judgments, for it would be necessary to find everything good, whether lechery, murder, or stealing,[16] and the worst crimes that we can imagine would have to be viewed as laudable works.

Therefore in order to discredit this view, these three consequences should be treated in succession and reproved by destroying the foundations on which they are mistakenly based.

14. *ce phantastique.*
15. *peneux* = *penaud.*
16. A possible allusion to the excesses at St. Gall.

14

On How We Ought to Understand the Providence of God[1] by Which He Does Everything, and How the Libertines Confound It All When Speaking of It. The First Consequence of the Preceding Article

For our part we do not deny that whatever comes to pass does so by the will of God.[2] In fact when we explain why He is called "all powerful," we attribute to Him a power active in all creatures, teaching that, having created the world, He also governs it, always keeping[3] His hand in the work in order to maintain everything in its true state and to dispose of things as it seems best to Him. To explain more clearly what this means, I believe[4] that we have to consider that God, when it comes to governing the world, works in a threefold manner.[5]

First of all, there is a universal operation[6] by which He guides[7] all creatures according to the condition and propriety which He

1. Calvin's discussion of providence and God's use of the works of the ungodly (*Institutes* 2.16, 17) is pertinent to this chapter.

2. *toutes choses ne se facent par la volonté de Dieu.* Literally, "All things happen only by God's will."

3. *ayant.* Literally, "having."

4. *dis.*

5. *besongne en trois sortes.* Literally, "works in three ways."

6. *une operation universelle.*

7. *conduict.*

had given each when He made them. This guidance[8] is nothing other than what we call "the order of nature." For whereas unbelievers only recognize in the arrangement of the world what their eyes see and thus view nature as a design or essence[9] that rules over all, we are compelled to give this praise to the will of God, as it alone governs and moderates all things.

Consequently, when we see the sun, the moon, and the stars making their course, let us realize that they do so in obedience to God, according to His commandment, and not only that, but that the hand of God guides them, and by virtue of His power are all things done. In the same way, then, when we observe the ordinary course of earthly events, let us be advised to attribute all of it to God and to think of creatures as instruments in His hand for Him to use in His work as it pleases Him.

This universal providence[10] is often touched upon in Scripture for us, to the end that we might glorify God in all His works. In particular the Lord enjoins us to recognize His own power in us in order to strip us of all presumption, which immediately arises in us whenever we fail to remember that we are in His hand.

Along these lines, Saint Paul says to the Athenians, "It is in Him that we live and move and have our being" (Acts 17:28). For herein God admonishes us that we could not last a single minute if He were not upholding us by His hand; for indeed it is in Him that we subsist. And as the soul, spreading its vigor throughout the body, affects the members, in the same way God vivifies us and gives us whatever faculties and power we have.[11]

Nevertheless, this universal operation of God's does not prevent each creature, heavenly or earthly, from having and retaining its own quality and nature and from following its own inclination.

The second way or manner in which God operates in His creatures is that He causes them to serve His goodness, righteousness,[12] and judgment according to His present will to help

8. *conduicte.*

9. *une deesse.*

10. *providence universelle.* This term is used as a synonym for *operation universelle.*

11. Note the analogy between the Aristotelian understanding of the soul as efficient cause and God's role as efficient cause in human life.

12. *iustice.*

His servants, to punish the wicked, and to test[13] the patience of His faithful, or to chastise them in His fatherly kindness.[14]

Accordingly, when it pleases Him to bless us with an abundance of good things, it rains in its season, He gives warmth and good weather through His sun, and He uses all of the other natural means as instruments of His benediction. But when He withdraws His hand, the sky becomes as iron and the earth as fire. So much is this so that it is He who thunders, hails, sleets, and causes storms and sterility.

Consequently, what pagans and the illiterate attribute to fortune we must assign to the providence of God, not simply because of this universal power,[15] of which we have spoken, but because of a special ordinance by which He guides all things in accordance with what He deems to be expedient.

This is what is meant when He says through his prophets (Isa. 45:7; Amos 3:6; Prov. 16:1–4, 9, 33) that He creates darkness and light, that He sends death and life, that good and evil come only by His hand, even going so far as to say that He directs all those other things that seem to be fortuitous. And if anyone is killed accidentally in the process, it is He who is the cause of his death, indeed, has willed it, to the end that we might realize that nothing happens by chance, but only in accordance with His counsel and judgment.[16] And He is sorely angry[17] whenever we think that these things occur by other means or whenever we fail to look up to Him, recognizing Him not only as the principal cause of everything, but also as the author, who by His counsel disposes as He wills.[18]

Therefore, let us adopt this resolution: that prosperity and adversity alike, rain, wind, sleet, hail, good weather, abundance, famine, war, and peace are all works of God's hand; and that creatures who constitute secondary causes[19] are only means by

13. *esprouver = prouver.*

14. paternellement. A hallmark of Calvin's theology is the emphasis he places on God's kindness. See the *Institutes* 2.8.4.

15. *ceste vertu universelle.*

16. *qu'il l'a determiné en son conseil.*

17. *se courrouce amerement.*

18. *ainsi ou ainsi.*

19. *les creatures qui en sont causes inferieures.* Literally, "creatures who form inferior causes." See Calvin's discussion of secondary causes in the *Institutes,* vol. 21 of the Library of Christian Classics, pp. 1643f.

which He fulfills His will; and consequently He commands and uses them as it pleases Him in order to bring them to that end which He has ordained should come to pass.

Furthermore, we should note that not only does He avail Himself of insensible creatures in this way, in order to govern them and to put into effect His will through them, but He also avails Himself of men and even of devils. So much is this so that Satan and evildoers are executors of His will. For example, He used the Egyptians to afflict His people. Later He raised up the Assyrians to chastise them when they had transgressed, and so forth.

As for the devil, we know how He used him to torment Saul (I Sam. 16:14; 18:10), to deceive Ahab (I Kings 22:22), and to carry out His judgments against all the iniquitous whenever that is necessary (Ps. 78:49), or indeed on the contrary to test the faithfulness of his own, as we have in the example of Job.

Now when the Libertines hear these passages, they rush to them heedlessly, and without thinking them through they conclude that creatures no longer act for themselves.[20] For not only do they thoroughly identify heaven and earth together, but also God and the devil.

This is owing to their failure to recognize two exceptions which are essential. The first is that Satan and evildoers are not so effectively[21] the instruments of God that they do not also act in their own behalf. For we must not suppose that God works in[22] an iniquitous man as if he were a stone or a piece of wood, but He uses him as a thinking creature,[23] according to the quality of his nature which He has given him. Thus when we say that God works in evildoers, that does not prevent them from working also in their own behalf.

What the Scripture shows us is as clear as it is wonderful. For at the same time that it declares that God "whistles" (Isa. 5:26), and almost rings the tambourine that makes unbelievers flee their arms, and hardens or inflames their hearts, it also never fails to recount these evildoers' own judgment and will, and it attributes to them the work which they have done by the ordinance of God.

20. *donc ne font plus rien.*
21. *tellement.*
22. *besongne = travaille, opère.*
23. *creature raisonnable.*

The second exception for which these wretches have no regard is the enormous diversity between God's work and that of an evil man's when God makes use of it as an instrument. For the wicked man is motivated either by his avarice, or ambition, or envy, or cruelty to do what he does, and he disregards any other end. Consequently, according to the root which motivates[24] his heart and the end toward which he strives, his work is qualified and with good reason is judged bad.

But God's intention[25] is completely different. For His aim is to exercise His justice for the salvation and preservation of good, to pour out His goodness and grace on His faithful, and to chastise those who need it. Hence that is how we ought to distinguish between God and men; by separating in the same work His justice, His goodness, and His judgment from the evil of both the devil and the ungodly.

Let us pick up a good clear mirror to see what I am saying. When Job received news of the loss of his goods, of the death of his children, and of all those calamities that befell him, he acknowledged that it was God who was visiting him, saying, "The Lord has given me all these and takes them away" (Job 1:21). And in truth, God had. But at the same time did he not know that the devil had deceived him? Was he not aware that the Chaldeans had stolen and plundered his flocks? Did he praise the thieves and brigands, or did he blame the devil for the affliction that God had brought upon him? No! For he knew there was a great difference. Therefore while condemning the evil he said, "Blessed be the name of God" (Job 1:21).

Equally, when David was being tormented by Shimei, he acknowledged it as coming from God (II Sam. 16:11f.) and well understood that this evil man was a rod by which God was chastising him. But later, when praising God, he did not hesitate to condemn Shimei (I Kings 2:9).

We shall come back to this again, but for the moment let it suffice us to see that God truly makes use of[26] His creatures and makes them serve His providence as instruments of which He avails Himself, though they may often be evil. And the fact that God turns the malice of Satan and of wicked men into good is

24. *qui est l'affection.* Literally, "which is the affection."

25. *regard = intention.*

26. *besongne = travaille, opère.*

not in order to excuse or sanctify them, though they might not have transgressed nor their works be evil or damnable. For every work is qualified by the intention of the one who performs it. And hence all who cannot discern this are like swine who uproot everything with their snouts and create a mire out of the most beautiful garden in the world.

Such are the Libertines, who not only make the devil God's companion, but who change him into God, making his works laudable under the pretext that he only does what God has ordained. And this heresy, if we believe the early church fathers,[27] originated with Simon the magician.[28]

On the contrary, we must observe that creatures here below do their works in accordance with their capacity, being judged good or evil based on whether they act in obedience to God or trespass against Him. Nonetheless, God is over all and directs things toward a good end and turns evil into good. Or at least He extracts good from what is evil, working according to His nature, that is, in [accordance with] justice and equity. And He avails Himself of the devil in such a way as not to mix with him or have anything in common with him. Or He envelops Himself in a society of evil, effacing the nature of evil by His righteousness.[29]

For in the same way that the sun shines on carrion and causes it to rot, neither being corrupted nor tainted by it, and by its purity is not the cause of the carrion's stench and infection, God also so truly performs His works through evildoers that His sanctity does not justify them nor does their infection contaminate anything in Him.

The third form of God's operation consists in the fact that He governs His faithful, living and reigning in them by His Holy Spirit. For inasmuch as we are corrupted by original sin, we are like a dry and barren ground that cannot produce any good fruit. For our judgment is perverse; our will is rebellious against God, inclined and given to evil: in sum, our entire nature is vicious.

Being such, not only do we not have the power to apply ourselves to good, but, still more, as Saint Paul says (II Cor. 3:5), we

27. *docteurs.* See Eusebius, *Church History,* p. 113.

28. It was Farel in his letter to Calvin of October 2, 1544, (Herminjard, *Correspondances,* vol. 9, p. 335, no. 1395) who suggested that the Quintinists were "disciples of Simon Magus."

29. *iustice.*

are incapable[30] of conceiving of a single good thought, rather all our sufficiency must come from Him. Consequently, it is He who works in us "both to will and to work" (Phil. 2:13); it is He who illumines us that we might come to His knowledge; it is He who draws us up; it is He who creates new hearts in us, softening our hardness; it is He who inspires us to pray; it is He who gives us the grace and the strength to resist all of Satan's temptations; it is He who causes us to walk in His commandments (Ezek. 36:27).

Nevertheless, we must note the nature of our choice[31] and will. For although they are both depraved by sin, our Lord reforms them and changes them from evil into good. Thus whatever we are able to discern, to will, and to do belongs to a natural gift. But whatever we cannot choose, desire, or but do wrong is the result of the corruption of sin. What we will to do well and have the power to effect comes from the supernatural grace of the Spirit, which regenerates us in a divine life.

That, accordingly, is how God works in His children. For in abolishing their perversity He guides them by His Spirit into His obedience.

Now these giddy people in warbling that God does everything make Him the author of all evil, then later, as if evil had changed nature, since it is covered under the cloak of God's name, they call it good. In doing so they blaspheme God more vilely than if they had transferred His power or justice elsewhere. For insofar as God has nothing more rightly than His goodness, it would be necessary for Him to deny Himself and to change Himself into the devil in order to perform the evil they attribute to Him. In fact their God is an idol, which we must consider more odious than any idol the pagans knew.

But they think that they have washed their hands clean when they reply, "We say that everything is good, since God has done it." As if it were in their power to change black into white! That is how they acquit themselves when, after having called God a brigand, a lecher, and a thief, they add that there is no evil in any of that.

But, lo, hasn't God Himself condemned murder, lechery, and

30. *pas idoines = pas capables.*
31. *election = choix.*

stealing? Hence on this ground we should have to call God a liar in His Word in order to excuse Him in His works.

But the Scripture, they answer, universally declares that God works "all things in all" (I Cor. 12:6). I reply that in this instance they maliciously and falsely apply Scripture. For when Saint Paul uses this phrase, he is speaking only of the gifts[32] of the Holy Spirit. In any event, the passage makes this clear. For it exhorts the Corinthians to make good use of the "gifts" since they are gifts of God. So much is this so, as it declares, that no one can say a word in praise of Jesus Christ unless he speaks by the Holy Spirit, from whom every good proceeds (I Cor. 12:3).

But where can they show that God robs like a thief? or that He murders the innocent like a brigand? Consequently the pretext they use does not purge blasphemy, but rather only redoubles it.

32. *des graces.*

15

On the Second Consequence Which Follows from Saying That God Does Everything, That Is, That One's Conscience Need No Longer Be Concerned About Anything

We have said above[1] that if one attributes everything to God, as the Libertines do, and says that man does nothing, then conscience ceases to be a matter of importance.[2] For this would not keep one from sinning, but rather would curtail[3] the work of God.

Now I do not merely say this because it would undermine[4] their first proposal so that we would no longer be under pressure to dispute if such is the meaning or not, but I only repeat what they themselves confess. In fact, it is the principal end toward which they strive, that is, to put consciences to sleep, in order that without worrying each person can do whatever comes to him and whatever his heart desires. As if God had given His law in vain for discerning between good and evil.

I ask of them if in the law we don't have the declaration of God's will. For there He declares that adultery,[5] stealing, murder,

1. See the end of chapter 13.

2. *il ne sera plus question de faire conscience de rien.* Literally, "It will no longer be a matter of making conscience of anything."

3. *reculler = reculer.*

4. Literally, "destroy."

5. *paillardise.*

and, by consequence, avarice, hatred, envy, ambition, and all similar things displease Him. Hence to say now that to Him these things are pleasing is contradictory. Moses solemnly affirms that the law has been given to us in order to teach us how to serve God, how to cling to Him, and how to obey His will, and how not to provoke His wrath by trespassing against Him (Deut. 4:10).

These wretches incite us to reject all such considerations. And to prevent us from seeing at all, they put this bandage over our eyes: that everything that happens does so by the will of God, and consequently nothing displeases Him. As if God were so changeable as to contradict Himself, or was a simulator when He says that He hates and despises what He wills and desires.

"Because of these things," says Saint Paul, "the wrath of God comes upon unbelievers" (Eph. 5:6). "You have grieved the Holy Spirit," says Isaiah (63:10). "You have transgressed against Me," says the Lord in another passage (Isa. 43:27). Again, "The Lord has poured out His anger upon him and His wrath has enveloped Israel" (Isa. 42:25).

I know quite well that God is not subject to human passions. But all these passages reveal that He reproves evil and condemns it. Consequently, sin is the cause of enmity between Him and us, and we cannot enjoy a covenant with Him when we do evil (Isa. 59:2; Ps. 5:5); rather He will punish us, seeing that He is a just judge who cannot tolerate iniquity.

One hardly sees anything else except these exhortations throughout Scripture: "Fear the Lord." "Beware lest you sin against Him." "Abstain from evil." But these madmen say to the contrary that it is a folly to be afraid of sinning against God, seeing that we do neither good nor evil since He does everything in us.

Saint Paul teaches[6] that even pagans, being without doctrine and without Scripture, have a law printed upon their hearts, which is their conscience, by which they are excused or condemned in the presence of God (Rom. 2:14). These wretches want to efface that, saying that there is nothing in which one can be accused, since God does everything. Ought they not to be ashamed of reversing Scripture, inasmuch as they try so ardently

6. *remonstre = enseigne.*

to deprive the human heart of this persuasion [i.e., the conscience] that God has engraved by nature in us all?

When we want to cite ignorance in an effort to excuse ourselves, God refers us to our conscience, which is sufficient to testify against us. But these frantic people,[7] in suppressing this voice, say that God would first of all have to accuse Himself if He wants to accuse us, seeing that He does everything in us.

Moses calls this "a root bearing poisonous and bitter fruit" (Deut. 29:18), whenever we attempt through flatteries to extinguish[8] all remorse and make believe that evil is only a joke.[9] And in truth, what worse and more deadly poison could there be in the world? He also calls this "adding drunkenness to thirst." And with good reason. For our natural affection is nothing other than an inordinate appetite, aflame to do evil.

Thus when we come to bless ourselves, as he says there, and we make believe that we shall find peace in doing evil, it's as if a strong man should change himself by becoming so drunk that he loses consciousness, instead of preventing such alteration by sobriety and abstinence. It is a perfect passage[10] for warning us against the gall that is hidden under the honey which these wretches offer us.

Nonetheless, they continually maintain this subterfuge: that nothing happens apart from the will of God. To this I reply that concerning our own works,[11] we need to ponder the will of God in accordance with His revelation of it to us. For example, He commands us to look after each other, without wronging or harming anyone.[12] That is His will as clear as it can be! Hence it is unnecessary to inquire further with respect to what pleases Him. For in doing this we know that we shall perform His will. Similarly, we know that the contrary displeases Him.[13] Thus if a man steals and later claims that he has done nothing but the will of God, he lies with impudence, inasmuch as he has acted

7. *phrenetiques.*

8. *assopir = éteindre.*

9. *ieu.*

10. Deuteronomy 29:19–20.

11. *les oeuvres que nous faisons.*

12. The "precept of love" is one of Calvin's favorite principles of interpretation. See the *Institutes* 2.8.55.

13. Calvin frequently defines a virtue by considering what the opposite of a vice would be and vice versa. See the *Institutes* 2.8.8.

contrary to the commandment by which he was taught not to steal.[14]

One might ask if we can ever do anything against God's will. I think not. But the whole of the matter is that we ought not inquire into His providence, which is a secret to us, since we know what He wants of us and what He approves and condemns.

Solomon is not without justification when he says that "he who seeks out too eagerly His majesty will be overwhelmed by His glory" (Prov. 25:27).[15] It is fitting that this should happen and that God should punish in such a way the arrogance of the presumptuous. And we have certainly experienced how those who, desiring to transcend the clouds in their search for God's will, instead of holding to the revelation which contains His will in the Holy Scripture, have fallen into such churlish absurdities that it is a horror to hear them speak of them.

14. *d'icelle.* Literally, "this."
15. The Hebrew of this passage is not clear.

16

On the Third Consequence Which the Libertines Deduce from the View That God Does Everything, That Is, That It Is Not Lawful to Condemn Anything

After they have relaxed the reins on each other for each to do what seems best to him under the pretext of being led by God, they deduce from this same principle that it is wrong to pass judgment. Now they could not have chosen a better doctrine for uncovering their abominations.

Indeed have they scored well when they have so truly bandaged the eyes of their hearers, or rather punctured them, that they are no longer willing to judge whether what they say or what they do is good or bad. But if we grant them this point, then what becomes of God's statement where He curses all "who call evil good" (Isa. 5:20)? That is God pronouncing woe on us if we justify what He finds to be evil.

But on the contrary these Libertines do not want to tolerate our condemning anything. If they were sovereign princes over God, whose function was to give grace to His judgments, that would be something to consider. But who wants to be condemned by God in order to be absolved by Quintin?

Whenever they want to promote this fine idea, they use this statement: "A Christian ought to profit from everything."[1] For as I

1. *qu'un Chrestien doit faire son profit de tout.*

said at the beginning, they never speak plainly enough to explain their intention flat out, but they indirectly circumvent a subject altogether.

Now I freely admit to them that "a Christian ought to profit from everything" in the sense in which the Scripture points this out. That is, in adversity, he should think about what Saint Paul says, that afflictions are sent upon the believer in order to help him conform to the image of Jesus Christ, and thus aid him in salvation, and therein will he be comforted (Rom. 8:29).

If he sees his neighbor fail, let that serve as a mirror to him in order to understand the weakness of human nature to the end that he might walk in greater fear. If it should come about that he himself should fall, let that serve as a warning to him in order that he might denounce his own strength, humble himself, and empty himself of all presumption, and let it spur[2] him to pray to God all the more ardently.

That is how a Christian may profit from everything, not by rejoicing in his evil deeds, nor by closing his eyes lest he see evil, but rather, in seeing that God is offended by himself and others, he becomes sorry and contrite and is taught repentance, humility, the fear of God, and solicitude in order to be on guard in the future.

That is how David profited from the sin which he committed, not by justifying it, but, after having received condemnation, by being confirmed[3] that much more in the goodness of God and by being warned never to fall again into such harm.

That is how Saint Paul admonishes us to profit from the sins which the children of Israel committed against God (I Cor. 10:11). That is, that in considering the punishments which came upon them we might be warned.

Finally, that is the reason why Scripture recalls for us all the sins[4] of both the faithful and the wicked and contemptuous of God. It is not in order to blind us so that we might not know what to say about them or how to define them, or should doubt if evil is good, but to the end that we might recognize evil and shun it. As it also declares to us how we should esteem it.

But the Libertines cite [the passage] where it is written, "Judge

2. *esquillon = aiguillon.*
3. *se conferment = se confirment.*
4. *fautes.*

not." True, our Lord uses these words "Judge not" (Matt. 7:1). But why? In order to reprove the temerity of those who usurp the authority of God by judging things which are not known to them.

This same argument is treated by Saint Paul in Romans 14:10, where he reproves those who want to condemn their brothers in indifferent matters. "We all have one judge," he says. It is to Him that we must render account. And to Him also belongs the function of passing judgment.[5] Consequently, let us not subject our neighbors to our judgment.

This is a sound and useful doctrine, that as there is only one single spiritual lawgiver, viz., God, so He alone is competent to judge our souls. Nevertheless, this is not to say that His judgments, which He has already rendered, are no longer valid. Hence when we judge lechery, larceny, blasphemy, drunkenness, and ambition to be evil things, we are not making a judgment of our own, but are only ratifying what God has rendered.

These riffraff, on the contrary, in pretending not to want to judge, make themselves judges superior to God. I ask of you, if, after a sovereign judge should have pronounced his sentence, an individual should say, "We should leave the matter in doubt, as if nothing had been decided about it, and should not consider the matter that has been condemned as evil," should he not deserve strict punishment as a seditious and mutinous person, who wants to rescind all order of justice?

Now these mad dogs, under the pretext of saying that we ought not to judge, revoke all the decisions[6] that God has made and published and say that all the condemnations that He has ever passed[7] are without effect.[8] Nevertheless, we see how it is not lawful for us to attempt to make judgments on our own,[9] but we should hold as good what God has judged and should ratify it by being in accord with it. Hence in order to testify in His behalf that He is a good and equitable judge, let us condemn with Him all wicked works, and equally, following His admonition, let us judge a tree's goodness or evil according to its fruits.

5. *qu'il appartient d'en determiner.*
6. *arrestz.*
7. *faictes.*
8. *frustratoires = sans effet, vains.*
9. *de nostre teste.*

They further cite this passage: "Hypocrite, first take the dust[10] out of your own eye and then you can take the straw[11] out of your brother's" (Matt. 7:5). But what do they hope to conclude from this? That warning is addressed to hypocrites who only see vices in others while hiding their own. As when He said to the accusers of the adulterous woman, "Whoever among you is without sin, let him cast the first stone at her" (John 8:7).

He does not mean that we ought not to punish malefactors. He only warns that when we reprove others we should begin with ourselves; when we correct offenders, we ought to be innocent of the crimes which we are correcting in them, in order to show that we are led by a true zeal for justice, hating evil in ourselves as much as in others, without excepting anyone.

Now there is a vast difference between not judging out of hypocrisy and not judging at all. Our Lord commands us to judge in truth, not being more severe on our neighbors than we are on ourselves. These scum, under that pretext, want to exclude and eliminate all judgments, however reasonable they might be. However, it does not follow that when a hypocrite reproves another by flattering him that a sinner is herein excused. For evil is always under condemnation. But the hypocrite's vice lies in his not keeping himself under an equal judgment, for while pardoning himself easily he employs an excessive rigor toward others.

Now, as I said at the beginning, it is not without cause that these clowns labor to gain this point, inasmuch as this would make a great starting place for them, once[12] they have persuaded the world that it is not necessary to find anything evil. Besides, it is wise to observe Satan's guile behind this and to remember to what end he strives.

In addition to the sins of our neighbors and the chastisements that God brings against them, we must be all the more warned not to provoke the wrath of God. There is also another matter required: that we ought to deem it evil and feel a sadness in our hearts for God to be transgressed against and for a sinner's soul to fall[13] into perdition. We should have such a zeal for the honor

10. *poultre = pouldre.*
11. *festu = fêtu.*
12. *quand.* Literally, "when."
13. *va.*

of God that when He is offended we feel an anguish burning in our hearts (Ps. 69:10). We should have such an affection for our neighbors that when we see them in danger of ruining themselves, and above all their souls, we should be moved with pity and compassion.

Satan through these wooers[14] would like to render the world stupid, to the end that whatever confusion we might see would no longer matter to us, and we would no longer be upset[15] to see God's name blasphemed, His holy commandments trespassed, souls lost, or iniquity reigning. For in truth these men are scoffers[16] who do nothing but mock at everything that happens, taking nothing to heart, afraid of being killed by melancholy, unless things happen according to their will. But if not, then they forget these grand notions of not condemning [anything], and they become a hundred times more biting and harsher than others. As for those who feed them, they mock them behind their very backs and stick their tongues out at them. For their only pleasure is to have a good time and to be without care.

They have heard of this passage from Solomon: "that a sad spirit dries up bones" (Prov. 17:22). Thus out of fear of becoming downcast,[17] they find it possible to have a good time and to surmount their anger by finding good whatever afflicts and torments God's children. That is how—in finding as much pleasure in evil as in good—they are able "to profit from everything."

Now Saint Paul says that it is the height of iniquity when a man not only performs evil but consents to it by approving of it (Rom. 1:32). That is why, if Saint Paul is to be believed, we must consider these wretches the most desperate in the world, who, not being content to slumber in their evil, overflow to the point of applauding the vices of others.

14. *galons;* the Latin reads, *nebulones,* "idle rascals."
15. *touchez.*
16. *gaudisseurs = bon vivants, railleurs.*
17. *maigres.* Literally, "lean," "skinny."

17

On the Libertines' View of Christ,[1] and How They Acknowledge Him as Their Redeemer

After having forged a God in their image, who is such a portraiture as to hide all their abominations, they forge a Jesus Christ in the same mold, who is not simply like an idol, falsely raised up against the Son of God, but a sack full of villainies and a public receptacle[2] for receiving every kind of filth.

First of all, they create Him out of the Spirit of God which is in us all and from what they call "suppositions [*cuider*],"[3] or the "world." That is the monster they invent for us instead of Him, who being the sole true and natural Son of God, of the same essence as the Father, took on our nature in order to have brotherly union with us.

Lest one think that I am only attributing this to them, two of them were executed at Valenciennes[4] for having said that Jesus Christ was not dead on the cross but only seemed to be.[5] Isn't that a fine beginning: to make Jesus Christ into a phantom about whom one knows nothing?

When they come to speak of His office and of the grace which we have received from Him, it is even worse. For they

1. *Quel est le Christ des Libertines.*

2. *retraict = lieu d'aisances.*

3. *cuider = une croyance, une opinion.* See Calvin's use of this word on p. 234, n. 4, and on p. 264, n. 11.

4. See the letters of Valérand Poullain, Pierre Viret, and William Farel of May 26, Sept. 5, and October 5, 1544, respectively (Herminjard, *Correspondances,* vol. 9, pp. 246ff., no. 1358; pp. 327ff., no. 1392; pp. 341ff., no. 1398).

5. *mais le cuider seulement.*

limit[6] all our redemption to this: that Jesus Christ was only like a model,[7] in whom we should contemplate those things which Scripture requires for our salvation.

It is true that in order to disguise the villainy of their teaching they use a number of high-sounding statements,[8] as they desire to enhance their doctrine's worth. But it all comes down to this: that what Christ has done and suffered is only a farce or a morality play, acted[9] out upon a stage, which represents the mystery of our salvation for us.

For example when they say that Jesus Christ has abolished sin, they mean that Jesus Christ represented this abolition in Himself.[10] When they say that death is vanquished, this is owing to Jesus Christ's having played on the cross the role of one who endured it. In His resurrection, He acted the role of a victorious captain. Moreover, according to their view we are all Christs, and what was done in Him He has performed in us. For as I have said, they make Jesus Christ into an image or a model who represents those things required for our salvation, yet they imagine that what was done in Him has also been done in us.

It is owing to this that Quintin becomes vexed whenever anyone asks him, "How are you doing?" He replies, "How can Jesus Christ not do well?"[11]

In fact, they explain[12] in the above manner[13] the words which the Lord Jesus uttered while dying: "All is finished" (John 19:30). For inasmuch as we are Jesus Christs, it is not necessary for what has already been accomplished[14] in us to be repeated.

In brief, Jesus Christ is nothing but an idol for them which they carry about to the end that they might pretend[15] that they are free[16] of God and of the world and are absolved from doing

6. *constituent.*

7. *patron = modèle.*

8. *belles sentences.*

9. *une moralité iouée.*

10. The French is awkward: *leur sens est, que c'est d'autant que Jesus Christ a representé ceste abolition en sa personne.*

11. This exchange of retorts is expressed in idiomatic French: "'How are you bearing yourself?' To which he replies, 'How is Jesus Christ able to bear evil?'"

12. *exposent = expliquent.*

13. *ainsi.* Literally, "accordingly," "hence."

14. *parfaict = parfait.*

15. *qu'ils se facent a croire.*

16. *quittes = laissés.*

any good. As for having to endure evil, they exempt themselves from it as much as they can. When others suffer afflictions, they appear robust, saying that it is blasphemy to complain or to appear to be feeling anything from it.

For example, I was once present when Quintin said to a very ill man who had only said, "Alas, my God, how ill I feel, help me!" "What are you saying? Is that any way to speak? To say that Christ isn't well? Hasn't all evil passed away in Him? Is He not in glory with His Father? Is this then all you have learned?"[17]

But when God tests them, they are completely surprised to discover in themselves men different from the Son of God, or at least surprised not to find in themselves this idol which they have forged in the air. As in the case of one who was tried[18] at Cologne,[19] who said while weeping, "Why must I still suffer, since 'all is finished'?"

That is how they profit from transforming the nature of things through their foul daydreams. And no doubt the Son of God avenges Himself of the harm they do Him by usurping His name and mocking Him in such a way.

As for ourselves, since we are warned that in their taking of Christ's name they maliciously profane it in order to make it serve their abominations, let us not be moved thereby when we hear them pronounce [it], except to view their sacrilege with the greatest horror.

17. Again Calvin has Quintin speak in patois: *Vore dia? est che bien parlé chela? de dire que Christ se porte mal? tou le ma n'est y mye passé en ly? n'est y mye en le gloire de sen pere? est che la tou che que vous avez aprin?* (*CO* 7, col. 199).

18. *un l'esté passé.*

19. Proponents of the Radical Reformation were tried, tortured, and executed in Cologne as early as 1529. See Williams, *Radical Reformation*, pp. 361f.

18

Wherein Is Shown the Significance with Which the Libertines Hold the Word *Regeneration*, and on the Contrary What It Means According to the Truth of Scripture[1]

They confess with us that we cannot become children of God unless, first of all, we are reborn. And on the surface it would seem advisable to hear them speak so that we should form a common accord. For they use the authentic words wonderfully well in order to magnify regeneration.

In fact, who can be offended when we hear these words resounding in their mouth: "If we are of God, then our old man should be crucified in us, the old Adam should die, our flesh should be mortified, the world should be destroyed, and sin should no longer reign in us"? For this is the pure teaching of Scripture and the principal point of the Christian life, so much so that with regard to these words we can only repeat them, as the angels of heaven do not speak any better. For God Himself has taught us to speak accordingly.

But when it comes to explaining[2] them, what they want these

1. The *Institutes* 3.3.1–14 is pertinent to Calvin's discussion of regeneration and repentance. Many themes in this present chapter (such as the need for self-denial as a part of repentance, the believer's continual warfare against sin, the persistence of sin in a believer's life in spite of the cessation of its reign, and the gospel's constitution of repentance and forgiveness) are later incorporated in the 1550 and 1559 editions of the *Institutes.* See the superscript letters in the *Institutes,* vol. 21 of the Library of Christian Classics, and the translator's explanation (p. xxiv).

2. *deschiffrer = raconter, exposer, faire connaître.*

words to mean corrupts everything. For they begin to disgorge their stinking and detestable blasphemies in order to overturn—I won't say all fear of God and holiness of life—but all uprightness,[3] which was even inviolable among pagans. And together they relax the reins on each other and permit[4] each other to prostitute themselves in every form of churlish concupiscence.

Now the principle they hold is this: that regeneration is to return to that innocent state which Adam enjoyed before he sinned. And in their view this innocent state sees neither white nor black,[5] because Adam's sin was to eat of the fruit of the *knowledge of good and evil.* Hence to mortify the old Adam means to cease having to make judgments, as if one had knowledge of evil but like a child lets himself be led by his natural sense.

They even interpret this innocence in light of the passages where childlikeness is recommended to us.[6] As if God's Spirit, in commanding us to become like children, did not at the same time mean this—not in the sense of having to resemble them—but in the sense of being gentle, sincere, and innocent (I Cor. 14:20). As if, furthermore, He did not exhort us to believe in Christ until we attain "mature manhood" (Eph. 4:13f.). As if it were not required of us to abound in spiritual prudence (Matt. 10:16). As if He did not warn us that we ought not walk heedlessly, but rather should understand "what the will of God is" (Eph. 5:17).

What clearer exposition could we want for censuring the impudence of these wicked persons in their bold attempt to falsify[7] Scripture? Hence let us return to their principal theme.

If they see a man who has scruples about[8] doing evil, they say, "O Adam, are you still about? Hasn't the old man been crucified in you yet?"[9] If they see a man who is afraid of the judgment of God, they say, "Still savoring the taste of the apple? Be careful

3. *honnesteté.*

4. *donner congé = donner permission.*

5. *ne voir goutte entre le blanc et le noir.* Calvin's point is that innocence transcends good and evil. See n. 11 below.

6. See p. 167, n. 34, and p. 170, n. 49.

7. *depraver = détourner du vrai sens.*

8. *qui face difficulté.*

9. Again the patois: *O Adam, . . . tu y voy encoire. l'Anchien homme n'et nyen encoire cruchifié en ty.*

that the morsel doesn't strangle your throat!"[10] If a man is displeased when he thinks of his sins and becomes contrite, they say that sin reigns in him and that he is being held captive by the senses of his flesh.

In order that one might more easily understand their villainy, it should be noted that for them "sin," "the world," "the flesh," and "the old man" are nothing more than what they call "distinctions" (*cuider*).[11] Hence, insofar as one no longer needs to make distinctions (*cuide*), one no longer sins in their view. Now under the word "distinctions" (*cuider*) they include all remorse of conscience and all scruples: in brief, all consciousness[12] that a man has of the judgment of God.

That is, I say, the great regeneration that one learns in their school: no longer to be touched in their hearts by anything whatsoever, but to live for pleasure without difficulty. And those who are no longer troubled by sin are called "new creatures," because they have been delivered from having to make distinctions,[13] and hence sin is no longer in them. That is what constitutes for them the entire benefit of the redemption accomplished in Jesus Christ: that He has destroyed this need to make distinctions[14] which entered the world through Adam's guilt.

When this need to make distinctions[15] is abolished, then in their view there is no longer any devil or world. For they have no other enemy to torment them than the devil. From which it appears that they will be in good company with Satan and the powers of hell, since they are [supposedly] no longer troubled by them.

Now God's Spirit speaks to us of a different sort of regeneration altogether. It is true that when we were without Scripture, human reason was sufficient enough. Now I do not mean that reason which is condemned as folly because of our blindness

10. The patois: *Tu sens, . . . encoire le gou de la pumme. Vuarde bien que che morcheau ne t'estranle le gosié.*

11. "Distinctions" or "suppositions" in the sense of having to make conscious acts of moral discernment. The use of *cuider* in this and subsequent passages is central to understanding what Calvin means by the term. *Cuider* properly means "belief," "opinion."

12. *sentiment.*

13. *cuider.*

14. *cuider.*

15. *cuider.*

owing to sin. But I mean that intelligence[16] that God implanted naturally in our hearts in order to render unbelievers inexcusable and to deny them every pretense of ignorance. This natural intelligence,[17] which is like an edict engraved in us by the hand of God, suggests and shows us quite well that the holy and virtuous life, which everyone confesses to be the fruit of Christian regeneration, does not ignore good and evil, but rather discerns between them in order to keep itself pure of all iniquity and to have a good conscience before God and to bear a good testimony in its works before men. That is the natural intelligence[18] that God gave from the very beginning to all pagans, as Saint Paul says (Rom. 2:15).

Scripture itself even more clearly teaches us what the state of the regenerate is. It is not one which makes us irresponsible[19] so that we might follow without discretion whatever we want to do, but on the contrary it makes us more vigilant than ever and makes us proceed with greater prudence and thoughtfulness than before. For it admonishes us that our enemy, the devil, is always nearby, prowling about for some prey (I Peter 5:8). Consequently we must always be watchful, afraid that he might surprise us; and we must resist his temptations (Eph. 6:12). Similarly, we must continually wage war against our flesh and those vicious concupiscences that lure us toward evil (Gal. 5:17), and resist the sin that dwells within us.

Nor is its[20] purpose to put us to sleep in order that we might be free of any further remorse or unhappiness over our sins. For the Scripture says that the righteous[21] accuse themselves, and it pronounces the man happy indeed whose heart is afraid, who remembers in meekness[22] the judgment of God, in order to humble and to take himself in hand (Prov. 28:14).

But still to have a brief and clear definition of it all, the teaching of the Scripture emphasizes[23] that regeneration consists in

16. *le sens.*

17. *le sens donc naturel.*

18. *le sens naturel.*

19. *nonchallans.*

20. "Its" refers to the state of the regenerate.

21. *iuste.*

22. *reduisant en memoire.* See Calvin's emphasis on the place of fear in the work of repentance (*Institutes* 3.3.7).

23. *est.*

repentance.[24] For repentance, properly speaking, is nothing other than our denying ourselves[25] in order to become new creatures who live according to God. Now everyone knows whether that implies living it up without worrying about anything by changing the names of things, or whether it means forcing our heart[26] away from its natural inclination and redirecting it toward the obedience of God, blaming ourselves for all our evil affections.

But in order to avoid longwindedness, to which out of necessity I would willingly give myself in order to discuss this material at length, I shall produce only a few scriptural passages that are so clear that even the least learned[27] will be able to understand and see with his eye that this word "regeneration," as misused by these wretches, is as contrary to true Christian regeneration as fire is to water.

In the first place, instead of what they babble about the Christian man being led by his affection without seeing sin again, Saint Paul exhorts all Christians to mortify their earthly members, i.e., as he also explains as their evil concupiscences, such as lechery,[28] avarice, ambition, and the like (Col. 3:5ff.). In order to make them fearful, he refers them to the judgment of God, saying that His wrath comes upon the rebellious for such things. He commands them to be renewed day by day, denying the old man (Eph. 4:23). He admonishes that they must walk soberly as children of light. He warns them not to be deceived by flattering words (Eph. 5:6ff.). He instructs them to walk in their calling "in fear and trembling" (Phil. 2:12; Eph. 4:1). He humbles them by reminding them that they are "not called to impurity,[29] but to holiness" (I Thess. 4:7).

These exhortations are as common in Scripture as anything else, to turn us away from evil and to do good. In fact, as I have said, what did our Lord command His apostles to preach except repentance and remission of sins[30] (Luke 24:47)? And this not

24. *penitence.* See Calvin's definition of repentance in the *Institutes* 3.3.5.

25. *de renoncer nous mesmes.* See Calvin's discussion of self-denial and repentance (*Institutes* 3.3.8).

26. *couraige = courage.*

27. *nul si idiot.*

28. *paillardise.*

29. *immondicité = impureté.*

30. *penitence et remission des pechez.* Calvin believes these two themes sum up the gospel (see the *Institutes* 3.3.1).

simply for a day or at the outset but until the end.[31] Consequently, Saint Paul, wishing to affirm that he has duly fulfilled his office, says that he has not ceased to teach both, as much among the Jews as among the Gentiles (Acts 20:21).

For this reason all who want to hold to the pure truth of God are advised to continue for the rest of their life in this doctrine of repentance,[32] which implies, as Saint Paul points out, that by virtue of God's Spirit and by His grace we should mortify "the works of the flesh" (Rom. 8:13), that sin should no longer reign in us (Rom. 6:14ff.), that we should be transformed in our understanding and own heart in order to be reformed[33] in the obedience of God, keeping ourselves from the defilements and corruptions of the world, in order to fulfill[34] our calling.

As for that "perfect innocence" which the Libertines imagine, pretending that the regenerate man is exempt and free[35] of all sin and that regeneration is like an angelic condition which man cannot help but attain,[36] if that were the case, what would become of the prayer that our Lord has taught us to pray: that it is God who forgives our sins? That is not said for the ungodly. But all who comprise the children of God must pray in that way, according to Jesus Christ's model (Matt. 6:12). [And] this prayer contains the affirmation[37] that all believers[38] are sinners. Whoever does not wish to be of this rank excludes himself from the number of God's children.

In order to cite a specific example, could we name a mortal man as perfect as Saint Paul, or of a holiness as excellent? Now he confesses that throughout his life he always had to battle against the sin that indwelled him, and being held back by his weakness, he did not do the good he willed to do. And in the end as a final conclusion he writes, "Wretched man, who will deliver me from this body of death?" (Rom. 7:18, 24). In so doing he indicates that there is no other means of being put into a state of perfection and of being rescued from the bondage of sin except

31. Calvin makes the same point in the *Institutes* 3.3.8.
32. *penitence.*
33. *reduictz.* Can mean "transformed," "subdued," "converted."
34. *nous entretenir.*
35. *pur.*
36. *ne puisse mal faire.*
37. *une protestation.*
38. *fideles.* Calvin emphasizes this in the *Institutes* 3.3.10, 11.

in departing from his body, where he was held captive as in a prison (II Cor. 5:6, 8; Phil. 1:23).

It is true that these mockers in altering[39] what Saint Paul discusses there have a term, saying that when they are reprimanded for their evil actions, this isn't their fault, but the fault of others.[40] Now although this is not in agreement with what they say about the perfect state of Christians, and although there is an obvious repugnance in their thesis, nevertheless it is still a detestable and villainous blasphemy to make such a shield out of this "fault of others" in order to absolve themselves of evil.

For when Saint Paul says, "It is not I who do evil, but sin that indwells me," he does so not in order to justify himself or in order to throw off the guilt of his sins by laughing at them, but he simply wants to point out that his principal affection should be his complete conformity to the will of God. And at the same time, if there is anything [more] to be said, it is not that he should become addicted to evil, but owing to the weakness of his flesh, he is so hampered that he cannot serve God as fully as he would like. According with what he later says, that those who are God's children ought to be led by His Spirit to the end that they cease to walk according to the flesh (Rom. 8:2).

Now certainly sin indwells the children of God as long as they live in this world, but it does not reign in them.[41] True, they are hampered and troubled by their flesh, but they do not pursue it in order to become vanquished by it. In any case, after Saint Paul said that he did not consent to evil, he nevertheless considered himself unfortunate for being its captive. What is more, he presents himself to us as a living image of the state of the regenerate, saying that it is as if the believer's life is divided into two parts: that is, inasmuch as he is reformed by God's grace, he concurs with the good; but owing to the fact that he still possesses relics of his nature, he feels a contradiction. So much is this so that his flesh, i.e., that part of him which still indwells him and which has not yet been reformed by God, pushes him in the wrong direction.

If we ask the source of this contradiction, he provides as his reason that the law is spiritual, that is, it requires a perfect holiness

39. *depravant = alterant.*
40. *"c'est baudet."*
41. Calvin strongly emphasizes this in the *Institutes* 3.3.10, 11.

and a pure and whole conscience, but we, on the contrary, are carnal (Rom. 7:14).

Hence let us accept what he concludes, which is that all believers during this life should obey the law of God in that they are renewed by His grace, but according to the flesh they are subject to sin. Hence Christian perfection, to put it in three words, is to have a sincere[42] affection to serve God, to be free of a double heart, and to possess a genuine openness,[43] so much so that one can affirm that his principal desire is to please God. Nevertheless, as Saint Augustine says,[44] the greatest perfection is to acknowledge and confess how imperfect one is and to confess without end one's weaknesses to God.

These fantastic people, however, to support their error arm themselves with this verse of Saint John's: "Let him who is born of God sin no more" (I John 3:9).[45] Now I readily concede that if there should be found a totally regenerated man, then there would not be any sin in him. But the point is to know whether regeneration has ever been perfected in a mortal life. I say that since the creation of the world not a single example has appeared.[46]

Thus Saint John's words mean nothing other than that insofar as man is regenerated by God, he no longer sins. But inasmuch as that only partially occurs, so long as we live in this world, let us not fret that we have not yet come to the end of that road on which we travel.[47]

Someone might reply that this advice seems to be contradictory, that is, to interpret Saint John's words in this way. And indeed it does appear that in context[48] Saint John's intention is different. To this I reply that Saint John does mean to signify that once a man is regenerate, sin no longer reigns. For the grace of God's Spirit ought to be superior to subdue carnal affection.

42. *sans feintise = sans hypocrisie.*

43. *une rondeur entiere.*

44. See *The City of God* 22. Cited in *CO* 7, col. 205, n. 2.

45. The Loists used this text similarly. See Williams, *Radical Reformation,* p. 352.

46. Calvin discusses the illusion of perfection in the *Institutes* 3.3.14.

47. *ne songeons point que nous soyons ia venus au but, ou nous sommes en chemin.*

48. *par la procedure.* The *Corpus Reformatorum* editors note that the Latin reads thus: *ex ipso contextu,* "from the context itself."

Nevertheless we must always come back to this point, that a man is free of the bondage of sin according to the measure of grace which he has received, which is more in some and less in others. But this measure is never full in anyone, whoever he might be.

In fact Saint John's task is only to expound this, which is sufficiently declared when he commands us all to pray for the forgiveness of our sins, saying that "if anyone believes that he is without sin, he deceives himself, and makes God a liar" (I John 1:8, 10).[49]

What I have said ought indeed to be sufficient to show what the true regeneration of the children of God involves, what their perfection in this world entails, and how contrary are all the daydreams of these wretches. For Scripture teaches us about both.[50] But whereas the Libertines base a believer's holiness on a churlish ignorance, pretending that the innocent state consists in governing oneself according to one's appetite, and that man is thus perfect when he has forgotten the judgment of God and no longer worries about good or evil, as long as everything happens according to His will, the Scripture thoroughly[51] repudiates this [view].

49. See p. 269, n. 45.
50. i.e., regeneration and perfection.
51. *bien.*

19

On Christian Liberty. How the Libertines Interpret[1] It and What on the Contrary the Scripture Means by It

Following this fine renewal which they invent for us, they next extend Christian liberty to include[2] everything lawful for man, without any exceptions. In fact, since man has been changed[3] into a beast, why shouldn't he be permitted to follow his sensual affection? Though we hold other beasts in check, or chain them up, or shut them up! But these fiends give man full liberty[4] so that nothing may hinder him or prevent him from having a good time.

Now to begin with, since according to the Scripture we have been set free from the curse[5] of the law in order that we might no longer be subject to that horrible sentence where it declares that God will punish all transgressors, these frantic people[6] without any distinction abolish all the law, saying that it is no longer necessary to keep it, since we have been set free from it.

I shall explain this point yet more easily. There are two things to consider in the law. That is to say, the teaching, which is the rule for right living.[7] For therein our Lord shows us what pleases

1. *prennent.* See Calvin's discussion of Christian freedom in the *Institutes* 3.19.1–16. Also relevant is Calvin's discussion of the law in 2.7.1–12.
2. *pour faire.*
3. *converty.*
4. *la bride sur le col* = *la bride sur le cou.*
5. *malediction.*
6. *phrenetiques.*
7. *bien vivre.* See the *Institutes* 2.7.1, 12.

Him and what He approves.[8] Hence the doctrine of the law exists to show us how our life ought to conform to the will of God.

The second point is its rigor,[9] since it declares to us that whoever fails in a single point will be cursed, and it promises salvation only to those who perfectly observe its commandments. As long as this rigor is in force, we are entirely bereft of the hope of life and are under the condemnation that the law announces. For there has never been found a single mortal man who has acquitted himself with respect to what it requires.

Hence if the law with its appendages has authority over us, then everyone is without hope. For to satisfy its requirements is impossible. Nor can its condemnation be avoided. For this reason, the only remedy that remains is to be set free from such a bondage. This deliverance is given to us in the gospel when it is said to us that we are no longer under the law.[10]

Now the dispute is this: that these frantic people understand by these words that the law has been so truly abolished that we no longer need to regard what it teaches but can let it sleep like a doctrine that has nothing to do with us.

Now there is no doubt that God's intention and the sense of Scripture are totally different from this. That is to say, the doctrine remains in effect[11] in order to guide in the right direction; only the curse is removed in such a way that[12] in spite of our weakness we do not cease to be pleasing to God, who does not cease[13] to accept the service which we render Him, although it is imperfect, inasmuch as He forgives us the shortcoming that is in us.

For Saint Paul, after having dealt with Christian liberty quite well in his letter to the Romans, and having said that we are free and absolved from the subjection of the law, nevertheless still leads us back to this doctrine, teaching that it is fitting for us to observe it. How then do we square these views: that the law no

8. See the *Institutes* 2.7.12.

9. See the *Institutes* 2.7.4, 6.

10. See Galatians 3:25; 4:4–7.

11. *demeure en son estat.*

12. *en sorte que* = *à la façon de.*

13. *et ne laisse.* The reading of the emended text of 1611 is preferred: *qui ne laisse* (*CO* 7, col. 207, n. 2).

longer holds us in bondage, yet its doctrine still remains in effect for governing our life?

We clearly see that this liberty only has to do with the law's curse or its rigor. Such is the way Paul treats it in his letter to the Galatians. For after intensively exhorting believers to stand fast in their liberty,[14] he immediately afterward commands them to observe love,[15] since it is the "fulfillment of the law" (Gal. 5:1, 13). In brief, there is not a letter in which he does not refer believers to the law[16] as a rule for right living, to which they must conform themselves. And if there should be nothing but this admonition, which he gives us in Galatians, [i.e.] not to abuse our liberty in order to overflow with carnal license, that would already be a sufficient enough restriction to check the impudence of these dogs who accordingly reject every yoke, giving themselves permission to live without law or rules.

Saint Peter makes the same remonstrance to us when he says that the spiritual liberty which the Lord Jesus has acquired for us must not become "a pretext for evil" [I Peter 2:16]. Now how can that be done, except by being delivered from the rigor of the law, in order not to be cursed by it before God, we live at the same time in accordance with it. For it does not cease to be a good and salutary doctrine, although[17] it no longer exercises such severity on us as it does the ungodly.

That is the fine beginning with which the Libertines treat Christian liberty.

Consequently the Scripture shows us that the ancient ceremonies have been abolished and that hence we are no longer required to observe them (Col. 2:16) and in general that our consciences are not restrained by external things, but rather they are entirely under our subjection; hence one cannot impose external things upon us as being necessary. [But] these giddy people hold to the doctrine in general as if it applied to everything, even to matters which our Lord requires of us strictly and without which no holiness or integrity of life can exist.

For a clearer explanation, we shall look at[18] the passages of

14. *de se maintenir en leur liberté.*

15. *de garder charité.* A reference to the "precept of love" principle of interpretation. See the *Institutes* 2.8.55.

16. *la.* Literally, "there."

17. *ia soit que = quoique.*

18. *prendrons.*

Scripture which they distort in their turning them to suit their fantasy. Saint Paul says that "all things are lawful" for him (I Cor. 6:12; 10:23). Now anyone of sound reason understands in what way. Moreover, the context of the passage shows this clearly. For it is referring to external matters: as whether to eat meat that has been consecrated to idols, seeing that idols are a matter of superstition. Although that is immaterial, Saint Paul says that it is lawful for him, but its usage should be subject to the rule of edification.

These demoniacs turn this into a general statement, holding this pretext that nothing is forbidden a Christian man. As if Saint Paul meant that it was lawful to commit adultery,[19] to rob, and to murder.[20] But what? Although they mock at all of Scripture whenever they please, they seem here to be dwelling upon its words. They say that the word "all" excludes nothing. But it would be proper to keep in mind the subject which he treats, not wander beyond it.

Saint Paul discusses there a matter which is neither good nor bad in itself, but only in its consequence. After having taught how he abstained from what was lawful and permitted by God for him to do in order to avoid any scandal, after having furthermore shown how the action which was in question involved great scandal, he offers his conclusion: saying that it is not a matter of what is lawful, but of what is expedient, indeed, for the edification of our brothers.

These wild beasts want to infer from this that everything without exception is lawful for us. But we must not be astonished by this impudence, inasmuch as they are not ashamed to cite along similar lines[21] what Paul later said: "Do not Barnabas and I have the right[22] to take along our wives?" (I Cor. 9:5).

They are, I say, so shameless in their use of this passage as a shield in order to eliminate any distinction between good and evil. But of what is Saint Paul speaking? It isn't of things which God has forbidden. It's of marriage which God permits and

19. *de paillarder.*

20. A possible allusion to the radical excesses at St. Gall. See Williams, *Radical Reformation,* pp. 127–134. See also Heinold Fast, "Die Sonderstellung der Täufer in St. Gallen und Appenzell," pp. 223–240. Kessler's *Sabbata* points out a unique murder (in *Schriften des Vereins für Reformationsgeschichte,* p. 51).

21. *à ce mesme propos.*

22. *puissance.*

approves of in any case. Saint Paul glories in not having used this right, or at least in not having brought his wife with him on the journeys which he was making, for fear that this might have impeded him. Even if he had done that, he would have done nothing wrong. But he voluntarily gave up that right, lest he support anyone's weakness.

Isn't it then a cock-and-bull story[23] to tear out this passage in order to prove that everything is permissible[24] to a Christian man and that nothing is forbidden him? These examples should suffice to warn readers how these riffraff impudently defame the Scripture in order to make it serve as a coverup for their diabolical liberty, which they attempt to advance.

They also cover under the cloak of this liberty the deception of consenting to every form of impiety and idolatry. For they permit a man to genuflect before an idol, to carry candles, to make pilgrimages, to sing Masses, and to go along with all the abominations of the papists,[25] even though he mocks them in his heart. If one replies to them that we ought to glorify God in our bodies (I Cor. 6:20), that we ought to confess Jesus Christ before men, that we ought to affirm our faith before the world (Matt. 10:32), instead of replying they simply put forward this shield of liberty.

Now because I have amply written of this matter in another tract,[26] I would rather refer readers to it than delay myself any longer at this point. At all events, this single warning is alone necessary to confound their impudence, that with regard to matters which God has commanded us or forbidden us to do, we are without liberty to change anything. For the necessity of those things[27] is inviolable. Other matters are immaterial and are within our liberty, but upon condition that we should always take care to use them for the purpose of edification.[28]

23. *saulté du cocq à l'asne.*

24. *bon.*

25. This could be an allusion to Nicodemism.

26. An allusion to his *Petite traite monstrant que c'est que doit faire un homme fidele connaissant la verite de l'Evangile: quand il est entre les papistes* (1543) (*CO* 6, cols. 537–588). *CO* 7 (col. 209, n. 2) adds that the allusion might also be to his *Excuse aux Nicodemites* (*CO* 6, cols. 589–614).

27. *y.*

28. See the *Institutes* 1.14.3 where Calvin develops his argument against speculative theology in favor of material that strengthens consciences and teaches "true, sure, and profitable" things.

20

On What the Libertines Understand by the Vocation[1] of Believers, and How Under This Guise They Excuse Every Form of Villainy

Saint Paul admonishes us that each person should continue in the vocation wherein he is called [I Cor. 7:17, 20, 24]. Now the word "vocation" signifies all kinds of living or estates which God has established and founded in His Word. For the Scripture, above all, wants us to have a recommendation concerning it, [viz.] to order our life not by choosing such a manner of work[2] as seems good to us, but by adopting[3] what God approves and by holding ourselves within the limits of His Word.

Thus the apostle's intention is that each should serve God in the estate in which he is called and should be content with it; that he should not desire to change; that he should not meddle in another person's calling;[4] and that he should not regret doing his own duty. For he was speaking of the estate of marriage and of virginity and by chance of other things as well. And with respect to it he concludes that each person ought to continue in his state and rank,[5] providing of course that it is a legitimate vocation.

These wretches [however] overturn this passage in order to

1. *vocation.* Calvin discusses the calling of believers in many places in the *Institutes:* 2.2.21; 3.6.2; 3.10.6; 3.14.19; 3.23.13; 3.24.10–11; 4.16–19 passim.

2. *faire.*

3. *suyvant.*

4. *office.*

5. *qualité.*

make it possible[6] for each person to follow the inclination of his own nature and to work and live according to what advances his profit or pleases his heart.[7] Although this proverb might be common in the world—"it is necessary to do as others do"[8]—nevertheless, even those who do, do not attempt to say that what they did was right, but they use the excuse, such as it is, in order to minimize their faults. These wretches [however] not only excuse iniquity by admitting that "to do as others do" is to be led astray by companions, but they also adorn it with the honorable title of "vocation," as if God were calling us to it.

Now we must note that this article contains three diabolical points. The first is that there is not a single manner of living in the world which they do not regard as good, in spite of the fact that God might condemn it in His Word.

For example, the papal priest[hood] is good in their view, and according to their fantasy a canon or another malefice[9] ought to continue in his calumny, devouring the offerings made to idols, nourishing himself on sacrileges, singing Masses, and doing similar things, for that's his calling! A monk must remain in his cloister, like a hog in its trough, for that's his calling! Which explains why Quintin, assisting one time at a cardinal's solemn Mass, said that he had seen the glory of God.

And not only under this guise do they approve of all these vocations,[10] which are repugnant to the truth of Scripture, but also of those which pagans condemn by their natural reason. Let a pimp, they say, do his job! Let a thief rob boldly! For it is right for everyone to pursue his calling. If anyone replies to the contrary how villainous these matters are, and that nature itself teaches us to regard them with horror, they respond that it is enough for everyone "to remain in his calling."[11]

Now we have already shown the means for overcoming[12] this

6. *faire trouver bon.*

7. *qu'il luy viendra a point pour son profit, ou que son cueur le portera.*

8. *qu'il faut uller avec les loups.* Literally, "It is necessary to howl with wolves." See the discussion of Calvin's use of proverbial wisdom in *Calvin's Commentary on Seneca's De Clementia,* ed. Ford Lewis Battles and A. M. Hugo, vol. 3 of the Renaissance Text Series (Leiden: E. J. Brill, 1969), pp. 100–104.

9. An apparent parody of "benefice." Also contains shades of Nicodemism.

10. *ces estatz.*

11. *que chacun doit vivre en sa vocation.* An obvious parody of I Corinthians 7:17, 20, 24.

12. *redarguer = convaincre de faute.*

blasphemy, which is to consider what God calls us to do and to take as a vocation any estate which He prizes and holds as legitimate. Any manner of life which does not have the support[13] of His will consider as not only uncertain and perilous but as an erroneous course, like one that a man has taken when he wanders off his road and does not know where he is going. Furthermore, whatever is repugnant to the Word of God can be taken as reproved by it and held as a certain roadway to hell.

The second point is that in all of the abuses and corruptions that reign in all the estates of the world there is no evil. We know today that the world is so depraved that in all estates, even in those that are legitimate, there are so many bad incidents[14] that it is a pity. Not because these estates cease to be good and legitimate, but because vices are not corrected.

For example, the nobility is full of vanity, of excessive pomp, of pride, of licentiousness and insolence, of blasphemy, and of ambition. Justice is full of favors, of avarice, of tricks, and even from time to time of fleecing people.[15] Merchandising is full of lies, of crooked deals, of perjury, of deceptions, and of rapine and cruelty. In brief, there is no vocation in which a great deal of abuse is not committed.

These great theologians[16] do not want anyone to distinguish between the pure ordinance of God and the corruption that results from the human side, but they want *everything* to pass under the title of "vocation." Hence according to their theology if a gentleman is insolent or indulges in adultery,[17] if he abandons himself to pomp and vanity, if he wraps himself in every form of folly, there is nothing to criticize. For his calling supports[18] it. Why? Because one governs oneself according to the world. As if the customs of men changed God's justice!

If an officer of justice sells the right[19] for hard cash, if he supports one person in order to wrong another, if he suppresses a good cause in order to favor one that is wrong, there is nothing

13. *tesmoignage.*
14. *accidents.*
15. *escorcherie = lieu ou l'on écorche.*
16. *bons docteurs.*
17. *dissolu en paillardise.*
18. *porte.* Literally, "carries," or perhaps, "includes."
19. *le droit.*

at fault. For it is right for everyone to pursue the train of his calling.

If merchants destroy the world through monopolies, if they counterfeit and disguise their merchandise, if they tell lies every hour in order to cheat and outwit, if they rob and devour anyone they can entrap, let it pass![20] For to speak out would be to blaspheme his calling from God.[21]

What are we to think, I beg of you, when such a detestable view is uttered by the mouth of a man, or by a man who is so beyond his senses that he dares to advance such absurd and villainous things? Nevertheless, they glorify in it as if it were some profound subtlety.

The third point is that every inclination in man, whether it is natural or a bad habit,[22] is a calling of God. As in the case of a man who is inclined toward drunkenness, it is not lawful to reprimand him for it. For that is his calling. If by nature someone is fond of playing, let it pass. For it is improper to deprive[23] him of his calling. In brief, they want each person to be governed by his own desires and for man's heart to be the master of his calling, according to where it leads him.

From this source the most villainous debauchery[24] which anyone has ever heard mentioned in the world has gone out. For they permit a man and a woman to unite with each other[25] in whatever form seems good to them. They call it a "spiritual marriage"[26] when anyone is content with the other. Hence if a man takes no pleasure in his wife, in their view he may provide for himself elsewhere to solve his problem. At the same time, lest the woman remain destitute, they also grant her permission to meet her need[27] and to accept it wherever it is offered to her.

If anyone asks, "What, then, will become of marriages that are held indissoluble, if it is lawful to retract them at will?" They reply that a marriage that has been contracted and solemnized

20. *que nul n'en parle.*
21. *la vocation de Dieu.*
22. *de mauvaise coustume.*
23. *retiter.*
24. *macquerelage = débauche.*
25. *s'accoupler.* Can also mean "to copulate."
26. See the relevant discussion of this subject on pp. 170–171.
27. *de chercher condition.*

before men is carnal, unless it contains a spirit of mutual compatibility.[28] For that reason the Christian man is not bound by it unless both are content with each other, which alone ought to be [the norm] held among Christians.

But even at that, this union is not permanent. For if, the day after tomorrow, a bawd should become angry with her pimp, she can make an exchange, provided he can offer her someone new who pleases her better.[29] Similarly, a philander can flirt about in order to acquire new "spiritual wives" and take them as he finds them. And they are so impudent as to cover such a villainy under the pretext of "calling," since they interpret it, as I have said, as following the inclination of the heart.

Now let everyone consider whether anything in the world will remain safe any longer. What order, loyalty, integrity, or assurance will remain if marriage, which is the holiest covenant and the one which ought to be the most faithfully kept, can be thus repudiated? For marriage, I say, as God instituted it (Gen. 2:24) and blessed it, transcends all natural unions, and should even be preferred to the union between a father and his son. Marriage, as Jesus Christ has promised, is indissoluble (Matt. 19:6). Marriage is consecrated in the name of God and is hence founded on His authority. Marriage is called a "divine covenant" by Solomon (Prov. 2:17) and is compared by Saint Paul to the spiritual union which we have with our Lord Jesus (Eph. 5:32). Must it not be that the devil surely possesses them when they dare to make such an enormous confusion as to jumble sky and earth together?

As for what they say about a marriage being carnal when a man's heart is not given to his wife or when a wife does not relish her husband, is it not an exceedingly villainous impudence to mock as they do a promise solemnly made in the name of God in the presence of the church?

As for what they say about a Christian man being no longer under obligation, I ask in what sense, then, was our Lord speaking when He said, "What God has joined together, let man

28. *bonne convenance.*

29. *Car du iour au lendemain, si une paillarde se fache de son rufien, elle peut faire eschange, s'il s'en offre quelque nouveau, lequel luy plaise mieux.*

not separate" (Matt. 19:6)? For He was not speaking[30] in that instance of this detestable pollution of "spiritual marriage."[31]

I ask in what sense does Saint Paul exhort husbands to love their wives and command both to persevere through life together until death (Eph. 5:25; Col. 3:19)? And if any dissension should come about, he forbids the wife to remarry again. And whereas these riffraff say that whenever the wife is angry with her husband, a marriage is carnal and consequently without valor, Paul commands the wife, whenever there is any problem or difference between them, to be reconciled to her husband (I Cor. 7:11).

But [the Libertines allege that] it is written that when God made man "He made them male and female" (Gen. 1:27); hence it only remains to choose, since we are all one body. As if it were in vain that the Scripture says that "the two shall become one flesh"! It does not say "three" or "four," but only "two," adding that "man shall leave his father and mother and cleave unto his wife" (Gen. 2:24; Mark 10:7). As if our Lord gave His law in vain when He forbids the coveting of another's wife (Exod. 20:14, 17)! As if He had condemned without purpose adulterers and lechers! As if Saint Paul had spoken in vain when he exhorts every man to be content with his wife (I Cor. 7:2)!

For this reason, in the same way that I have shown above that this wretched sect has a license to commit every form of brigandage and murder against the body, to steal, pillage, and plunder the goods of others, as being so much prey, we also see at the present how it constitutes an opening for defiling every bed and home, exterminating every form of chastity in the world.[32]

30. *nouvelle.*

31. See p. 279, n. 26.

32. It is possible that the Libertine view of marriage as Calvin depicts it is a highly distorted form of Bernhard Rothmann's position, stated in his *Restitution rechter und gesunden christlichen Lehre* (1534). E. C. Neff reports that Rothmann's *Restitution* "proclaims that a man has the liberty of having more than one wife; this teaching is based in part on the Old Testament example and the creation, in part on the idea that a man should be allowed to express himself with a good conscience!" ("Rothmann," in *Mennonite Encyclopedia,* vol. 4, p. 368). Rothmann (c. 1495–1535) was a Münsterite.

21

On the Fellowship of Believers According to the Fantasy of the Libertines

We have already seen how these wretches profane marriage, mingling men and women like dumb animals according to the lusts[1] that drive them. And how, under the name of "spiritual marriage," they disguise this churlish corruption, labeling[2] as a "spiritual movement" that wild impetuosity that goads and inflames a man like a bull and a woman like a dog in heat.

Now in order not to leave any order among men, they create a similar confusion with respect to goods, saying that the communion of saints exists where no one possesses anything of his own but each may take whatever he is able to get.[3] At the beginning, there were indeed a few giddy Anabaptists[4] who spoke like

1. *leur concupiscence.*

2. *appellant.*

3. *où il en pourra avoir.* This phrase could also be translated as "he will be able to have," or "he will be permitted to have," or "he will have power to have." The first two translations would bring Calvin's interpretation closer to the Swiss Brethren's view (see n. 4). But Calvin is attacking the radical form of this position and obviously intends the last interpretation. Note 18 (p. 285) cites a sentence where the context favors the interpretation, "whatever he is able to get."

4. It is helpful to keep in mind that Calvin has focused on the most radical of possible positions (see n. 3). Michael Sattler held a modified view: "Of all the brothers and sisters of this congregation none shall have anything of his own, but rather, as the Christians in the time of the apostles held all in common, and especially stored up a common fund, from which aid can be given to the poor, according as each will have need, and as in the apostles' time permit no brother to be in need" ("Congregational Order," in *The Legacy of Michael Sattler,* ed. John H. Yoder, p. 45). Yoder explains that Sattler's view does not represent "total communism." Ulrich Stadler (d. 1540), a Hutterite, espoused a more radical view

this. But because such an absurdity was repudiated by everyone as repugnant to human intelligence, so much so that even the first authors[5] were ashamed of it, these Libertines have held it as a kind of refuge,[6] since their sect is a cesspool,[7] or a sewer,[8] for receiving all the world's dung.

It is true that on the surface they have a good pretext in complaining about the avarice of those who are called Christians, since we see each so truly in pursuit of gain that the majority are generally like insatiable pits[9] or greedy beasts. In fact, there is no doubt that our Lord permits and almost relaxes the reins on Satan in order to give birth[10] to such furious persons who attempt thus to put goods in common[11] in order to punish the ingratitude of those who abuse them—which is to say almost everyone.

---

of communism. See *Cherished Instructions on Sin, Excommunication, and the Community of Goods* (1537), in *Spiritual and Anabaptist Writers*, ed. Williams and Mergal, p. 278.

Bernhard Rothmann, a Münsterite, taught a still more radical sharing of goods (see *Bekenntnis von beiden Sakramenten* [1533]), which he based on the *Chronica* of Sebastian Franck (1499–1543). Rothmann's program led to a community where the sharing of goods and wives was compulsory (he took nine wives). Its consequences were tragic for those involved and maligned Anabaptists in general (see *Mennonite Encyclopedia*, vol. 1, pp. 659f.).

5. Michael Sattler actually denounces the libertinism and excesses of "some false brothers" in his cover letter to *The Schleitheim Confession* (Yoder, *Sattler*, pp. 35–36). However, neither Sattler nor Stadler softened his views, nor did the Hutterites mitigate their position. Some Swiss Brethren rejected the Hutterite program and favored a more moderate view, especially Conrad Grebel (c. 1498–1526), George Blaurock (1492–1529), and Balthasar Hubmaier (1480?–1528). In his *Gespräch auf Meister Zwinglis Taufbüchlein* (1526) Hubmaier explains, "Concerning community of goods I have always taught that a man should have a concern for the other man, that the hungry be fed, the thirsty receive drink, etc. For we are not the masters of our possessions but stewards and distributors only. No one would say, take away what a man has and make it common. Rather he would say, let the coat go together with the mantle . . ." (quoted in *Mennonite Encyclopedia*, vol. 1, p. 659).

6. *refuge = échappatoire.* Can mean "loop-hole," or "hedge."

7. *retraict.*

8. *esgout.*

9. *gouffres.*

10. *susciter = faire naître.*

11. *à mettre ainsi les biens en proye.* Literally, "to put in this way goods in prey [prize or booty]." This could refer to the Anabaptist-Libertine practice under attack or to the practice of Christian hypocrites.

We know how those who possess goods devour them all alone, or hold on to them tightly, without having pity on their poor brothers in order to provide for their indigence by sharing with them what they have in their hand. We do not want to hear the remonstrances that God makes to us in their behalf. It is right, then, that the devil should stir the coals of hell in order to double the disorder which we do not correct, concerning which God admonishes us.

For this reason it is necessary to begin at this point that we might know what attitude[12] our Lord wants us to have with respect to goods, what the legitimate means are for acquiring them, and in what their right and lawful usage consists.

Hence the first point is that we should not desire the world's goods through covetousness; that if we are in poverty we should bear it patiently; if we have riches, we should not put our heart or confidence in them; that we should be ready to give them up when that seems good to God; that, having them or not having them, we should mistrust them as fading things, esteeming more the blessing of God than the entire world and seeking the spiritual kingdom of Jesus Christ, without enveloping ourselves in wicked lusts.

The second point is that we should work with integrity[13] in order to gain our life; that we should accept the gain that comes to us as coming from God's hand, not using evil means in order to take away another's goods, but serving our neighbors in good conscience; that we should enjoy the *profit of our labor as a just salary;*[14] that in *buying and selling* we should not employ fraud, deceitful tricks, or lies, but we should go briskly about our business with honesty, in the same way that we require it of others.

12. *affection.*

13. *honnestement.*

14. Calvin seems to espouse this more as a norm than he does the radical form of the community of goods. E. C. Neff cites the following passage from Rothmann's *Restitution:* "We have not only made all our possessions common by placing them into the hands of the deacons, but are also ready to promote one another with service of all kinds. All that has served selfishness and possession, *buying and selling, working for money, income* and interest, misusing our neighbors by fattening ourselves by their labor, etc., has been completely done away ("Rothmann," in *Mennonite Encyclopedia,* vol. 4, p. 367). Note the italicized words in both Calvin's and Rothmann's texts.

The third point is that whoever has hardly anything should thank God and eat his bread with contentment; that whoever has a great deal should not misuse it by squandering it, or by being intemperate or sumptuous, or by [acquiring] superfluous things out of pride and vanity. Rather by using it moderately he should employ the property that has been given to him in order to help and to provide for his neighbors, seeing himself as God's steward[15] who possesses the goods he has on condition that he must one day render an account, continually keeping in mind the comparison which Saint Paul makes between the world's goods and manna (II Cor. 8:15), that is, that whoever has a great quantity of it should only take enough to eat so that whoever has hardly enough might not be in want.

In brief, as Jesus Christ has given Himself to us, we too out of charity should share with our neighbors the benefits[16] which He has given us, contributing by this means to their indigence, inasmuch as in doing so we help them. That is how we should proceed and that is the means we should use.

But because we do not do this, let us acknowledge that it is a just vengeance on God's part that these madmen should thus appear to overthrow all order, wanting to eliminate all differences of property,[17] turning all the world into a brigand's forest, where without counting or paying each takes on his own what he is able to get.[18]

Now there are so many scriptural references that reprove this villainous confusion that if I wanted to recite them all there would be no end to the matter. Thus let us be content that our Lord does not command us to give up[19] everything or that whoever has goods must abandon[20] them, but simply exhorts us to use them well. He does not forbid human contracts and

15. *recepveur* = *receveur.* Literally, "receiver," "collector."

16. *les graces.*

17. *toute distinction de biens.*

18. *chacun prenne comme sien ce qu'il pourra avoir.* Again, Calvin either did not want to dignify the Anabaptist position or knew of gross abuses among the Libertines that justified his repugnance for and caricature of their position. See pp. 282–283, nn. 4, 5.

19. *de quitter.*

20. *placque* = *plaque.* In this and the subsequent sentence Calvin rejects the political theology of the sixth article of *The Schleitheim Confession.*

political means which men use among themselves in order to gain their life, but only redirects them toward justice and truth.

It would be, then, a superfluous exercise to cite here many references concerning this subject, since the entire Scripture is so clear on the matter that no one can be ignorant of the subject. But these frantic people, in order to cover up their error, cite what the monks have alleged in order to prove that their estate was perfect and angelic, i.e., they cite what our Lord said to the young man who had asked Him what he must do in order to enter the kingdom of God: "Go and sell all that you have, and give it to the poor, and follow Me" (Matt. 19:21).

But the solution is simple. For our Lord in that passage is not proclaiming a general statement that is applicable to everyone, but only to the person with whom He is speaking. For inasmuch as he thought himself to be acquitted before God by observing all the commandments of the law, and thereby had deceived himself in hypocrisy, our Lord uncovers for him his hidden malady. For he was rich and had his heart on his goods[21] and did not recognize that that was a vice. Hence our Lord reproached him for his vice[22] to the end that he might recognize his fault[23] and stop boasting that from his childhood he had fulfilled all the commandments of the law. Which in reality[24] was a long time! Hence it is sheer folly[25] to extract a universal doctrine from a passage that was meant to test the heart of a particular man.[26]

Furthermore, it is quite right for each of us to be ready not simply "to sell" but "to loose" what we have for the honor of God. And let those who have an abundance of goods in hand be at the same time poor in heart. But we know quite well that the actuality of having to sell one's goods is not required of all whom our Lord instructs in Christian perfection, that is to say, that they cannot be Christians unless they rid themselves of all their goods.

21. *son affection à ses biens.*

22. *gratter sur sa ronge = reprocher son vice.*

23. *mal.*

24. *dequoy = la realité,* as opposed to hope.

25. *une lourde sottise.*

26. A reference to Aristotelian logic, which permits one to argue from the universal to the particular (subalternation) but not the converse. See Aristotle's *Analytica Posteriora* 1.4, 24. Quirinus Breen describes Calvin's use of Aristotelian and medieval logic in "John Calvin and the Rhetorical Tradition," *Church History* 26, no. 1 (1957): 3–21.

They[27] also cite[28] what is written in Acts 4:32ff., that "none of the disciples said that what he had was his own, but all brought their substance to the feet of the apostles. Even those who had fields and possessions sold them in order to make money to provide for the indigence of the poor." This is certainly a fine illustration, provided it is applied well. And would to God that there were today such an affection of charity in all those who are called Christians. Then everyone would be provided what is necessary, and the goods which God gives us would be distributed in a better way than they presently are. But these fools imagine it to mean something other than Luke intended to say. For this reason, in order not to fall into this illusion with which they deceive themselves and trouble the world, let us be advised as to what Saint Luke means by "the distribution of goods"[29] when he says that "no one called what he possessed his own."

It is a manner of speaking common to all languages to say, when referring to a generous man, that he has "nothing of his own," since he always has an open hand in order to assist those in need. By an even stronger reason, when you have a company of friends of such a sound accord that one does not wish to fail another in need, but each is ready to help his neighbor, one could say that these people have "nothing of their own." And this would be true though each should hold onto his house, enjoy his goods, and retain the management of his possessions and natural riches,[30] without any of it being placed in such a pile of confusion. Such was the fellowship of believers[31] of which Saint Luke speaks. Each retained his household goods and governed them by himself. But they had such a fellowship[32] that none suffered indigence.

Now, as I have said, this is a true mirror of Christian love[33] and indeed one with which we ought to bring ourselves into conformity. And would to God that Quintin and his accomplices could be put again under such a reformation! I would not oppose them.

27. The "they" are "these frantic people," who could be either Anabaptists or Libertines.

28. *ont.*

29. *communication.*

30. *de sa chevance.*

31. *la congregation des fideles.*

32. *fraternité.*

33. *la dilection Chrestienne.*

But this is not what they seek to do nor what they aspire to. Their goal is to put everything into confusion. For they insist on this point: that no one may have anything of his own. And in place of accepting the explanation which I have made, they reply that it is written next[34] that "those who had possessions sold them." Thus according to their fantasy no one can be a Christian unless he lays aside everything he has.

To this I reply that they are doubly mistaken. First of all, Saint Luke does not say that *everyone*[35] sold [his possessions]. And as for those who did sell, he does not say that they sold *everything* without leaving themselves something.

Now lest anyone allege that I am inventing a solution out of my head, I beg of you, is it very likely that if everyone had sold [his possessions], Saint Luke would have only given us two examples, of whom one was even a hypocrite who wanted to deceive God? [Rather] he mentions Barnabas,[36] who sold a field truly out of a sincere affection. The second he mentions did it for vainglory and only brought part of the proceeds. Are we to believe that among the six thousand believers or thereabouts who were present then, that all who had possessions[37] sold them, and that Saint Luke only produced one as an example?

In the second place I reply that even the believers who sold their possessions at that time in order to aid their poor brothers did not so effectively sell everything as to have had nothing left. For each did not cease owning his house, or feeding his family, or using the goods which God had given him.

In any case, it is said afterwards that Tabitha, a woman who excelled others in the excellence of charity, gave great alms (Acts 9:36).[38] Whence could she have made them, if she had given up all her goods? It is said that Saint Peter lodged at the home of Simon the tanner (Acts 10:6). This could not have been possible, if Simon had not had a house and a family. The same holds true for what is said next of Mary, John [Mark]'s mother, i.e., that Saint Peter, being miraculously delivered from the prison by the

34. *qu'il ensuit apres.* Literally, "that it follows next."

35. Italics for emphasis.

36. *Ioses Cyprien.* See Acts 4:36.

37. *heritaiges.*

38. One should note that the examples Calvin cites are taken from the Acts of the Apostles, the very book that had in part inspired the concept of the community of goods which Calvin is seeking to refute.

angel, went into her house (Acts 12:12). The same for Lydia (Acts 16:15). For after being converted to Jesus Christ, she not only lodged the apostles once, but after they were released from prison, they returned to her house.

These people of whom I speak were the most perfect[39] among the Christians. Nevertheless, they did not practice[40] a confused "community of goods" among themselves. But it would be a superfluous matter and [would require] far too much time to collect all the specific examples in order to show that when the believers brought[41] their goods together they did not mix into a pile[42] what they had, but each retaining what was his in his own hands, they distributed them according as demand necessitated.[43]

Hence we have [here] the general doctrine, with which it is always best to stop in order to be on the safe side. Only I shall produce one more specific example, and then we shall arrive at the conclusion, which follows from this general doctrine, which is the true rule by which we ought to measure everything else.

There is Philemon, whom Saint Paul rightly calls his companion in arms in the work of the Lord and whom he praises because of his faith and excellent love, known by all, toward God and toward all the saints [v. 5]. Nevertheless, he continues to possess not only his estate and his household goods but also his serfs and servants, who in those days were like slaves. For they were not servants whom one hires, but one owned them in order to be served by them all one's life, or in order to sell them and transfer them. Hence it would have been something quite strange for a master to have considered his servants, along with the rest of his goods, as anything more than natural possessions.[44]

Now Saint Paul does not require him whatsoever to cast this

39. Possibly an attack against the Anabaptists' belief that their movement best represented the primitive apostolic community's virtuous ethics and call to be perfect. See Frank Littell, *Origins of Sectarian Protestantism,* pp. 46–78. The Swiss Brethren also rejected the more radical Hutterite view. See p. 283, n. 5.

40. *il n'y avoit point.* Literally, "There was not."

41. *communiquant.*

42. *ne mesloyent point en confus.*

43. *l'exigence de la necessité.*

44. Literally, "This was hence a thing indeed more strange, that a master should enjoy such a condition of his serfs than to retain the rest of his goods as natural riches or possessions."

aside, but he begs him to receive Onesimus his serf, who had fled from him. If a man, who is like a mirror of perfection for others, enjoyed his possessions in good conscience in this way and is approved by Saint Paul for doing so, who will dare impose a completely different law on Christians?

Let us come to the general[45] doctrine wherein lies the true solution.[46] Saint Paul does not teach Timothy to require[47] the world's rich to give up everything, but only not to be puffed up, not to put their hope in corruptible riches, and to be rich in good works (I Tim. 6:17). He [Paul] does not require masters to dismiss their slaves but only to treat them reasonably and with humanity (Eph. 6:9; Col. 4:1). He does not forbid any more buying or selling but only that we not outwit or cheat our neighbors when buying or selling (I Thess. 4:6). For example, "Let those who buy be as those not buying" (I Cor. 7:30). He does not require the renunciation of property, but only that it be possessed as not being possessed. Finally, when speaking of alms, he does not require us to toss everything into a heap[48] in order that each might take out what he needs, but says that each should give according to the devotion of his heart (II Cor. 9:7): "not reluctantly or out of necessity, but out of a free and generous heart"; not that he who has goods should ruin himself in order to supply others, but in order to provide for his neighbor's want out of his abundance. Those are the very words of Paul. What more can we ask?

Thus let us learn to participate with decency and order[49] in the fellowship which believers exercise concerning goods, and consequently to reject and hold in abomination this diabolical delusion of wanting to heap all goods into a pile in order to introduce not only a labyrinth into the world but a terrible brigandage, as we can conceive it and would be able more clearly to see from experience.

As for Saint Luke's passages cited above, it appears that they

45. *commun.*

46. *decision.*

47. *commande.*

48. *en un tas.* Literally, "heap," "pile."

49. *ordre et police.* Perhaps Calvin has in mind Geneva's hospital and the manner in which "procurators" and "hospitallers" were elected to care for the needs of the indigent and the sick. See *Draft Ecclesiastical Ordinances* (1541), in *Theological Treatises,* trans. J. K. S. Reid (London: SCM, 1954), vol. 22 of the Library of Christian Classics, pp. 64–66.

no more serve these fantastics than they do monks who want to feather their own nests in order to found their lovely communities of swine, such as we find in their cloisters. I neglect to say that their charity does not extend as far. For they hardly make their own condition worse in order to do good to others. Rather they are content to divest themselves in order to seize the goods of others. The only thing they understand is to give nothing to others.

For this reason I am wont to call them "theologians of passive charity,"[50] since they allow one to do as much good for them as one can. And still when one has done everything, they are never content but murmur continually. But when it comes to giving [in return], try to find the person who does! That isn't part of their understanding.[51] And they are so far from being able to teach "active charity" by example that one would never be able to learn it from them. In fact what they would teach would only point out the affection from which they operate.

I shall not pursue the matter beyond this point. I am satisfied with having shown how the doctrine in itself is wicked and damnable.

50. *docteurs de la charité passive.* See Calvin's attacks against monks in the *Institutes* 4.14.8–16.

51. Literally, "This cannot enter into their understanding."

22

On the Libertines' View of the Resurrection[1]

Saint Paul makes mention of Philetus and Hymenaeus (II Tim. 2:17f.), who were already saying in their time that "the resurrection is past," saying that this position is a wicked heresy that overturns faith. Nevertheless these dogs, in the face of such a clear statement, continue to maintain this detestable error. For they scorn all our hope of being raised, saying that what we await has already occurred.

If we ask them how, it is [owing to the fact] that man knows that his soul is nothing other than immortal spirit which is always living in heaven, and that Jesus Christ in His death has abolished the need to make judgments between good and evil,[2] and has thereby restored[3] us to life, which means to know that we shall not die.

That is how these wretches, along with their predecessors Hymenaeus and Philetus, overturn the principal foundation of our faith, without which the gospel, as Saint Paul says (I Cor. 15:14), would consist of nothing. For outside the resurrection, what will continue our life? And to reduce it [i.e., the resurrection] to such an idea[4] would indeed be to eliminate it by destroying its truth.

Now it is certainly true that "whoever believes never dies, but has passed from death to life" (John 11:26; 5:24), that he is no longer under condemnation, nor does death reign any more, because the Spirit that raised Christ resides in him and is an

1. *De la resurrection que tiennent les Libertines.* Cf. Calvin's tract *Against the Anabaptists,* chapter 6, "On the state of the soul."

2. *le cuider.* See p. 234, n. 4, p. 263, n. 5, and p. 264, n. 11.

3. *restitué.* See pp. 296–297, n. 15.

4. *une telle imagination.*

immortal seed in him. But from this it does not follow that the beatitude which we await has already been revealed, that we are enjoying it, and that we have entered into the actual possession of our inheritance.

But it is important to note the passage of Scripture with which they dazzle the eyes of the simple in order to believe that they have been raised. Solomon, speaking on death in his Ecclesiastes, says that "the spirit of man will return to God who made it, while the body will return to the earth from whence it came" (Eccles. 12:7). From this they conclude that the spirit is reunited with the essence of God, so much so that only a single spirit lives on.

But whom are they trying to persuade by such an interpretation: that the human soul upon returning to God becomes God? Our Lord Jesus when dying clearly said, "Father, I commend My spirit into Your hands" (Luke 23:46). Saint Stephen also made a similar prayer: "Lord Jesus, receive my spirit" (Acts 7:59). But far from favoring their error, these passages suffice to conquer them, purely and plainly. For they expressly point out that God receives our souls into His keeping and preserves them until the time that they shall be reunited with their bodies.

If we ask in what condition and estate He holds them, it is shown to us clearly enough from other passages that He gives them joy and consolation, causes them to rest from all their miseries, and satisfies them with His blessings. That is [what it teaches] with respect to souls.

As for our bodies, Saint Paul, desiring to magnify the benefits[5] which we have received through Jesus Christ, says that "we are members of the household of God, citizens of His kingdom with the saints, seated in heavenly places" (Eph. 2.19). And in another passage (Col. 3:1) he says that "we are raised with Him." But they forget to speak of the end [of the passage] where he adds that "we are citizens of paradise, already having our residence there, in truth by hope" [Eph. 2:19, 22].

Hence everything that is said about the present happiness of Christians we must regard[6] as something which God assuredly gives them in their hearts, but we must not understand it as something which they already hold, or whose effects they see.

5. *les graces.*
6. *rapportez.*

For it is fitting that what Saint Paul says elsewhere should be true: "that our salvation is still hidden, since our hope is based on things that are absent and yet to come" (Col. 3:3). Again, "that in appearance we are dead, and our life will not be manifested until Jesus Christ comes in judgment" [v. 4].

Thus we are confident of everything that God promises us. But we still await it.

As Saint John says, "Indeed we know that we are children of God, but this has not yet appeared" (I John 3:2). For this reason it is said that we carry the decree of life in our hearts, "while God's Spirit testifies to us that we are children of God" (II Cor. 1:22; Rom. 8:16; Eph. 1:14). As for what Saint Paul says about our being raised, it is not in reference to the glorious life which has been promised us—and hence does not mean that we are already enjoying it—but only refers to regeneration, as the context seems to indicate.

Thus what are we to say? Nothing else, unless it is that in denying the world we should aspire to a heavenly life, meditating on the kingdom of God and seeking only to conform ourselves to His will.

And how can that possibly destroy the hope of the resurrection which God has given us? Is it likely that Saint Paul wanted to turn us away from it? He who condemns overtly as heretics those who held such a view? Or does he do so in order to speak to us of the novelty[7] of life? Certainly not! That is too impudent to attribute to him.

Therefore let us realize that as God has elected us and adopted us as His children before the creation of the world (Eph. 1:4), so also He confirms in us the testimony of our adoption through His gospel, and even partially[8] introduces us into our inheritance, but only through hope. And so long as we live in this world we are like strangers, who anticipate that the blessings which we have been promised will be revealed to us in effect and that we shall see face to face what we now behold in a mirror and in dim figures, as Saint Paul says (I Cor. 13:12). "We are away from God," as he says in another passage (II Cor. 5:7), inasmuch as "we walk by faith and not by sight" and actual joy.

Hence we labor, hoping for rest after death. We battle, hoping

7. *nouveauté.*
8. *aucunement.*

later to receive the fruit of our victory. We suffer, while awaiting our joy and consolation.

In brief, inasmuch as we should be the most unhappy people in the world if our hope were confined to this present life (I Cor. 15:19f.), we hope in this highest happiness which transcends human understanding, in this happy life indeed into which our Lord Jesus has entered in order to guide us when our time comes.[9] At the same time we believe what is said by Saint Paul, that "when this earthly house is destroyed, we shall have an eternal house in the heavens" (II Cor. 5:1f.). We also know that that is where the gospel calls us. That is why we long to leave this prison in order to be with the Lord. We know that being in His presence we shall have true contentment and fruition of all that is best.[10]

Furthermore, insofar as the Scripture constantly directs us toward this last day, in which it promises that Jesus Christ will come to judge the world, our highest hope also lies in it. For even though the souls of believers, which are currently separated from their bodies, live with God and abide in the happy joy of His kingdom, nevertheless both the glory and the perfect happiness of all the children of God are different with the second coming of Christ. So much is this so that Abel, Noah, Abraham, and all the ancient fathers await us, "not having received their crowns, in order that we might be crowned together" (Heb. 11:40).

Hence it is imperative that the understanding of believers should be entirely pinned on this day and that their hearts should cling to it. For as we see, the Scripture is full of such exhortations. What then do these wretches want to say, who deny[11] us the principal point of our Christianity? The Scripture cries loud and clear (Luke 21:28) that if we want to contemplate our salvation, then we should lift up our hearts to the last day. These dogs yelp that such is in vain and that we are already raised, without there being any further resurrection.

The references are so clear that nothing more [is needed] to show that our bodies, which are presently corruptible and subject to every form of weakness, will be raised in glorious

9. *en nostre ordre.*

10. *biens.*

11. *ostent.* Literally, "take away from."

immortality, and that equally those of unbelievers will be raised in perpetual ignominy (John 5:29). If there were no resurrection for us, says Saint Paul (I Cor. 15:14, 17), it would follow that Jesus Christ is not raised, that the gospel is only a lie, and that our faith is empty.[12]

In a similar way the following doctrine is continually reiterated: that the Lord Jesus will then come in majesty with His angels in order to call the children of God into their full possession of their heavenly inheritance, and to send the wicked into hell in order to separate the goats from the sheep so that He might fulfill in His members the work of redemption which He has accomplished (Matt. 25:31).[13]

These swine, on the contrary, uproot this entire doctrine with their snouts, saying that nothing else remains once the need to make judgments between good and evil[14] has been abolished. Thus it is sufficient for the spirit, upon leaving the body, to return to God. For that, in their view, constitutes its proper place and perfection.

By this we see that they achieve with equal perversity what they began. For in the same way that they confuse God with the devil when they speak of the creation of men and of all God's works, so also when it comes to the *restitution*[15] of everything,

12. *la foy est aneantie.*

13. Although not to be associated with the Libertines' eschatological position under attack in this chapter, Hofmann, Rothmann, and Jakob Hutter (d. 1536) all held chiliastic views. Hofmann was imprisoned for a decade (1533–1543) in Strassburg, overlapping the time that Pocquet, Perceval, and Bertrand of Moulins were staying at Bucer's home there, and that Calvin was sojourning in Strassburg. See Williams, *Radical Reformation,* p. 599. For more details, see *Mennonite Encyclopedia,* vol. 2, pp. 782–784, 851–853; vol. 4, pp. 367–370. See n. 15.

14. *le cuider.*

15. *restitution.* Italics for emphasis. The term "restitution" was associated by sixteenth-century Anabaptists with the restoration of the church to its original state from which it had fallen during the time of Constantine (A.D. 313). Williams notes that the idea was so widespread among the Anabaptists that it "may be said to be one of the marks of the Radical Reformation" (*Radical Reformation,* pp. 375ff.). In Williams's view Evangelical Anabaptists (Stadler, Hubmaier, Sattler) stressed the restoration of the ancient church, whereas the Spiritualists emphasized the future and sought to shape it. Rothmann represented the second trend. In his *Restitution* (1534) he identified a series of falls and restorations, seeing the final restoration as having begun with Erasmus and Luther and to climax in John Beukels's theocracy at Münster.

Several sources discuss the concept of restitution more thoroughly: Littell,

they completely overturn what is said in the Scripture concerning the hope of our salvation, leaving us nothing but the present life, in order to pass on and then cease to be.[16]

For this reason, being aware of this detestable blasphemy, let us live in the hope which God gives us so clearly and so certainly throughout Scripture. And that is that the Lord Jesus will appear in the heavens *in His time,*[17] and that those who have died beforehand, whose bodies have rotted in the ground, will all be raised at the sound of the trumpet, i.e., by the voice of the archangel who will accompany them at the judgment, and that those who are still alive will be changed in an instant, and that all of them together, being resuscitated, will come before the judge in order to present themselves before His majesty (I Thess. 4:16f.; I Cor. 15:51). Then, at that time, the children of God will receive the reward of their hope, and the beatitude which they presently await will be revealed to them. They will see it fully, I say, face to face; whereas it is currently hidden to the human senses. Then, at that time, we shall enter into the possession of our inheritance, which is promised to us in the gospel [Matt. 25:21, 23, 34]. At that time we shall enjoy full happiness, whereas we are currently in misery. Then we shall be with God and we shall see God such as He is, whereas we currently know Him only by faith. Then our bodies, which are presently subject to corruption and putrefaction, will be transfigured into the glory of our Lord Jesus.

Hence let us think of our resurrection to come as conforming to His.[18] That is, that as He was raised in immortality, so also we should not doubt that when the time comes the same will be done in us as in His members. And let us be assured, according to the testimony of the apostle (Heb. 11.40), that all the holy fathers and prophets and other believers are awaiting us, not having yet received the crown of glory which God has prepared

Origins, pp. 50ff.; Frank J. Wray, "The Anabaptist Doctrine of Restitution of the Church," pp. 186–196; *Mennonite Encyclopedia,* vol. 4, pp. 302–304. The *Mennonite Encyclopedia* lists the sixteenth-century theologians who used the term either to advance the concept or to refute it. The term is derived from Acts 3:21, "the restoration of all things," translated in the Vulgate as *restitutio omnium.*

16. *puis n'estre rien.*

17. Italics for emphasis. This section refutes a spiritualized eschatology.

18. *en la sienne.*

for them, in order that we might all receive it together. And not only that, but also that all creatures unite in company with us, as Saint Paul says (Rom. 8:19ff.), "longing for the day of our redemption," in order to be returned to their original state[19] and to be delivered from their present bondage because of our sins.

Hence we all the better perceive how insane these miserable people are, since they have less understanding than dumb animals, or even than rocks, I say, and blocks of wood. Therein let us understand what it means to be made reprobate,[20] and let us learn to fear the judgment of God.[21]

19. *premier estate.*
20. *mis en sense reprouve.*
21. A thorough rejection of the Libertine notion of *cuider.*

23

Wherein What Has Been Said About Both the Style and the False and Damnable Impiety of the Libertines Is Almost Demonstrated to the Letter[1] in a Certain Cock-and-Bull Story by Monsieur Anthony Pocquet, One of the Proponents of the Sect

Since the things which I have inferred above (concerning both the detestable errors of the Quintinists and the cunning with which they obscure under disguised words the venom of their wicked and pernicious doctrine) can be much better understood when seen through examples, I have decided to inform the reader more amply by inserting here the ramblings of Monsieur Anthony Pocquet, the little priest of whom I spoke at the beginning, adding a few admonitions to alert the simple of things of which they might not possibly be able to warn themselves. I call these ramblings a "cock and bull story" because the proposals treated within it are maintained in any event as goat dung,[2] as each will be able to see.

Now it should be noted that his ramblings are a sort of enticement for the purpose of attracting the uneducated. For he does not expose the great mysteries which they are accustomed to sharing[3] only with those who have already come to them to be instructed in their school. But as I said earlier, in the same way that monks, hoping to allure a poor simple novice, take care not

1. *au doigt.*
2. *crottes de chievres.* Literally, "filth or dung of goats."
3. *d'entamer.*

to reveal to him the secrets of their order but begin by treating him as the greatest person in town, only divulging pleasant and sweet matters until they have entrapped him in their noose, so also these riffraff at first cover themselves with pretty make-up in order to give a flavor of their doctrine to the simple. And they never expose the hidden side[4] of their abominations until they are confident that a man is sufficiently seduced[5] to consent to their illusions.

Hence in the same way that poor novices after being bound in perpetual bondage by their promises find that the cloisters are a true hell and the honey has been changed into gall, so too these poor simple people, equally having thought at first that this loathsome sect was their gateway to paradise, are thrown into ruin before having caught sight of evil.[6] Consequently, to the end that no one may be deceived for want of being warned, let us listen a little while this great theologian, Monsieur Anthony Pocquet, harangues us in their accustomed manner.

> God be praised that in these last days it has pleased Him to make known to me by His instrument the great error in which I stood, desiring to reprove and correct you, where it is written, "They shall all be taught by God" (Isa. 54:13; John 6:45).

Note that his principal wisdom consists in letting each person walk according to his own intelligence.[7] Hence it is fitting that all teaching and admonition should cease between men, which is the reverse of what Saint Paul says to all believers: "Mutually teach and admonish one another" (Col. 3:16). Again, "You are full of wisdom in order to admonish each other" (Rom. 15:14). Again, "Convince, admonish, rebuke" (II Tim. 4:2). Again, as our Lord says, "If your brother has sinned, correct him between you and him" (Matt. 18:15).

He continues,[8]

> And when I presume to understand, I understand nothing.[9] For God is my understanding, my strength, and my salvation. Even if I

4. *le pasté.*
5. *embabouiné* = *séduit.*
6. This passage is reminiscent of Calvin's efforts in Strassburg to reconvert Anabaptists to Protestantism. See Williams, *Radical Reformation,* pp. 590f.
7. *sens.*
8. The rubric throughout the text is, *Il s'ensuit,* "It follows."
9. *et cuidoye entendre, et n'entens rien.*

> should want to judge you or murmur against you, keeping a close lookout on my neighbor and not on myself, that is forbidden. For He has made the nations of the world capable of salvation.

What does it mean to say that whoever has God for his understanding understands nothing? For if this were so, God would be making us blind, whereas His office is to enlighten us. It is true that a believer does not think of himself [alone] as coming to understand anything.[10] But does this mean that he must close his eyes in order not to see anything, as this insane Pocquet pretends?

As for keeping an eye on our neighbor but not on ourselves, that is forbidden. But our Lord does not forbid us from doing both. Besides, let us carefully note the "sound" reason he adds: "All nations are capable of salvation." Hence it is not lawful to care about your neighbor. But I conclude the opposite. For since we are ministers of God and His fellow workers for the purpose of edifying our neighbors in salvation, it is fitting that we should work unceasingly in their behalf.

He continues,

> In the first place I do not understand how we are created out of nothing and how our bodies will be reconstituted from extinguished ashes, while the spirit will be as clean air and dispersed as clouds, nor do I understand how I am [made] of an earthly species, that is to say, from him who was first of all made as a living soul (God does nothing without a purpose),[11] and how we are born from the womb of our mother earth, where all is woe. For this reason Job said (5:18f.), "God wounds and then heals; He brings one to hell and then retrieves; He delivers from six tribulations and no evil will touch you on the seventh."

I beg of you, is there any more substance to this proposal than there is to the daydreams of a man suffering from a high fever? Moreover he already begins to enter into this beautiful philosophy which we have already treated: that the spirit reenters God when man dies, when he says that it will be dispersed as the clouds.

He continues,

10. An echo of Augustine's doctrine of illumination. See the *Soliloquies* 1.1.3; 1.8.15.

11. Parentheses added for clarity.

> For it was my living soul that so presumed to speak. But thanks to God, by this spirit of renewal I am raised from death and revived with Christ, and I am dead to the works of the law,[12] and I am called with the angels and made a son of God and an inheritor of immortality and a member of Christ, and our bodies [are made] temples of the Holy Spirit, and our souls the images and secret dwelling places of divinity. And this horrible beast, the serpent, called the devil, to whom we were obligated and serfs and from whom it was impossible for us to free ourselves, this then was pride or avarice or the world, which has already come to an end by fire, as I shall explain more clearly.

Now he begins to "froth at the mouth," as Saint Jude says (v. 16), that is, he uses boastful words which have the appearance of a wonderful spirituality. For who would not say that on the surface Monsieur Anthony Pocquet has become a demiangel, hearing him speak in such a lofty manner, as if he no longer had sensations of anything except heavenly matters?[13]

But when all this is said, it is nothing but a lie and a lot of wind,[14] except that under the bombast of his froth are already hidden many of their blasphemies. For he already wants to introduce this fantastic resurrection of which I have spoken. And although he mentions the devil, nevertheless he denotes that this is only by way of imagination, explaining that he means nothing other than "pride," or "avarice," or "the world," which is their notion of *cuider*,[15] which I have already treated. Hence that is what the devil means to them.

Finally, by taking what is said about the consummation of the world by fire as a silly allegory, he completely destroys that article of our faith which is so well expressed in Scripture, and removes our hope of the renewal of all creatures.

He continues,

> The same is true of what is written about the transfiguration, where Jesus Christ was in the middle of Moses and Elijah. Moses was the ancient law, hard and unbearable. Jesus Christ was the law,

12. *me sont passées.*

13. Calvin does not seem to be accusing Pocquet of glossolalia but of speculative theology.

14. *ce ne sont que vessies bien confles en apparence, et au reste pleines de vent.* The expression *vessies confles* literally means "inflated bladders."

15. *leur cuider.* See p. 234, n. 4, p. 263, n. 5, p. 264, n. 11.

> gentle, gracious,[16] tractable. Elijah was the last, meaning the end of the world, as he demonstrated by his departure in his fiery chariot, full of flames, called "double spirit,"[17] and by which we are consummated outside of this earthly world. And nevertheless, as Jesus Christ said through Saint John, "I see a new heaven and a new earth." This was the world, which has already ended, not so entirely as not to be present, but the world has ended for those who are in Christ and who no longer live according to the flesh. For the wisdom of the flesh is dead and full of death.

You see the audacity of this rascal who shamelessly pretends to be a great theologian by recounting fables from the book of old wives' tales for mystical expositions of the Scripture. But Jesus Christ is shown in glory in the middle of Moses and Elijah (Matt. 17:3), i.e., of the law and the prophets, in order to denote that Moses and the prophets have witnessed to Him and that He is the true end toward which all their teaching ought to refer, and that He is in the middle, as a place of the highest honor, to demonstrate that He is the master of the house, as the apostle says (Heb. 3:2, 5), and that the others have only been His servants.

But this swine, overturning this beautiful mystery with his snout so that Christ is no longer the end at all, places Elijah in the highest position and makes him the perfection of everything, attributing nothing to Jesus Christ unless it is that He leads us up to the halfway point[18]—which is Muhammad's doctrine.

As for what he says about the world having already ended, he disguises this blasphemy still more clearly in both their perfection which they imagine and in the resurrection which they preach. That is, that since it is an accomplished event,[19] they are more glorious than the angels of paradise.

As for their interpreting[20] the fiery chariot, in which Elijah was carried away from this world, as "double spirit," in the first place it is a manifest falsification of the text in which it is only stated that Elisha asked his master if after him he could have a double portion of God's Spirit, adding that this was granted to him (II Kings 2:9). Second, in this word ["double"] is hidden the

16. *gratieuse.* Literally, "freely given."
17. See Calvin's rebuttal below.
18. *jusque au milieu de chemin.* Literally, "up to the middle of the road."
19. *elle est ia faicte.*
20. Literally, "making."

abomination, which they practice[21] in their sect, of disguising themselves and feigning, whether in their words, jests, or works, saying that Christian perfection consists in being double [i.e., "two-faced"], to the end that one neither knows how to take them nor can attribute any substance or certainty to them.

He continues,

> For it is written, "I have been made every man."[22] Since He has been made every man[23] by taking on human nature and is dead, can He still die here below? It would be a grave mistake to believe so. For He is dead and raised, and it is necessary to believe that He has not left any of His members without being dead and also raised with Him. Thus for this reason it is written that "we are all members of Christ."[24]

Where is what he alleges written? It is a blatant lie! For we do not find any such statement in Scripture. But above all let us note the consequence which he deduces from this false allegation, i.e., that we shall never again die, as if we should not differ in any way from Jesus Christ.

It is true that with respect to leading a holy life if we are members of Christ we should already be dead and raised, denying, I say, ourselves and living to God. But is that it? On the contrary, all of Scripture attests that that is only a part of it.

Is this to say that natural death has been abolished? Is this to say that there is no longer any hope of resurrection? On the contrary, Saint Paul says that the last enemy to be overcome on the last day will be death (I Cor. 15:26).

This "venerable" Monsieur Anthony seems quite pleased to prove all his silly notions by saying that we are "members of Christ," but he overlooks the fact that God extends His mercies within limits,[25] granting each of us his portion in this world according to the excellence[26] of each member, as Saint Paul says (I Cor. 12:7). Consequently, as Jesus Christ is not yet fully in us, so

21. *ont.*

22. *i'ay esté faict tout homme.* The context seems to suggest that "all men" are represented in Christ's humanity, a possible Libertine interpretation of Philippians 2:7, 8; John 1:14; and I Corinthians 6:15.

23. *tout homme.*

24. This could allude to I Corinthians 6:15.

25. *ses graces par mesure.*

26. *qualité.*

also His benefits and gifts are far from being entirely in us. Hence let us return again to what is written in another passage: that each will come to the resurrection quite happily "in his own order" (I Cor. 15:23).[27]

He continues,

> It is also written, "Bear one another's weaknesses." For if we criticize each other,[28] we will be siding with the serpent, called "the devil," accusing believers by constantly assuming them to be acting in pride.[29] But God elevates the small and the humble and humbles the great and the proud. For this reason those who are in Christ, who have the wisdom of faith, recognize the works of God everywhere and are astonished at nothing, benefiting from everything, realizing that everything is [caused by] the will and providence of God.

Our Lord certainly commands us to "bear" the weaknesses of our brothers (Rom. 15:1), but not "to approve of" them; rather He wants us to correct them as vices. Now in order to eliminate any reprehension this evildoer says that it is not proper for us to be like the devil. How so? "By criticizing," he answers.

I concur. But isn't there a great difference between criticizing our neighbor and reprimanding him for his shortcomings with the intention of helping[30] him? Whenever we falsely slander our neighbor, or rail against him through backbiting, we are imitators of the devil. But when we reprimand the shortcomings which we see, in simplicity of heart, we are imitators of God.

Now this rogue overflows still more, adding that it is the wisdom of faith to judge everything good, as the work of God. He says that we ought not find fault with anything. The reason, he adds, is because nothing can be evil.

That is how he absolves murder, robbery, and adultery,[31] under the ruse that we ought not to criticize. And what is worse, he commits the outrage of attributing all this malice to God in order to find it good.

27. Note the biblical perspicuity and simplicity with which Calvin rejects Pocquet's radical eschatology.

28. *sommes detracteurs.*

29. *pour cuider estre tousiours en leur orgueil.*

30. *l'amender = bénéficier.* See Calvin's discussion of the ends and processes of discipline (*Institutes* 4.14.1–7).

31. Note the apparent allusion to the violent excesses associated with the Anabaptist (Spiritualist) movement at St. Gall.

He continues,

> For it is written, "Everything is pure to the pure" (Titus 1:15). And whoever is purified by faith is totally acceptable to God. But he must be careful not to be ruined by his weak brother. For this reason it is written, "Love your neighbor and be joined to him by faith, without wishing to be avenged."[32] For whoever wants to be avenged will find the vengeance of the Lord who will remember his sins. For this reason it is said, "Forgive your neighbor who harms you. And when you pray, your sins will be forgiven you."[33] For a man must not make his petition[34] in anger. For how can he ask for forgiveness if he has no mercy on men like himself, if he is still in the flesh, not yet having memory of the last days, for he would continue to be the enemy, i.e., the devil, not having memory of the new covenant that shows him how to abstain from quarreling and contention, that abolishes all sin, and teaches him not to be concerned for his neighbor's ignorance?[35] For the Lord has said, "I wound and heal; I put to death and make alive."[36] Hence trust my words and be renewed in the renewal of your minds[37] in order to understand the will of God, not returning evil for evil, but overcoming evil with good. For if you love your neighbor, you fulfill the law. The love of neighbor causes no evil. For it is the fulfillment of the law.

We see here with what impudence they confuse good with evil. Saint Paul, speaking in reference to foods, says that nothing is "unclean" or "to be rejected," "since they are good creations of God" (I Tim. 4:4). This scab[38] applies this statement to robbery, adultery, and murder[39] in order to find them clean and holy.

What follows is a confused jumble of impertinent statements. But in all events, underneath it contains hidden malice, since in saying that we ought to forgive their sins he means that we ought to flatter our neighbors. And he confuses the word "vengeance" with "reprehension," thus concluding that it is not lawful

32. A possible allusion to Luke 6:27.
33. A possible allusion to Matthew 6:14.
34. *ne doit requerir.*
35. Literally, "being still in flesh, not having yet memory of the last days, seeing that he does not cease to be an enemy, that is to say, the devil, not having memory of the last testament, which shows how to abstain from noise and contention, abolishing all sin, and not looking after the ignorance of his neighbor."
36. A possible allusion to Job 5:18.
37. *sens.*
38. *pouacre = rogneux.*
39. See p. 305, n. 31.

to condemn anyone for his evil, since we must forgive those who have trespassed against us. True! But the forgiveness we must render refers to love.[40] But we are not to usurp the authority of God in order to call evil good.

Thus we see how these dogs make use of our Lord's Holy Word by their blasphemies.

He continues,

> That is why it was written that there would come forth one who would deliver from the bondage[41] of Jacob, saying, "I will give them a new covenant[42] when I remove their sins" (Jer. 31:33). For it is written that "God has consigned all men[43] to disobedience in order to be merciful to all" (Rom. 11:32). "For His judgments are unsearchable" [v. 33]. "For from Him and in Him and by Him are all things done" (Rom. 11:36).
>
> Moses says (Exod. 33:19), "I will have mercy on whom I will have mercy." Consequently the Lord is merciful when it pleases Him and hardens when it pleases Him. Jesus also says, "Without me you can do nothing" (John 15:5). "And no one can come to Me unless it is given to Him by My Father" (John 6:44).
>
> Isn't this the infallible truth, seeing who has spoken it? Who, then, wants to contradict His Word? Is it not written that God knew, before He even created us, whether we would be bad or good? and knew everything present and to come?

That is their lovely theology, to say that Jesus Christ came into the world that sin might be no more. It is true that He abolishes sin in His believers, but He does so by mortifying them through the grace of His Spirit in order that they might follow good and eschew evil. He also abolishes the curse of sin, so that it is not imputed to us before God. But this does not mean that believers do not sin or should not be condemned for their evil in order to obtain absolution from God; nor equally that they ought not correct one another in order to reclaim each other from sins.

"God has consigned everyone under unbelief" (Rom. 11:32)—that is, holds all men [as] confounded and damned by their unbelief, so much so that none is saved except by His mercy, which He gives, as Moses says (Exod. 33:19), to whom it pleases Him. But this does not mean that by forgiving sin He justifies it.

40. *charité.*

41. *infirmité.*

42. *souverain.*

43. Note in *CO* 7 (col. 232, n. 3) indicates that "all men" was missing in the first edition.

Besides, I beg of you, what purpose is served by his amassing all these statements without order or reason, unless it is so to dazzle his readers' eyes that they cease to know where they are? [Making them] quite like a man who having strayed from his road, and having neither path nor track before him, travels aimlessly and tortuously about.

He continues,

> It is written, "You shall not be adulterers of the Word, as some have."[44] And such was I. But all is forgiven. For it is written, "Abstain from unchastity so that you might enjoy your vessel[45] in holiness and honor" (I Thess. 4:3f.). For since we are dead to the law through the body of Christ in order that we might be[long] to another, who has been raised from the dead so that we might bear fruit to the living God (Rom. 7:4), you are hence no longer in the flesh. The wisdom of the flesh is God's enemy and does not know how to please God (Rom. 8:7f.).
>
> Now if the Spirit of Christ is not in you, how can you be in Him? But if He is, though the body is dead because of sin, the spirit lives because of justification. That is to say, He has justified us since we are all of the same Spirit. Hence, the Spirit of Him who raised Jesus Christ from the dead lives in you. For He died for all and, as it is said, He became every man[46] and "died for all that those who live might no longer live for themselves but for Him who died for all and was raised for all" (II Cor. 5:15).[47]

It hardly troubles Monsieur Anthony to cite Scripture in this way, falsifying one passage, corrupting another, and inventing in his head whatever seems good to him, pretending that whatever he imagines is [actually] written and astonishing all as if the Scripture existed in order to build a gross structure[48] from every crude and ill-designed piece.

Saint Paul says to the Corinthians (II Cor. 2:17) that he did not adulterate the Word, as some, i.e., that he did not disguise it as "peddlers" do their merchandise in order to make it serve his own advantage. This stupid ass[49] connects this passage with

44. The French is awkward at best: *Tu ne seras tirant à mal, toy gardont d'adulterer en la parolle, comme plusieurs.* See II Corinthians 2:17.

45. *vaisseau.* The Thessalonian passage reads, "wife."

46. *tout homme.*

47. This passage is ambiguous in the French, thus reflecting Calvin's charge that the Libertines expressed themselves in a somewhat obscure manner.

48. *un bastiment confus.*

49. *beste.*

what the apostle says to the Thessalonians with respect to chastity, then he jumps to Romans 8 in order to pervert the holy exhortations which are contained for us there. For instead of admonishing us, as Saint Paul does, to live in holiness and to renounce the world and the lusts of the flesh, this wretch attempts to cajole the simple into accepting his infernal spirituality, which consists in basing all their perfection on finding nothing wrong under the ruse that in their view they possess the Spirit of Christ. For this is what he says in the end, falsifying the words of Saint Paul, when he says that Christ justified us because we are of His same Spirit, instead of what Saint Paul says, that God's Spirit is life in us because of the righteousness He gives us.

He continues,

> For this reason "we now no longer regard anyone according to the flesh, and even though we knew Christ according to the flesh, we now no longer regard Him thus, because we are reigning and have been made new creatures in Christ" (II Cor. 5:16f.). "Therefore the old and sterile have passed away, because all things have become renewed, and all these things are from God who has reconciled us to Himself through Christ. For God was in Christ reconciling the world to Himself, not counting their sin against them." Thus it is written, "Whoever sees sin, sin remains in him, and the truth is not in him" (John 9:41). And a little farther over still again: "Whoever fails in one [point], fails in all [the law]" (James 2:10).

Saint Paul, desiring to combat the pride of those who glory in external appearances, says that it is improper for us to regard any man "according to the flesh" in order to emphasize what he had said above. Rather we should regard with esteem those who are new creatures.

This seducer pretends to carry the simple away by imagining that they should no longer discern between good and evil, as if that would be judging "according to the flesh." And in order better to confirm his proposal, he falsifies without shame Saint John's passage where our Lord says to the Pharisees, "Because you say, 'We see,' your sin remains." And he completely changes it by saying, "Whoever sees sin, sin remains in him."

Indeed, up to this point has he [not] frothed with his lofty and inflated notions, so that now he has defined in a word what the fine innocence and holiness of their sect is? That is, to be no more conscious[50] than swine.

He continues,

> But when you behold God[51] you no longer see all these things. For sin does not dwell in God, yet He makes all things and everything He makes is good,[52] and man's knowledge is folly to God. Will you thus behold in man, that is to say in the flesh, what is not in God? Indeed they are not [in God].

We see here how in attributing evil to God, in order to judge it good, they blaspheme God as well as detract from His righteousness. And because there is no sensible human who would be villainous enough to say that since God creates everything there is no sin, he alleges that human knowledge[53] is folly. With this I agree, but I say to condemn evil and to see sin in order to hate it is the knowledge of God,[54] unless he thinks that the devil spoke through Holy Scripture.

He continues,

> And because everything that is outside of God is nothing, the Scripture says that all that we do or know to do is vanity. Thus it is said, "Deny yourself, and take up My cross, and follow Me. Whoever walks with Me is not in darkness but walks in light" (John 8:12).

There is no passage, however sacred, in Scripture that this impudent wretch does not misuse to suit his churlish affections in order to permit each to live as one pleases. But when the Scripture says that there is nothing but vanity in us and that we can do nothing good without Christ, its purpose in condemning us is that we might pray to God for Him to work in us by His grace.[55]

This wretch derives a completely different conclusion: that we should do nothing, and that it suffices to think that God does

50. *n'avoir non plus de sentiment.*

51. *regardez en Dieu.*

52. Possibly these words are influenced by Augustine's Neoplatonism and by the words of Genesis 1, "And God saw that it was good."

53. *la science de l'homme.*

54. A true knowledge of man is inseparable from the knowledge of God. See the *Institutes* 1.1.1–3.

55. See the *Institutes* 2.7.1–11.

everything, and that we are not doing any evil when we attribute everything to God.

He continues,

> Remember the time that the disciple asked Elijah for a double [portion of] spirit. Such was the case when Jesus Christ said to His apostles, "I yet have something to give you, but now you are not able to bear it" (John 16:12). "But when the Spirit of truth comes, He will teach you the whole truth. For He will not speak of Himself but He will speak what He has heard and will declare to you the things that are to come; He will clarify Me. For He will take what is Mine and declare it to you, so that[56] you will be as incorruptible as I. Moreover, I shall not speak again until that time comes."

It is quite necessary to guess in order to fathom the end of Monsieur Anthony's proposals. For it seems that he jumps from the first item of his Mass to the second. But we must note that herein he pretends to save[57] the world from the simple and pure teaching of the Scripture, as if it were the wisdom of Christians to inquire into new revelations. And he now calls it "a double [portion of] spirit" to pass beyond the contents of Scripture.[58] Still, whenever it suits them, they interpret Scripture in a totally different sense.

Furthermore, he maliciously falsifies Saint John's passage in order to confirm his blasphemy. For instead of our Lord Jesus saying to His apostles that the Spirit will enable them to understand what they have heard from His mouth, this clown has our Lord say[59] that He will "declare things to come." And then he makes Jesus say what He never thought by imposing his own ideas on Him.

But this is how they reverence the Scripture. For by pretending to use it they mislead poor simple people who do not know what it contains.

He continues,

> Behold how God planted the luxurious garden and then set man in the midst of it to cultivate and keep it. And when God had created him he fell asleep, and God took one of his ribs and

56. *par lequel.* Literally, "by which," or perhaps, "which will make."
57. *retirer.* Literally, "to pull," "to snatch back."
58. Calvin opposes such a rejection of the principle of *sola Scriptura.*
59. *change.*

created woman from it to accompany man, then He said to them, "Be fruitful and multiply on the earth." That is the first law that God ordained, which was called "the law of nature."

Now understand how Saint John shows us in his Apocalypse seven time periods,[60] as in the seven candlesticks and seven stars [Rev. 1:12, 16, 20], and how the fifth will plunge us into darkness, saying that the first was holy and the last of the same solemnity as the first.

Now we are in the last time, which is the true bond, made in the tree of the cross, which we call "marriage," and which was accordingly asleep and whose side was opened in order to replace the rib, or the woman, that is, the church and the union of all human nature, and to be made all one member, of which Jesus Christ is the head.

For this reason let us leave to [the] mortal what is mortal and corruptible. For the kingdom and excellence of our soul does not lie here below unless soiled and tainted.

Let us consider then how the church was made and formed and that it was prefigured in Adam and Eve. Consequently Jesus Christ is the Bridegroom and we are the bride. As it is written in the Song of Songs, "Come my sister and my bride."[61]

Whereas Saint Paul uses this simile of Adam and Eve to commend to us the spiritual union which we enjoy with our Lord Jesus in order to participate both in Him and in His benefits, this wicked seducer twists it to [suit] their diabolical imagination, viz., that we are the same person as Jesus Christ.

Moreover what he calls "the natural law of growing and multiplying," and what he adds about our having to return to that in order to experience original innocence,[62] follows from their doctrine of "spiritual marriage," i.e., that each should unite[63] with the other wherever it suits.

What he interpolates from the Apocalypse is purely cock and bull. And while he perverts the meaning of the passage by placing the consummation of the reign of God in the present time, for whose coming we daily pray, we confess that it is still to be accomplished.

He continues,

60. *temps.*

61. See Williams's analysis of Pocquet's periodization of history and view of the cross (*Radical Reformation*, pp. 345f.). Williams examines this specific text.

62. *la premiere innocence.*

63. Can also mean "to copulate." It is possible that this is the meaning Calvin intended readers to understand.

> But we continue in sin unless we enter the garden of paradise[64] where it is still forbidden to want to do anything but to let ourselves be led by the will of God, otherwise we shall not be divested of the old serpent, which is our first father Adam, and we will see sin as he and his wife saw it, though they thought they were covering their nakedness and sin, which they had just committed. And earlier they had not seen their will and were not ashamed of their nakedness. They had not seen their sin, but when they saw sin, sin was necessarily imputed to them and everything was changed. For their happiness was changed into labor and misery, and the earth and all that it produces was cursed. Man was changed into vanity.

Herein we see the kind of mortification these seducers teach, i.e., that man should be free to follow his own desire, without troubling his conscience in anything. For lo, in their opinion, God works in us when we cease to say that the work is ours.

We further see this blasphemy reiterated: that one must remove all scruples and that their entire innocence consists in closing their eyes so that they no longer see any good or evil, which, as Solomon says (Prov. 28:5), is the height of all iniquity. And Saint Paul also says that when a man no longer has any compunction or regrets, it is a sign of his complete alienation from God (Eph. 4:19).

Furthermore, we must note how they overturn everything when they conclude that the origin of evil and man's perdition is the result of his having seen his sin, whereas his evil was the result of his unfaithfulness and disobedience which he had committed, and his awareness of his shame was an accompanying punishment, which our Lord nonetheless has changed into salvation.

Hence we see the impudence involved when this villain says that he saw sin and as a result sin was ascribed to him. For on the contrary, the moment he saw sin he began to obtain grace, as in truth it is required that the sinner must condemn himself in order to receive forgiveness from God. In fact, what would become of repentance, which all Christians must practice[65] until death?

Besides, there is another malicious point to note: that Adam and the serpent are one, which according to their view means

64. *le iardin de volupté.*
65. *mediter.*

that sin, the devil, the world, the living soul and his conscious acts[66] are all the same.

He continues,

> Consequently, let us leave the old Adam, i.e., our living soul, and let us come to higher things, i.e., the spirit. For it was said of Adam that he would die. And he is dead. Now we are vivified with the second Adam, who is Christ, no longer seeing sin, since it is dead. For grace was made from sin by our Father in Jesus Christ. Whence then comes this fear and terror of death and of being cast into hell? In reality one can set it aside as an error; one can make fun of it as a vain thought.

We see here how these serpents twist the terms "old man" and "spirit." For whereas the Scripture means by "old man" the corruption that reigns in us due to sin, they mean "the living soul" which was given to man from the first moment of creation, before it had sinned or had acquired any vice.

"Spirit" to them is not derived from the grace of regeneration. Rather it is the fantasy that God is in us and that we must permit Him to do whatever He wants.

We also see what they mean by the life which we have in Jesus Christ: i.e., that everything is lawful, and there is no evil, provided we are not conscious of it.

It is indeed true that a believer ought to fear neither death nor hell, truly realizing that he has been set free from both through his redemption in Jesus Christ, but not through a stupidity [such] as these wicked people claim, nor by eliminating the ideas of death and hell as if they were childish threats. For that is where Monsieur Anthony wants to come out, according to the common teaching of their sect.

He continues,

> For when Jesus Christ descended from heaven into the earth—where for some He is still confined—He completely vanquished the devils, who were the world, and who were astonished that this King was so glorious, and sending His light into the darkness and its infernal jaws He said, "Lift up your heads, O gates! etc." For as I have already said before, He takes us there and brings us back.
>
> But He is always with us. Indeed we cannot be without Him, nor He without us. For as I have said, He married us on the cross

66. *le cuider.*

and has been so attached that He neither can nor would want to separate Himself from us, because of the great love He has for us.

It is true that it would be quite difficult to expound everything Monsieur Anthony says. For this would be to look for reasons where none exists. But he does continually return to these two points: to make us into Jesus Christ so that we need not be afraid of sinning against God, having nothing in us but righteousness, and to argue that everything has been consummated so that we need not anticipate either paradise or hell. And further, we ought constantly note that for him the devil is nothing but the world, that is to say, his *cuider* [i.e., man's capacity to make judgments and to distinguish between good and evil].

As for the passage where he cites David (Ps. 24:7), we can forgive him this fault since all his knowledge is in his breviary[67] and since he has seen Palm Sunday acted out as a farce in his village, whereupon the priest strikes [the gates] with the cross, pretending to break the gates of hell.

Now in David's text there is nothing of this sort. For he addresses his words to the temple's gates, saying, "Lift up your heads that God might enter!" Consequently, it would be more appropriate if Monsieur Anthony would say his breviary, sing his Mass, and, after having raised the cloth, would lick up the plates in the kitchen, than try to be a theologian.

He continues,

> And this love profits in everything without seeking its profit, and it exists not for itself but for all: it prays for its enemies and even gives them what they lack and covers a multitude of sins without seeing sin. For it has destroyed everything by the highest commandment which Christ said and decreed, viz., "Love one another as I have loved you. For I have not come for Myself but for all of you who believe in Me. And I will be in you and you in Me. As My Father and I are one, so shall you and I be one. You know that I have come[68] from the Father and have come into the world. But I am leaving the world and am going to the Father again. Nevertheless I am not alone. For My Father is with me."

Although he distorts his ideas in accordance with his custom, nevertheless his intended meaning briefly is this: that there is no

67. A prayer book. Pocquet was a former Catholic priest and doctor in canon law. He served as a chaplain in Marguerite of Angoulême's court. See p. 202.

68. *issu.*

longer any sin, since it has been forgiven by the love of God, and we ought not ascribe sins [to ourselves and others], since love covers a multitude of sins between men.

Now it is true that God indeed covers our sins, provided we have our refuge in His mercy, but this does not mean that we do not sin. Otherwise what would forgiveness be if there were no sins? Nor does this mean that we ought not be conscious of our sins, since faith cannot exist without repentance.

I equally confess that the love of believers covers a multitude of their neighbors' sins, but Saint Paul did not cease to have love though he sharply reprimanded the vices of his brothers. Nor was he acting contrary to love when he said that he was glad to have saddened the Corinthians and to have caused them grief when he led them to repentance (II Cor. 7:8f.).

Hence it is blasphemy to say that love is blind to sin.[69]

He continues,

> "I have said these things to you that you might have peace with one another, that is to say, in Me. In the world you have tribulations. Have confidence, I have overcome the world." But those who are in the flesh cannot see God. For it is written, "Flesh and blood shall not inherit the kingdom of God." Then it is said, "Blessed are the pure in heart, for they shall see God."

His conclusion is similar to all the rest: i.e., a mass of statements badly stitched [together]. Nevertheless the end is that we do not have to be in the flesh to see God. By which they mean that we do not have to trouble our conscience about anything but only need to consider ourselves already in paradise, since Jesus Christ, who is in us, is there.

Now in order to confirm such a silly suggestion he cites Saint Paul's reference that "flesh and blood cannot inherit the kingdom of God" (I Cor. 15:50) completely contrary to the apostle's intention. For Paul was speaking there of the last resurrection. And this beggar[70] refers to it as if it were already an accomplished event. But we should not be astonished, since it is the principal foundation of their sect, as I have said, that "all is finished,"[71] since we are in Jesus Christ and no longer have a carnal soul but

69. Literally, "does not see sin."
70. *belistre* = *mendiant.*
71. See chapters 17 and 22.

the vivifying Spirit, in which not only our righteousness but also our resurrection and glory consist.

For this reason anyone can see and almost touch with his fingers how I have spoken the truth about these enraged beasts, without ascribing anything to them by way of calumny, in order to render them odious. For this grand masterpiece of Monsieur Anthony Pocquet's testifies both to their lofty rhetoric and manner of speaking as well as to their pretended meaning and intention.

On the other hand, those whom this mass-mouthing[72] villain would like to seduce by his nonsense have a good lesson here for being warned as to what sort of spirit he represents. And not only him but also all those of his gang—although it is necessary that he should be specifically singled out from among the others, after his father Quintin. For beyond the access to many people, which some give him,[73] so that he might sow his poison, and beyond the fact that he indeed diligently runs about everywhere in order to trouble poor souls wherever he can serve the devil without danger [to himself], he hides under the name of a Vaudois[74] so that he might have better access among uneducated and God-fearing people who know the bounty of the people there.

Hence, since he is a wolf in sheepskin in order to devour and destroy, it is quite right to deprive him of this guise, as I think I have so effectively done that anyone can perceive what sort of a beast he is. Furthermore, we should not allow this wicked man to bring such shame on a Christian people who follow the pure teaching of the gospel in the simplicity of their hearts by calling himself one of them in order to discredit them and to commit slander among both the true servants of God and the ignorant. Indeed, it would even be a blasphemy to think that the Vaudois had anything in common with such a dog!

72. *missatier* = *messotier,* i.e., a priest who says the Mass.

73. *qu'on luy donne.* An apparent reference to Marguerite of Angoulême.

74. *Vaudois.* A *Vaudois* is technically an inhabitant of the Swiss canton of Vaud, immediately north of Geneva. But *Vaudois* could also refer to the Waldensians, whom Calvin respected (Étienne de la Forge was one). See H. S. Bender and Christian Neff's article, "Waldenses," *Mennonite Encyclopedia,* vol. 4, pp. 874–876.

24

Wherein Readers Are Warned About Certain Printed Books Which Help the Libertines, Although They Are Not Written at All for Them

Inasmuch as once your mind[1] is confused by silly illusions one evil customarily leads to another, it seems wise[2] that all faithful readers should be warned about certain printed booklets, which are infected with fantastic opinions, which can serve as a gateway and an introduction to the Libertines' sect—as indeed they do serve to mislead the simple, making them even more vulnerable later.

Among others there is a little tract of only one sheet, falsely entitled, *Instruction and salutary admonition for living perfectly in this world and how in all our adversity we can be patient.*[3]

If you ask me what I find objectionable,[4] I would say first of all that the entire argument is so extravagant that one would not know how to take any clear resolve from it. Secondly, it contains silly and absurd speculations which only serve to unsettle minds and afterwards leave them suspended in the air. Thirdly, it contains proposals that far exceed the bounds of reason.[5] For

1. *l'esprit.*
2. *est bon.*
3. *Instruction et salutaire admonition, pour parfaictement vivre en ce monde, et comment en toute nostre adversité serons patiens.*
4. *mauvais.*
5. Note that all three of Calvin's objections share the criterion that sound theology must be accountable to reason.

example, that a believer is as comfortable in hell as he is in paradise, and similar such things. More could be said, but it is enough to have mentioned it, since my intention is not to argue against it.

There is another longer [tract], about fourteen quires[6] in length, entitled, *A Christian Telescope*,[7] which in truth is more likely to hinder than to enhance the view. Now it is true that whoever wrote it is not as great an ass as Quintin or Monsieur Anthony Pocquet, neither outwardly nor in effect, except for their ruse of using jargon[8] in order to achieve a reputation[9] by their obscurity. But its author is a man of some intelligence[10] and know-how and uses several methods of teaching.[11] So much is this so that his work could have been quite prodigious were it not [for the fact] that he clutters[12] it with foolish and pernicious ideas. But when everything is taken into consideration,[13] the entire book, from beginning to end, does not contain a great deal of substance. And it would have nothing to present were it not for the silly daydreams with which it is crammed.

As a fine beginning, the author denies that the afflictions which we endure in this world are punishments[14] from God. To prove this he adds that they are "spiritual medicaments"[15] which purge our vices. But this reason is invalid. For why does a father chastise his child except to improve it? Hence it is not inappropriate for the rod to be a remedy.

Furthermore we ought to note that as God chastises His faithful through war, pestilence, famine, and other adversities in order to improve and save them, so also He punishes unbelievers and the contemptuous, using His righteous vengeance against them. Hence in the same way that fire purges gold and silver

6. *quayers* = *cayers.* A quire contains 24 sheets, hence 14 quires are 336 pages. However, the 1611 edition reads "four," not "fourteen," making the tract 96 pages. See *CO* 7, col. 242, n. 5.

7. *la lunette des Chrestiens.*

8. *gergonner* = *jargonner.*

9. *bruit* = *réputation.*

10. *esprit.*

11. *traditive* = *tradition.* Cotgrave defines *traditive* as "a method of teaching."

12. *entremesle.* Literally, "intersperses," "intermingles."

13. *compté et rabbatu.*

14. *verges.* Literally, "rods."

15. *medecines spirituelles.*

and consumes straw and chaff, so also afflictions purge the good and destroy the reprobate.

Next he says that those who are members of Christ no longer live a corporal life,[16] which is an exaggeration and reflects his delusion. I neglect to say that he badly expounds the passage in Saint John's letter on which he bases his principal thesis.

Then on the one hand he condemns all affairs of state that protect property, and on the other hand [the practice of] medicine which preserves corporal life. And although in a few places he attempts to correct or at least moderate slightly his temerity, nonetheless he so perseveres in his course that all human laws concerning affairs of state are nothing but diabolical inventions and medicine nothing but an idolatry.

If he would take back the abuses he commits, I would be quite in accord with him and would have nothing more to say or add. But in reprimanding good and holy things he blasphemes God from whom they proceed.

Next he condemns in general all wars, without discerning if they are the result of a just cause or not, even when a prince should only go to war in defense of his people, without being driven by ambition or avarice, but only out of the duty of his office. To confirm this he cites that we are commanded to give way to wrath (Rom. 12:19). But by the word "wrath," Saint Paul means "the vengeance of God" and His just punishment which He has commanded princes to exercise.

With regard to the wars of the Old Testament, he says that it is not fitting for us to continue them, since we are under the law of love, as if that law did not exist then. In saying this he causes great injury not only to the holy fathers but to God who instructed them.

And he does not use simple and moderate reprimands, but he cries and storms as if he were battling against the devils of hell. For to him it is a detestable blasphemy, a great outrage against God, a wicked act of infidelity to make use of human laws for governing the world. And why? Because it is enough for God to govern us by His providence. True. But the providence of God cries in Solomon (Prov. 8:15) that human laws[17] come from His

16. Zwingli records a conversation in which a Spiritualist said to him, "For as we have one spirit so also we have one body" (*Refutation of the Tricks of the Baptists,* in *Ulrich Zwingli: Selected Works,* ed. Samuel Macauley Jackson, p. 172).

17. *cela.* Literally, "that."

providence and that princes and their counselors make ordinances and statutes.

It is Satan, he says, who has put [it] in princes' hearts to arrogate to themselves what belongs to God alone, i.e., to put God's will into effect—as if human laws existed to serve some end other than to hold the world in good order and justice. For God has ordained the governing authorities,[18] says Saint Paul (Rom. 13:1), to achieve what He wants and commands.

[But] the office of princes, he says, is not to hear their subjects' disputes, nor to decide lawsuits; for wherever lawsuits exist, transgressions exist on both sides.

First of all, I deny him this reason. For it is quite possible that one [of the party] might have a just cause, as [in the case of] a person who defends his right, having been unjustly assailed. And moreover I say that if evil exists it is proper for it to be settled.[19]

He ascribes the cause of all the children of Israel's sufferings to the fact that they asked for a king—as if beforehand the people had not been afflicted as they were later. Hence we see the thoughtlessness with which he speaks and how great his ignorance of history is.

Still I ask him whether there wasn't previously a political order instituted by God similar to the one he condemns today. I ask him whether Moses and the judges did not hear the people's disputes and decide them. What sort of a scatterbrained man is it who plunges across country on the basis of badly founded speculations?

I only wanted to touch on this matter in passing so that one could herein judge what the entire book is like. I say "touch on" because it would require too much time to criticize the book completely and fully. Moreover it would seem to me to be superfluous to reiterate here what I have treated in my *Institutes*.[20] Besides, his daydreams are so silly and absurd that among sane, intelligent people it is enough to have pointed them out so that one can be on guard.

As for the subject of medicine,[21] he overflows even more, grinding his teeth and storming against it, in the manner of

18. *les principautez au monde.*

19. See Calvin's discussion of the Christian use of law courts (*Institutes* 4.20.17).

20. See Calvin's section on civil government (*Institutes* 4.20).

21. See "Medicine," *Mennonite Encyclopedia*, vol. 3, pp. 550–553.

frantic people who hit, scratch, and bite those who are trying to help them for their own good. Now to list here all the praises of medicine and to explain in detail how it is not only a good and godly art but worthy of praise and honor would be too long a task. Equally to respond to all the scandalous things he brings against it would constitute too long a project to undertake. But fortunately there is no need to be longwinded to disprove the foolish reasons he musters and to maintain so certain and clear a cause as the one he impugns.

To begin with, it is a shame that he errs by debating[22] with those who call themselves Christians and who want to be esteemed such and who, even more, want to theologize on a matter which since the time of the pagans has been completely settled. For among the pagans it was a common proposition that medicine is a gift of God. However, I do not ask that this should prejudice his case, since the truth is clear to anyone.

He says that medicine came into the world through the suggestion of the evil spirit. I say and, what is more, I can prove that it came from God, inasmuch as it is a knowledge of carefully using the gifts of creation[23] which He gives us according to the necessities to which He subjects us. For in the same way that God, having subjected our bodies to hunger and thirst, provides us with an ability to eat and drink in order to overcome our need, and, having subjected us to cold and heat, provides us with means of remedying the problem, He equally, having subjected us to maladies, provides us with the capacity to attend to our illnesses.[24]

Whoever would deny that maladies proceed from vicious qualities in the body and from accidents and tragic events[25] which come about elsewhere deserves to be rejected by everyone as an insane man. The [healing] power of plants and other things is known through experience, so much so that anyone with an ounce of brains can see it with his eyes. The Scripture says that Solomon wrote a book in which he describes such things[26] (I Kings 4:33).

22. *faille debattre.*
23. *des creatures.*
24. *y prouvoir = y pourvoir.*
25. *exces.* Literally, "violent [acts]."
26. *les.*

Must such a natural knowledge that exists in clear reason and is approved by the Holy Scripture be taken as an enchantment and illusion of Satan? When Saint Paul mentions Saint Luke he calls him a "physician." He writes, "Luke the physician greets you" (Col. 4:14). Did he mean to dishonor him by this title, as if he had called him a bandit or thief?

I therefore ask this master corrector for the proof of his saying that medicine is the invention of the devil. He claims that we ought be occupied night and day with meditating on God's law, and consequently we would find neither time nor leisure to devote to the knowledge of plants, since such is the speculation of useless people.

Such a fantastic person ought to be locked up in a room with his Bible, without food or clothing, to see how he would apply himself night and day to the reading of God's Word, without thinking of anything else.

He would say that we are allowed to eat. [But] I would reply that that would not be the case if he believed in his folly. For what a distraction cultivating the ground, sowing, harvesting, beating the wheat, pounding it into flour, and cooking it can be! Think of how much time is required to learn the skills that are necessary for this present life and how much more time is required to engage in them!

Nevertheless I do not mean to detract from this meditation on God's Word, which is rightfully[27] commended to us, but I am only showing that such notions were never intended by this injunction. For our Lord does not forbid us to engage in those occupations which are required for the maintenance of this earthly life, provided we always aspire toward the higher and do not subordinate it by making other things our principal goal.

To show that we do not tempt God by scorning medicine, he says that it is a diabolical word, [capable of] ruining all Christendom. And his reason? Because whoever puts his whole confidence in God does not tempt Him.

I agree. But I say that whoever does not take account of the means which God has ordained does not have confidence in Him but is puffed up with false pride and temerity.

Those are his grand arguments for condemning the gifts of

27. *tant.*

creation[28] to the dishonor of Him who destined them to our usage so that we might receive them with praise and thanksgiving.

I refrain from commenting on many [other] foolish and absurd propositions which abound in this book. As when he says that our Lord Jesus is the only man in whom we all are,[29] and since He is the last there is no other man than He—which approaches the blasphemy of the Libertines which we have already reviewed[30] above. Or again, that the living soul only resides in man after sin.[31] As if it were not this very same soul which earlier had been endowed with the gifts of God[32] and is now repaired through Jesus Christ.

Or again, that it is a terrible blasphemy against the bounty of God to love our parents more than others. As if these commandments were given in vain: "Honor your father and mother"; "Husbands, love your wives; and equally, wives, love your husbands" (Exod. 20:12; Matt. 15:4; Eph. 5:25 etc.). Rather he says we have "a spiritual fellowship"[33] which is more valuable. I concur, but neither detracts from the other so long as each stays within its bounds.

Or again, when he says that we are not obligated to do God's commandments because He commands us to do them, rather He was only giving us examples. Or again, when he says that to bear our cross is to bear patiently being made into vessels of ignominy. Whereas on the contrary God continually sets this consolation before us in order to exhort us to patience, as the cross which we endure forms a fellowship with Jesus Christ[34] so that being conformed to His image we might share in His glorious resurrection, and consequently might be made into vessels of honor, not of ignominy.

I doubt if there is anyone who cannot see why such books, infected with such fantastic opinions, are to be avoided. That is all I wanted to point out, nothing more.

28. *les bonnes creatures de Dieu.*

29. *auquel nous sommes tous.*

30. *deduict.*

31. *qu'il n'est demeuré que l'ame vivante a l'homme apres le peché.* Literally, "that the living soul is only lodged in man after sin." The point seems to be that the present "living soul" is inactive, passive, only a lodger, ancillary to man's life.

32. *graces de Dieu.*

33. *une fraternité spirituelle.*

34. *est une societé avec celle de Iesus Christ.*

Conclusion of the Present Book

Now I pray that all those who seek God with their heart[1] and who love to be obedient to His truth will consider, as if looking here into a mirror, what a pernicious plague it is to allow oneself to be diverted from the pure simplicity[2] of Jesus Christ. For it is a frightful example of God's wrath to see men, who are rational creatures and who have even been illuminated with some gifts of intelligence,[3] fall into such terrible darkness as to make themselves similar to dumb beasts.

To avoid such a possibility, let us be warned to pursue our calling in fear and anxiety,[4] to take the trouble to learn from good and useful doctrine, having above all this end: that we hunger to know nothing except what it has pleased God to reveal to us in His Scripture. Let us not subject the sacred Word of God to our judgments[5] or lusts, but rather let us align[6] ourselves entirely with what it says to us.

Let us be on guard against profaning ourselves, since it has already pleased God to call us into sanctification. Do not covet new things and have tingling ears (II Tim. 4:3) that carry you away with curiosity, but seek what is profitable and edifying. Let us not be so fickle and unstable as to long each day for some change, but keeping to the true road, let us follow it; possessing the truth of God, let us firmly cling to it.

Moreover, let no one marvel at, or even bother to see, these

1. *d'affection.*

2. Note the stark contrast between the simple truth of the gospel and the vain speculations of an irresponsible theology.

3. *bonne intelligence.*

4. *solicitude = inquiétude, souci.*

5. *sens.*

6. *rengeons.*

errors which are so strange and devoid of all reason.[7] Let no one be shaken loose or withdraw from the gospel. But rather let us seek to be in conformity with it so that it might be a perpetual, sure, and faithful buttress for us, able to sustain us in the midst of all the troubles and scandals that can possibly assail us.

I do not ask for people to agree with[8] me, or with my opinion, or my words, unless they have first of all realized that what I am teaching is useful. I do not ask for them to reprove this loathsome teaching, against which I have written, unless they see that it is not only repugnant to God, but so full of detestable errors as to make one's hair stand on end.

In sum, let us use our eyes only to be on guard against it. For certainly no one would [then] be able to be seduced by it, or be made blind to God and numbered[9] among the reprobate for having scorned His Word and not having honored it.

It is for this reason that I have so strongly exhorted all believers constantly to remember the end of their calling so that they might never fall from it, as well as to consider why the Scripture has been given to us and how we are supposed to use it, so that we might not profane it by subjecting it to usages which God never ordained.

7. See p. 318, n. 5.
8. *s'arreste.*
9. *mis.*

Subject Index

Scripture Index